Making sense of social movements

Making sense of social movements

Nick Crossley

Open University Press
Buckingham · Philadelphia

Open University Press
Celtic Court
22 Ballmoor
Buckingham
MK 18 1XW

email: enquiries@openup.co.uk
world wide web: www.openup.co.uk

and

325 Chestnut Street
Philadelphia, PA 19106, USA

First Published 2002

A catalogue record of this book is available from the British Library

ISBN   0 335 20602 6 (pb)   0 335 20603 4 (hb)

Library of Congress Cataloging-in-Publication Data
Crossley, Nick, 1968-
    Making sense of social movements/Nick Crossley.
        p. cm.
    Includes bibliographical references and index.
    ISBN 0-335-20603-4 – ISBN 0-335-20602-6 (pbk.)
    1. Social movements–Philosophy.   I. Title.
    HM881 .C76 2002
    303.48'4'01–dc21   2001035927

Typeset by Graphicraft Limited, Hong Kong
Printed in Great Britain by Biddles Limited, Guildford and King's Lynn

Contents

	Acknowledgements	vii
1	Introduction	1
2	Social unrest, movement culture and identity: the symbolic interactionists	17
3	Smelser's value-added approach	39
4	Rational actor theory	56
5	Resources, networks and organizations	77
6	Opportunities, cognition and biography	105
7	Repertoires, frames and cycles	127
8	New social movements	149
9	Social movements and the theory of practice: a new synthesis	168
	References	192
	Index	201

Acknowledgements

I have benefited from conversations with a great many movement scholars. In particular, however, I would like to thank Colin Barker, who has pointed me down many interesting avenues and whose annual Alternative Futures and Popular Protest conferences are always a treat. I would also like to thank my wife, Michele, who has been happy to 'talk movements' with me and more generally put up with my garbled mutterings. The postgraduate students on my 1999/2000 and 2000/01 Social Movements course also deserve a mention here. More than a little of our lively debates and discussion is reflected in the final version of this book.

chapter one

Introduction

This book is about social movements, or rather about the ways in which we can make sense of them sociologically. I review the main strands of sociological thought on movements and suggest some new pathways for development. I explain how I plan to tackle this task shortly. Before doing so, however, I address a number of more basic questions:

- What are social movements?
- Why are they important, sociologically?
- What is the sociology of social movements about?

It is only when we have answered these questions that we can progress to the broader concerns of the book as a whole.

What are social movements?

As with any sociological phenomenon there is no neat answer to this question. We can find a relatively easy way in, however, by considering some examples of movements. There are many to pick from, some of which will be quite familiar to many people. We might include:

- the women's movement or feminism;
- the labour and trade union movements;
- fascist movements;
- anti-fascist and anti-racist movements;
- the anti-psychiatry and psychiatric survivor movements;
- nationalist movements;
- the (Polish) Solidarity movement;
- the environmental or green movement;
- pro- and anti-abortion movements;

- animal rights movements;
- the peace movement.

The list could go on but we have enough examples to take the next crucial step of considering the properties that these movements share and which make them social movements. This is where the difficulties begin. Many definitions have been offered in the literature but all are problematic. Some are too broad, such that they include phenomena which we would not wish to call social movements, and yet any attempt to narrow the definition down seems destined to exclude certain movements or at least the range of their forms and activities. In addition, every definition includes terms which themselves require definition. We would all agree that social movements are 'collective' ventures, for example, but what makes a venture count as collective? Is it a matter of numbers? If so, how many? Is it a matter of a type of interconnection between people, an organization or network? If so, how is that interconnection itself defined? Does 'wearing the badge' and 'buying the T-shirt' make one part of a movement or must one attend monthly meetings and engage in protest? And if the latter, what counts as protest? Would wearing the aforementioned badge count as a protest or must one stand in a group of three or more people waving a placard? There can be no decisive answers to these questions. Social movements manifest what Wittgenstein (1953) refers to as a 'family resemblance'. Each movement shares some features in common with some other movements, without any feature being both sufficiently inclusive and sufficiently exclusive to demarcate and identify the set. What all movements share in common they tend to share with things other than movements and yet those characteristics which are unique to some are not shared by all. Even within the same movement we find diversity, and all movements change. Furthermore, we cannot define the terms of our definition, other than arbitrarily, because 'collective', 'protest' and other such terms, like 'social movement' itself, belong to our everyday language and derive meaning from their diverse uses in specific contexts. Sometimes they are used this way, sometimes that. Their definition obeys the 'fuzzy logic' of social practice (Bourdieu 1992a). This does not mean that we cannot or should not opt for arbitrary closure, for the purposes of specific projects. Precise definition is necessary to scientific research. But it does preclude a precise definition that will work for general purposes.

Having said this, we cannot dispense with general definitions altogether. Though they may beg more questions than they answer, they at least introduce us to the movements 'family' and allow us to reflect upon the sorts of characteristics, as well as the divergences and differences, we can expect to find within this family. They raise questions and pose problems, thereby enabling us to begin the process of reflecting upon and analytically dissecting movements. With these purposes in mind I will briefly consider four important definitions. The first is from Blumer:

Social movements can be viewed as collective enterprises seeking to establish a new order of life. They have their inception in a condition of unrest, and derive their motive power on one hand from dissatisfaction with the current form of life, and on the other hand, from wishes and hopes for a new system of living. The career of a social movement depicts the emergence of a new order of life.

(Blumer 1969: 99)

A few points need to be drawn out of this definition. First, Blumer defines movements as '*collective enterprises*', that is to say, they entail social agents working together in various ways, sharing in a common project. Nobody would seriously disagree with this clause of Blumer's definition. As Blumer himself acknowledges, however, many or most phenomena in the social world are collective, such that being so is hardly definitive of movements. To the notion of collective enterprises, therefore, he adds both that movements *emerge out of dissatisfaction with a 'form of life'* and that they *seek to establish a new form of life*. This reference to the establishment of a new form of life is important, assumedly, in order to distinguish movements from forms of collective action, such as panics or mass hysteria, which react to conditions of collective discontent but do not seek to rebuild social life in such a way as to resolve whatever is at the root of this problem. Again, many movement analysts would agree with this clause. The notion that movements arise out of unrest and dissatisfaction, however, at least hints at a central controversy in the literature. Many contemporary movement analysts, as we will soon learn, are very sceptical of the notion that there is a direct link between dissatisfaction and movement emergence. Finally, note Blumer's use of the term '*career*'. This is a central concept in the symbolic interactionist tradition to which he belongs. It indicates that movements follow a temporal trajectory, that they do indeed 'move' or change.

At one level, Blumer's is a very broad and inclusive definition. Both political parties and religious movements may fit within its remit, for example. This accords with some strands in the literature. Certain central papers and studies do focus upon either parties or religious cults (for example, Michels 1949; Snow *et al.* 1980). There are other strands in the literature, however, where movements are sharply differentiated from both religions and parties (for example, Offe 1985; Byrne 1997). From this point of view Blumer's definition would be too inclusive. On the other hand, Blumer's definition seemingly excludes more conservative and reactionary movements from its remit, that is, groups who resist change and attempt to maintain the status quo. At least some work has been done on these types of movements, and the question therefore arises whether Blumer is not too exclusive in his definition. As noted above, there is no correct answer to these questions of exclusiveness and inclusiveness. What is more important is that we appreciate the complexities that are glossed by this seemingly straightforward concept, 'social movements'. We do not need a simple definition of movements if we remain alert to the problems that any such definition would create.

The second definition we can consider comes from Eyerman and Jamison:

> Social movements are . . . best conceived of as temporary public spaces, as moments of collective creation that provide societies with ideas, identities, and even ideals.
>
> (Eyerman and Jamison 1991: 4)

This definition adds at least two further points to that of Blumer. First, it specifies more clearly that movements are *a source of creativity* and that what they tend to create are identities, ideas and even ideals. Second, Eyerman and Jamison make reference to '*public spaces*', a phrase which is more or less equivalent to the notion of a 'public sphere'. This is an interesting and useful clause in the definition as it conjures an image of previously privatized individuals being drawn into a public debate over matters of common concern. It raises certain problems, however, partly because the concept of the public sphere is itself contentious (see Calhoun 1994) and partly because we can imagine esoteric movements and secret societies which are by no means 'public' in the full-blown sense of the word. Indeed, within the environmental movements that Eyerman and Jamison themselves have studied, the role that science has played in defining otherwise often invisible problems has meant that a good deal of debate has been esoteric and relatively inaccessible for the public (Jamison *et al.* 1990; Beck 1992). If we wanted to pick further at Eyerman and Jamison's definition we might question their emphasis upon the temporary nature of movements. This not only raises the inevitable and unanswerable question of how long we mean by 'temporary', it also invites the response that even those movements we still call 'new social movements' (e.g. environmentalism, post-sixties feminism, etc.) are all in their late forties now and hardly seem temporary.

In contrast to the emphasis upon temporariness in Eyerman and Jamison's definition, our third definition, from Tarrow, emphasizes the relative durability of movements:

> Contentious politics occurs when ordinary people, often in league with more influential citizens, join forces in confrontation with elites, authorities and opponents . . . When backed by dense social networks and galvanised by culturally resonant, action-oriented symbols, contentious politics leads to sustained interaction with opponents. The result is the social movement.
>
> (Tarrow 1998: 2)

This identification of '*sustained interaction with opponents*' is intended to distinguish social movements from singular protest events, while also linking them to protest, and thus does not contradict the notion that they might be temporary when judged from a longer term perspective. They exist for a longer duration than the individual protest events in which they engage but not for as long as certain other forms of organization or institution. Duration is not the only noteworthy feature of Tarrow's definition, however. He adds a number of useful points. First, he makes reference to *social networks*, consolidating our sense of the collective nature of movements by specifying how they are collectivized. Moreover, he pushes the notion of the cultural element mentioned by Eyerman and Jamison, in the form of ideas, identities and ideals, by suggesting that these have a *direct function within the context of struggle*. The culture created by movements 'backs' and otherwise 'supports' their struggle. Finally, and somewhat more controversially, he specifies '*elites, authorities and opponents*' who are confronted in struggle. This is a useful clause, in some respects, as it aids our imagination in trying to think about what resistance to 'the status quo' might look like. One can readily visualize movements struggling against real individuals and groups, such as their bosses or the police. However, many contemporary movements struggle against more abstract targets, which are not so easily identified in this way: e.g. 'institutionalized racism' or 'patriarchy'. Such targets are always embodied, often in the behaviour of specific agents, but they do not always assume the form of an 'opponent'. Many contemporary movements involve at least a partial focus upon the complicity of their own participants in unacceptable states of affairs, for example. They attempt to initiate social change by way of self-change. The anti-psychiatry movement of the 1960s, for example, involved psychiatrists turning back upon and criticizing their own role in processes of social control, and attempting to transform their practice (Crossley 1998a). Similarly, black and feminist consciousness raising has focused upon the complicity of women and blacks in their own subordination, building new ways of acting and thinking (Rowbotham 1973). Finally, a strong strand of both the animal rights and environmental movements has identified the way in which changes in ordinary, everyday behaviour can make a strong contribution towards achieving change. The notion of 'opponents' and 'elites' who are opposed should be treated with caution therefore.

This point also problematizes the concept of protest. Do all movements seek to bring about change by way of protest? Is that all that they do? The work of Melucci (1986, 1996) is particularly interesting in relation to this question as he has sought out and explored the manifold 'experiments in living' and alternative forms of practice that so-called 'new social movements' engage in when they are not protesting (see also Crossley 1999b). Movements do much besides and sometimes instead of protesting, Melucci argues, such that protest can be a poor indicator of the life or existence of a movement. Blumer (1969) takes this one step further when he suggests that some movements consist of little more than a 'cultural drift', that is, a discernible and coherent yet decentred and unorganized shift in particular ways of thinking, acting and perceiving. Drifts are 'movements' but they entail no protest. Again, then, although protest is inevitably going to be central in our attempt to make sense of social movements, we must be careful not to pre-empt our understanding of the latter in terms of the former. It is also worth adding here, as Tarrow's definition suggests, that we can have protests without movements, such that our understanding of the latter should not be allowed to pre-empt our attempts to understand the former.

Protest is also central to our final definition. Della Porta and Diani argue that social movements are:

1 informal networks, based on
2 shared beliefs and solidarity, which mobilise about
3 conflictual issues, through
4 the frequent use of various forms of protest.

(Della Porta and Diani 1999: 16)

This definition agrees with that of Tarrow insofar as it highlights networks, protest and conflict. It adds a further point, however, only alluded to by Tarrow, concerning *shared beliefs and solidarity*. At one level this clause of their definition expresses a truism. Members of any movement, in order to qualify as such, must assumedly subscribe to a set of beliefs which are distinct from those of the wider population and sufficiently homogeneous for us to describe them as those of a single movement. Furthermore, those who subscribe to those beliefs must feel some degree of affinity with others who do so, relative to those who don't, at least if they hold those beliefs with any degree of passion. Nevertheless, as the aforementioned notion of public spheres suggests, movements may be sites of argument and internal disagreement. Movement members often disagree and fall out.

It may be responded here that a certain amount of tacit agreement between movement participants is required in order for them to disagree and that this is what marks them out. They must at least agree over what they are in disagreement about. However, the same is true with respect to the relation of the movement to wider society. The arguments which a movement levels at the social order it opposes only have any leverage, insofar as they do, because they assume widely shared assumptions and beliefs. Anti-nuclear protestors, for example, assume that others share their desire to avoid mass destruction and perhaps also their mistrust of political and military elites. Similarly, feminist and black campaigners assume that the wider public aspire to the value of justice and equality. Thus, the sharing of basic assumptions is by no means exclusive to members of a movement, and is always, as in all social relations, a matter of degree. In addition, disagreements within movements can create schisms and conflicts which are no less vehement, and perhaps more so, than that between the movement and the wider society. One need only have been accosted by the members of a specific factional group within a movement and informed to ignore the dogmatism or whatever of another faction to see this. Koopmans

(1993) picks up on this point when he argues that: 'Social movements are characterised by a low degree of institutionalisation, high heterogeneity, a lack of clearly defined boundaries and decision making structures, a volatility matched by few other social phenomena' (Koopmans 1993: 637); and Offe (1985) is similarly suggestive of it when he argues that social movements are condemned to less institutionalized forms of political involvement because they lack the internal homogeneity for them to be able to engage in binding negotiations. Whatever 'leaders' they may have, he notes, have no mandate to talk on behalf of the movement as a whole because they cannot assume that fellow movement activists share their specific perspective on events. This is not to say that solidarity is never evident in movements but to suggest, rather, that we cannot take it for granted as a stable and self-evident feature. To return to Blumer's point, we need to bear in mind that movements are *in movement* and that their characteristics will consequently change.

None of the definitions we have considered is watertight but then we could not expect this. As I have said, social movements share a family resemblance rather than a fixed essence and their definition inevitably rests upon the fuzzy logic of ordinary language use. I hope that my brief discussion of these various definitions has not been in vain, however. Both the definitions discussed and the problems identified with them should have served to bring the issue of social movements alive and into question for us. With this task achieved we can turn to our next question.

Why are social movements important, sociologically?

Though there are doubtless many reasons, I will focus upon three. In the first instance, social movements are extremely prevalent in contemporary western societies. Evidence of their activities is everywhere. Protests are one very obvious example of this. One can seldom open a newspaper or turn on the TV news without being informed of an act of protest somewhere in the world. On the day that I sat down to write this opening chapter, for example, my local radio station was reporting a story of a 24-year-old woman, calling herself 'Fungus', who had climbed naked into a tree in protest at the building of a new airport runway. She had cocooned herself in a large polythene bag and padlocked herself by the neck to the tree because she and her fellow protestors claimed the new runway would destroy the habitat of local wildlife. In a fashion now common among 'eco-warriors', she and her associates had initially resisted the runway by constructing occupied tree-houses and underground tunnels in the path of the workmen who were to clear the ground for the runway, but the residents of this 'protest village' had been evicted by this morning and Fungus's act of defiance was a final symbolic gesture. This is one incident but many others, equally dramatic, were beamed into my home by the media in the same year: e.g. a hunger strike by an imprisoned animal rights activist; the accompanying threat by his colleagues in the Animal Liberation Front that they planned to assassinate ten well-known vivisectionists if he died; a 'Carnival Against Capitalism' which ended in rioting and trapped London's stockmarket traders in their buildings; a series of attacks on fields of genetically modified crops; sabotage of a nuclear submarine; and regular road blockages by truckers protesting at VAT on fuel, which culminated in a week-long blockade of fuel depots that almost brought UK society to a halt.

In addition to protest, movements permeate the smaller crevices of our lifeworld in a multitude of ways. Most social science students, for example, will at some time have confronted the 'nature or nurture?' question in relation to specific aspects of behaviour, such as gender roles. For some this may have seemed like a formal academic exercise but it can hardly have escaped the attention of many that these debates were provoked by the work of feminist writers, that is, writers who belong to a social movement and who have brought their movement concerns to bear in their academic work. Similarly, many students will at one time or another have had to confront the choice of whether to use female or male pronouns in their work, and 'he or she' will be aware that this dilemma has been provoked by the work of feminist authors who have sought to challenge the dominant masculine norm.[1] When writing up some work I have done on mental health movements, to give another example, I was struck at my own uncertainty over what to call my 'subjects'. I could hardly call them 'patients' or 'the mentally ill' when an integral aspect of their struggle had been to shift conceptions of their experiences and behaviours away from such labels. Finally, outside the academy, many of us have cultivated the habits of, for example, taking a portion of our household rubbish to recycling centres, using our cars less or buying an anti-perspirant which does not contain harmful CFC gasses. This is a small gesture but it is one very much shaped by the activities of the environmental movement. Indeed, it is an activity of the environmental movement. Part of the 'movement' in social movements is a transformation in the habits, including linguistic and basic domestic habits, that shape our everyday lives.

This prevalence makes social movements important for sociology because it demonstrates that movements are an important constituent element in the world that we seek to investigate and explain. A science of society and social relations can no more omit to study movements than it could the family, economy or state.

At a more specific level, movements are important because *they are key agents for bringing about change within societies*. Immediately this conjures up an image of revolution or major legislative change. This happens but it is comparatively rare and the kinds of changes movements achieve

---

1 I have tended to opt here for the feminine norm.

are more often local and cultural in nature (McAdam 1994). Movements problematize the ways in which we live our lives and, as noted above, call for changes in our habits of thought, action and interpretation. More to the point, they are, in themselves, manifestations of social change. Societies are not static or stable. They flow. And social movements are key currents within this flow. Not that changes are always intended. Movement actions trigger chains of events which cannot always be foreseen or controlled and they sometimes provoke backlashes and other unintended responses. These processes of change and movement are important from a sociological point of view because the discipline revolves around questions of stability and change: the problem of order and the problem of transformation. Social movements are not the only cause of change – or, for that matter, in the case of conservative movements, order – but it would be foolhardy to ignore them if these issues are of importance to us.

There is another aspect to this question of change. The question of change, particularly change by way of movement politics, is a question about the difference which social agents themselves can make to the various structural dimensions of their life, a question about the form and distribution of power in society and the adequacy and limits of democracy. Social movements are, in effect, natural experiments in power, legitimation and democracy. *Their existence, successes, failures and more generally their dynamics*, though all incredibly difficult to read and interpret, *allow us to gauge the workings of the broader political structures of our society*. This is the third reason why movements are important.

What is the 'sociology' of social movements about?

Social movements, new and old, potentially raise a multitude of questions for sociologists. And as the field of movement analysis has grown more of these questions have been opened up. I could attempt to list these questions but any list would be incomplete. What is more relevant is the principle upon which we determine the issues. This too could be an issue of debate and disagreement but I believe that Neil Smelser speaks for many sociologists when he says:

> [Movements and protests] occur with regularity. They cluster in time; they cluster in certain cultural areas; they occur with greater frequency amongst certain social groupings . . . This skewing in time and place invites explanation: Why do collective episodes occur *where* they do, *when* they do, and *in the ways* they do?
>
> (Smelser 1962: 1)

We could extend this point. Why do certain movements last? Why do some succeed where others fail? Why do some clusters of movements emerge at certain points in time? However, the point is clear enough. The dynamics and properties of social movements or movement clusters are not random, even if their pattern and cause is not obvious, and the point of a sociological analysis is to get beneath the appearance of randomness to reveal the pattern and posit its explanation. This begs our next question.

How do social scientists explain and make sense of social movements?

This is the key question for this book as a whole and I cannot hope to do justice to it in a few paragraphs. However, it would be useful briefly to map out the terrain. For purposes of exposition we can split the field into four camps, divided along two axes (see Figure 1.1). The two columns in Figure 1.1 map out a well-worn distinction between American and European schools of movement analysis. Any attempt to distinguish these two is likely both to offend and to sound over-simplified but for purposes of exposition I suggest the following. The European trajectory has been more firmly framed by the Marxist/Hegelian tradition of the philosophy of history, while the American tradition, if equally indebted to Marx in certain respects, has adopted a more empirical, scientific and, to a degree, empiricist frame.

Even when doggedly empirical, European debates have typically been as much about the constitutive structure and type of society in which modern movements emerge, the relation of those movements to that society and their 'historical role' therein, as they have been about the movements themselves. There has been an assumption that societies centre upon certain key conflicts or contradictions and that these conflicts generate particular movements, perhaps even a singular key movement, which seeks to address them. European scholars have asked, 'What are the key conflicts of our time?' and, 'Who are the parties to them?' In the American literature, by contrast, one finds reference to a vast range of different movements and groups, from the black civil rights movement to Mothers Against Drunk Driving, and

	USA	Europe
Pre-1970s	Collective behaviour	Marxism
1970s onwards	Resource mobilization/ political process	New social movements

Figure 1.1 Four traditions of movement analysis

there is much less concern to pin these movements to the dialectics of history or a specific type of society. Rather, researchers have sought out the specific empirical conditions which facilitate and inhibit the development and flourishing of movements.

The main focus of the recent European literature has been the so-called 'new social movements', that is, the various movements which emerged in western societies in the wake of the 1960s, including environmentalism, the peace movement, second-wave feminism, animal rights, anti-psychiatry, etc. This notion of 'new social movements' is a 'post-Marxist' notion. Much of European political sociology and social theory during the second half of the twentieth century was a debate with Marx about, for example, the likelihood of proletarian revolution, the reasons for its non-materialization, etc. New social movement theories are an outgrowth of this. They entail a view that contemporary western societies have outgrown the model of capitalist society suggested by Marx, rejecting the priority he affords to class struggle and to classes as agents of historical change. New social movement theorists attempt to identify the central conflicts and movements definitive of the new era.

Figure 1.1 maps out a parallel paradigm shift within the American trajectory, from 'collective behaviour' approaches to resource mobilization and political process approaches. Contemporary retrospective accounts of what the collective behaviour approach entailed tend towards a gruesome caricature, reducing the model to little more than a foil for the newer theories. I do not subscribe to this straw model but it has uses so I will briefly outline it. According to many contemporary accounts (e.g. Oberschall 1973; Tilly 1978; McAdam 1982; Jenkins 1983; McAdam et al. 1988), the collective behaviour approach:

- portrays movement emergence as a reflex response to 'grievances', deprivations', 'anomie', 'structural strains' or other such forms of hardship. The stereotypical collective behaviour theorist believes that objective hardships are both a necessary and a sufficient cause of protest and movement formation;
- portrays the protests and movements triggered by these hardships as irrational psychological responses; manifestations of 'mob psychology' or collective hysteria;
- portrays those who become involved in these 'mobs' as (previously) isolated individuals who are often not very well integrated into society;
- lumps social movements together with other assorted forms of 'collective behaviour', such as fashions, crazes and panics, without any due consideration for their distinctness and properly 'political' nature.

Following Tilly's (1978) lead, many critics of the collective behaviour approach seem to view it as Durkheimian in inspiration, given Durkheim's interest in both collective psychology and the causes and consequences of anomie. There has therefore been a fair degree of Durkheim bashing in the more recent literature.

The critique of this straw model of collective behaviour theory has been multifaceted. On one hand it has involved straightforward empirical refutation. Many studies have shown, for example, that objective increases in hardship do not lead to increases in protest or movement activity (e.g. Snyder and Tilly 1972). Indeed, protests very often seem to increase during periods of reform and economic upturn (Eisinger 1973). In a more theoretical vein, this observation has been bolstered by the claim that strains and conflicts are a constant factor in social life and, as such, cannot explain protests and movements, which are variable in their rates of both occurrence and intensity. For example, there were structural conflicts and tensions between blacks and whites in the USA long before the rise of the civil rights movement. In addition, it is noted that studies have failed to show that movements recruit from the less well integrated members of society. On the contrary, movements often seem to form around pre-existing networks. The black civil rights movement in the USA formed around and out of the black churches, for example. In a different vein, theorists have challenged the tendency to view movement behaviour and beliefs as 'irrational'. Against this it is argued that we can only understand movement activity if we assume the behaviour of activists to be rational. This point hints at a further source of disagreement with the collective behaviour approach, which is more normative in orientation. The new American paradigm of movement theory emerged, like new social movement theories, in the wake of the struggles of the 1960s, and many of its advocates had taken part in those struggles. They therefore tend to have a sympathetic attitude towards movements and want to develop theories which are helpful to them and do not brand them as strange or irrational.

The emergence of the new replacement paradigm has come in a number of stages. Early developments tended to centre upon two key elements. First, a rational actor model of the social agent was appropriated, along with an economistic focus upon exchange relations in social life and the effects of the movement of resources between agents. Second, a structural 'network' model of social relations and social life was adopted. With these elements movement theorists from within the 'resource mobilization' approach were able to examine the balance of costs, rewards and incentives that provided agents with the motivation to become involved in struggle, and they were able to focus upon the block mobilization of whole communities. Many features of this resource mobilization approach have persisted in American movement analysis but by the 1980s they had been added to by a consideration of the ways in which political systems and processes variously open up and close down opportunities for protest, thereby affecting the flow of activism itself. Rational actors, it was argued, will tend to act when the opportunities for doing so effectively are greatest. This insight has provided the basis for a later development of the new paradigm, sometimes referred to as the political process approach.

The political process approach itself has undergone some degree of change too, however, in recent years. Many of its advocates have noted its neglect of such issues as identity, emotion, culture and various social–psychological factors. Thus the new paradigm has seemingly entered a third phase, focused upon these particular issues. Some writers have portrayed this as a dialogue between the American paradigm and the new social movements paradigm from Europe. That paradigm too focuses upon identity and culture. However, it is as true to say that this third phase of the new American paradigm involves a partial return to some of the more fruitful themes and issues of the collective behaviour approach. The repressed is returning.

The argument and plan of this book

One of the main tasks of this book is to provide a relatively clear introduction to the field of movements analysis. I will be going over the positions and developments discussed above, in detail. However, introduction and exposition are only one half of the picture. I also intend to use the book to advance a number of claims about movement theory and to make a contribution to it. My position is summed up in Chapter 9, but a few pointers would be instructive at this stage. In the first instance I seek to contribute to the growing body of criticism directed at the 'new' American paradigm. I have three broad lines of critique, each centred upon rational actor theory (RAT). The first concerns its intrinsic plausibility. There is something undeniable and very attractive about RAT. Social agents do, for the most part, pursue specific goals in a purposive manner, avoiding unnecessary costs and, where possible, maximizing their gains. Furthermore, recognizing this opens the door for a systematic and predictive approach to explanatory theory. Having said that, one would be hard pushed to find a social theory which denied this. Most theories make some such claim or presupposition. What distinguishes RAT is a range of more problematic assumptions which frame this claim. I identify and critique these assumptions in Chapter 4.

My second key criticism is that the minimalism of the RAT model precludes many important issues from analysis, including the origin and distribution of preferences, movement identities and culture, and the role of emotion. Rational actor theory is not capable of addressing these issues and recommends that we do not clutter our analysis with them. Such minimalism can have advantages. It is attractive because it promises parsimony and prediction. In the final analysis, however, it proves too minimal to explain anything; it requires us to ignore a great deal of empirical and phenomenological data; and it ultimately has to become quite convoluted to address even the simplest of questions.

Although some theories of movements have been affected by these problems of rational choice theory, many have recognized them and sought to correct them. However, this has created a third problem. In seeking to compensate for the deficiencies of rational choice theory, movement analysts have tended to violate the 'sacred' assumptions of the approach, thereby leaving themselves in an ambiguous and unspecified theoretical limbo, somewhere between RAT and a more adequate sociological model. One cannot modify RAT without abandoning it, in my view, and as I have no equivocation about abandoning it this is what I suggest that we do.

One of the key emphases of the new American paradigm has been 'structure'. In practice this has translated variously as 'network' and as 'structure of political opportunities', a reflection upon the institutional political arrangements in society which variously facilitate and constrain political activity. These ideas are important but it is my contention that they entail a very thin notion of 'structure' and that they fail to connect with broader and wider conceptions of *the* structure of society. There are two very clear senses in which this is so. First, the emphasis of much of the research in the tradition is on political structures, narrowly defined, to the detriment of a proper consideration of other structural fields of society or, more broadly, of the differentiated nature of contemporary societies. While many of the more recent writers in the paradigm acknowledge the importance of the media, for example, they fail to reflect upon the fact that the media field is a distinct and relatively autonomous social field with its own 'rules', dynamics, agents, rhythms, etc. For this reason it has tended to be overlooked that political opportunity structures are but one set of opportunity structures for movements, alongside media structures and also, of course, legal, academic and many other types of structure. I attempt to remedy this problem, in the book, by reference to Bourdieu's concept of social fields (see below). Second, the new paradigm, on account of its critique of the collective behaviour approach, has tended to demonize the issue of stresses and grievances to the point where it has had very little to say with regard to them at all. This is problematic on a number of levels but most particularly because it detracts attention away from the underlying structural patterns of society which give rise to specific sorts of movements at specific times. In fact, it has seemingly detracted attention away from any such deeper notion of social structure and any attempt to link movement formation to the 'contradictions', 'stresses' or 'conflicts' generated by a particular societal type. The theorists of new social movements, whether wrong or right in their claims, represent an important corrective to this and I explore their work, in Chapter 8, as a way of demonstrating this. The central claim of the new social movements theorists is that societies of the post 1960s era have entered a new stage of development in their history in which the contradictions which dogged earlier eras have been displaced into new forms of conflict.

It is also my intention, in this book, to open up the space for a possible re-evaluation of the collective behaviour approach. It will be apparent that I am not persuaded by the straw model of collective behaviour described above. There are many collective behaviour approaches and by no means all of them are guilty as charged. More to the point, some still have a great deal to offer movement theory. In particular I believe that Smelser's 'value-added' model of movement emergence provides the most adequate frame by which to think of the various interconnecting conditions which lead to movement emergence. I also believe that Blumer's account of 'social unrest' and movement formation offers a strong starting place for thinking about questions of movement culture, identity, emotion, and their various connections to purposive social action. Finally, I offer a reassessment of Durkheim. Tilly (1978) claims to find no use for Durkheim in his attempts to make sense of protest and many have toed this line, never uttering the 'D word' except in contempt. It is surprising, however, just how many Durkheimian notions, unacknowledged as such, seem to have found a place within contemporary debates. Concerns with solidarity and collective identity have a very obvious Durkheimian feel, for example, while, as Barker (1999) has noted, the new and important concept of 'cycles of contention', which identifies those creative periods in history when conflict 'speeds up' and new political actors and themes emerge, bears more than a superficial resemblance to Durkheim's ([1912] 1915, [1924] 1974) 'collective effervescence'. Durkheim has been read very one-sidedly in social movement theory, as a prophet of anomie and social disintegration. This book seeks, albeit in small measure, to draw out his other side and thereby to reveal his considerable potential for movement analysis.

In addition to reviving these old figures, I seek to draw in the ideas of a more recent social theorist: Pierre Bourdieu. The origin of this aspect of my argument, if I am honest, is partly accidental. My own first attempts at empirical research in the movements field, on anti-psychiatric and mental health movements, were conducted at a time when I was far more familiar with Bourdieu's theories than those outlined in this book, hence my own way of thinking about movements tended to follow the path that his theory laid out. Notwithstanding this accident of birth, however, having caught up with movement theory I remain convinced that Bourdieu's framework has much to offer movement analysis. Indeed, it is my contention that, though Bourdieu seldom deals directly with the issue of movements, his theory of practice provides the most fruitful conceptual framework for anchoring the sociology of social movements and allows us to overcome many of the key problems that are evident in the more usual approaches. A Bourdieu-inspired approach to movement analysis has much to learn from the other major movement perspectives, and it is my intention to draw out just exactly what that is, but it offers a much more cogent and coherent theoretical starting place for movement analysis than these other perspectives, and I intend to show that too.

I examine Bourdieu's work in the final chapter of the book, having discussed the various alternatives in the chapters which precede it. My aim, in this final chapter, is twofold and has a twofold bearing on the arguments elsewhere in the book. First, I argue in that chapter that a great many of the problems of the various other theories discussed in the book revolve around questions of agency and structure, and I suggest that Bourdieu offers us a framework for resolving these problems. In this respect Bourdieu's work is posited as a solution to persistent theoretical problems in the movements field. However, second, I argue that Bourdieu's own work on movements manifests many of the problems which movement theories have identified and criticized, and I thus argue the case for improving Bourdieu's own account of movements through an incorporation of many of the ideas discussed earlier in the book. Thus, while Bourdieu's approach may suffice to ground movement analysis, it must also be prepared to learn from it. This is not merely a matter of improving on Bourdieu, however. What I also seek to show in the final chapter is that Bourdieu's relatively simple theoretical framework allows us to pull together a range of scattered insights that we will have encountered in the main body of the book, into a persuasive, parsimonious and coherent perspective. By centring my conclusion on Bourdieu, in other words, and building what for the sake of argument we can call a 'Bourdieuian' approach to social movement analysis, I seek to pull together the many insights of movement analysis discussed elsewhere in the book, without lapsing into an unhelpful and incoherent eclectic mishmash. I use Bourdieu's theory of practice to give structure to the diverse insights I want to hold on to. There is a real danger in 'post-RAT' movement analysis that theory will give way to eclecticism and empiricism (i.e. the bundling together of interesting empirical observations) and I hope to pre-empt this by way of Bourdieu.

The chapter plan for the book is as follows. Chapters 2 and 3 focus upon two of the main advocates of the collective behaviour approach: Herbert Blumer and Neil Smelser. I am critical of both but argue that each has an invaluable contribution to make to contemporary thought about movements, which has been overlooked. This is followed by four chapters which explore various aspects of the new American paradigm. I start, in Chapter 4, with a discussion of RAT and its 'collective action problem'. Then, in Chapters 5 and 6, I discuss the basic ideas of the resource mobilization and political process approaches. Finally, in Chapter 7, I consider three very important concepts which have come out of this approach: 'repertoires of contention', 'frames' and 'cycles of contention'. This gives the book a very American bias. In Chapter 8, however, I offer a sustained engagement with one key version of new social movements theory, that of Jurgen Habermas (1987), in an effort to bring the concerns and issues of the European schools of movement analysis more squarely into the picture. The details of the final chapter of the book, Chapter 9, have already been discussed.

chapter two

Social unrest, movement culture and identity: the symbolic interactionists

In this chapter I outline and assess Herbert Blumer's (1969) theory of social movements. This theory belongs to the 'collective behaviour' (CB) camp of movement theory, referred to in my Introduction, and it is often cited in the blanket condemnations that approach receives in the contemporary literature. In my evaluation I will suggest that there is, indeed, much that is problematic in Blumer's account but I will also attempt to draw out some valuable insights that have been buried by critiques of CB. In particular Blumer's account raises important issues relating to identity, meaning and culture within social movements, which, having been neglected in the work of the critics of CB, are now re-emerging as central issues in and for movement analysis. More to the point, Blumer offers us a solid and insightful basis for thinking about these issues which is still superior, in many respects, to those advocated in the more recent literature. His work deserves a re-evaluation and it is my intention to do just this.

Blumer's work is rooted in the perspective of G.H. Mead (1967). Many critiques of his work within the social movements literature fail to recognize this and, as a consequence, do his work an injustice. I hope to right that wrong here by beginning with a reasonably detailed, if brief, overview of the main tenets of Mead's approach (see also Joas 1985; Crossley 1996, 2001c). Having done this I spend two sections of the chapter examining Blumer's account of social movements and their formation. Finally, I offer a critical evaluation of the contribution which Blumer's account can make to a contemporary analysis of social movements.

Mead and symbolic interactionism

Mead's work engages with a number of important sources, including the works of Hegel, Kant, Dewey, James and Darwin (Joas 1985; Honneth 1995). However, for our purposes his critique of psychological behaviourism is the most fruitful point of departure. Behaviourism sought to refocus psychology. It opposed the dualism which conceives of an immaterial 'mind', distinct and separate from the physical body. Psychological life is the life of the body, the behaviourists argued. It consists in embodied behaviours. Furthermore, they sought to explain human behaviour in terms of basic *physical* causation. Behaviour, they argued, is a mechanical–physical response caused by fixed *physical* stimuli. Indeed all behaviour is rooted in a complex of reflex actions, such as the knee-jerk reaction which straightens an individual's bent leg when the leg is tapped, below the knee, on the patella tendon. Some reflexes, behaviourists argued, are innate, particularly the more fundamental ones. But these 'hard wired' reflexes form a basis upon which new stimulus–response pathways can be forged, by way of learning or 'conditioning', thus giving rise to a range of acquired reflexes.

Mead shares the behaviourist's critique of dualism. He too seeks to locate psychological life and agency at the level of embodied behaviour (or praxis). However, his conception of behaviour is radically different to that of the behaviourists. He has two immediate criticisms of their stimulus–response model of behaviour (see also Dewey 1896). On one hand, dealing with the response side of the equation, he notes that whatever identity may be discerned in an individual's repeated responses to a fixed stimulus is an identity of *purpose*, not, as behaviourism suggests, of mechanical *movement*. The same stimulus very rarely elicits the same mechanical movement, he observes. What *may* remain constant across situations is the end towards which a response is oriented, its meaning or purpose. Every time the phone rings, for example, I answer it. My response is 'the same' in that respect. But what that entails *physically* will vary markedly across situations depending upon where and how I am located relative to the phone. In strictly physical and mechanical terms my actions will, contrary to what behaviourism must predict, vary widely. This reveals that behaviour is, at the very least, a purposive or goal-oriented 'reply' to a stimulus rather than a mechanical reflex response.

Similarly, from the 'stimulus' side of the equation, Mead notes that identical stimuli can occasion quite different 'replies' according to the context in which they are presented and the current activities of the agent to whom they are presented. This indicates, for Mead, that it is *not the physical properties* of the stimuli which bring about any given effect, but rather their *meaning* and the level of priority they may claim in relation to the on-going activities and interests of the agent. The same stimuli may mean something very different, according to the context in which they are presented and what the agent is otherwise doing, and, as a consequence, may call for a very different reply. If the phone rings in the middle of the night or following a job interview, for example, its effect upon me and the way I react to it will be quite different to the routine daytime call. It 'means' something different because of the time at which it occurs, and provokes a different reaction from me, even though it is physically identical to any other instance of ringing from the same phone.

It follows from this that if we want to understand how agents act in a particular situation, it is insufficient for us to take an outside perspective upon the 'objective' situation (or stimulation) they are in. We must consider the meaning which the situation has for them or, as some interactionists put it, the way in which they 'define their situation'. And we must view their action as a meaningful and purposive 'reply' to the meaning of that situation; that is, an element in an interaction.

The 'meanings' to which Mead refers in this context may operate at a very basic level of perception. Human beings are disposed towards 'typification', which allows natural objects to become meaningful symbols or signs: thunder may come to mean the imminence of rain, for example, while large footprints may signify the possible presence of a large animal and thus danger. Mead is particularly concerned, however, with the higher level symbolic systems which human agents have collectively constructed within the context of communal life, giving rise to a 'virtual reality' of symbolic culture within the very heart of the natural world. Such symbolic systems are, of course, embodied and depend upon the biological capacities of the species. And yet they spread a new layer of meaning over the world which is often quite independent of any natural exigencies. There are many such 'sign systems' in the human world, as pioneers of semiotics, such as Roland Barthes (1973), have demonstrated admirably. Mead focuses particularly upon language, however. The human world, in his view, is a linguistically constituted world.

Innovation, communication and habit

Mead identifies a dual tendency within behaviour: sometimes towards creation and innovation, other times towards conservation and habituation (see also Dewey [1922] 1988). Innovation and modification are common, but not so common that they are denied the chance to sediment in the form of habits, that is, flexible and intelligent dispositions which constitute the necessary background for characteristically human ways of perceiving and acting in the world:

> Our past stays with us in terms of those changes which have resulted from our experience and which are in some sense registered there. The peculiar intelligence of the human form lies in this elaborate control

gained through the past. The human animal's past is constantly present in the facility with which he acts . . .

(Mead 1967: 116)

This is complemented by physical transformation of the natural world, which endows aspects of it with a use, symbolic meaning and often an exchange value also. Thus, human behaviour or praxis creates a 'world' which it then inhabits, a world of both physical artefacts and symbolic meanings. However, this is not an individual matter. Human life is group life and human action is generally social interaction. The process of world building, in this respect, is a collective and collaborative venture achieved through human interaction. Individual habits find a corollary in shared cultures and traditions.

What Mead means by interaction, in this context, is very broad. The behaviour of another person may communicate to me and thereby affect my behaviour without their even being aware of my existence. However, much interaction is both linguistic and mutually oriented towards. Mead puts a special emphasis upon such 'symbolic' forms of interaction. Symbolic interaction is special for two reasons. First, the versatility and power of language as a communicative system, not to mention its shared nature, enables, encourages and even necessitates that agents form collective definitions of the situations they are in and collective plans for action. In this way social situations and the social world are collectively constructed. Second, the use of symbols not only facilitates communication between agents, but actually generates a situation in which agents communicate back to themselves. They hear or read their own utterances and in this way become aware of their own thoughts. Moreover, having spoken to themselves they are inclined to reply. In this way agents assume a dialogical relationship to themselves and it is this dialogical relationship which is definitive of the reflective intelligence of human beings, in Mead's view. Our capacity and tendency to 'talk', either to ourselves or to others, is the basis of our capacity to reflect, plan, make decisions, etc.

At one level Mead views self-interaction as a 'complication' of group interaction; agents interact simultaneously with both self and other. They respond both to the other and to their own previous actions and communications. He also elaborates the notion, however, so as to include situations where individuals simply interact with themselves. When they make a solitary decision, for example, they will 'discuss' the pros and cons of various ways of acting to themselves, as if debating them with others. This, moreover, amounts to a form of 'self-stimulation'. The formulation of a decision, as Mead conceives of it, is effectively a way in which agents act upon themselves and thereby 'cause' themselves to act in a particular way.

This is not quite so solitary as it may at first appear. To dialogue with themselves, agents must have acquired language: language is the vehicle of dialogue. And language is a social structure which embodies the forms of practical consciousness of the society which has given birth to it. When individuals speak and think they do so by way of the (linguistic) tools of thought forged by their ancestors. Furthermore, Mead adds that agents must have learned, in early life, to substitute certain immediate responses to a situation with a linguistic formulation. They must have acquired the habit of formulating courses of action in words before acting, so that the process of reflection can take place. This is another respect in which the capacity for solitary thought presupposes collective social experience, as the disposition towards linguistic substitution, like the capacity to speak itself, is acquired through social interaction. More importantly, however, Mead argues that to dialogue with themselves, agents must assume the 'role' of another person. When individuals dialogue with themselves, he argues, they reply to themselves as other people they know would reply. In the absence of a parent who might point out the folly of a proposed course of action, for example, they point it out to themselves in the manner of the parent. And they learn to do this by actually acting out roles, particularly the roles of 'significant others', in early childhood. Through imaginative role-play they incorporate the role of other people within their habitual behavioural repertoire, at a most fundamental level. And they continue to replay those roles to themselves, throughout their lives. This is enhanced later when children begin to play games. Through this process children learn to take the role of the 'generalized other', that is, the view of the (or a) community as a whole. They learn to view their actions from the point of view of the team, the rules and the very structure of 'the game' itself. In the context of a solitary decision, therefore, agents bring the perspective of others to bear upon their own utterances, and perhaps even the perspective of the whole community.

Self

What Mead is discussing here is the process whereby an agent becomes self-conscious. Initially, he argues, human agents are conscious only of the world around them. We are not self-aware. This is our fundamental state and an element of it, which Mead designates with the label 'I', always remains. Through interaction with others, however, and specifically the incorporation of their roles, the I learns to turn back upon itself and to form a conception of itself, which Mead terms 'me'. I and me do not coincide. The me is an image of itself which the I constructs retrospectively, and if the I should attempt to catch up with itself it would be like a dog chasing its own tail – it would never catch up with itself for the simple reason that the most penetrating act of self-reflection always necessarily excludes itself from reflection. The relationship of I to me does constitute a form of self-consciousness, however, and, as such, it has important implications which we must briefly outline.

At one level Mead believes that self-consciousness is a form of social control which makes society possible. The ability to reflect upon one's actions and to bring the perspective (e.g. norms, beliefs and values) of one's community to bear upon one's actions and decisions is a basic prerequisite for social integration and harmony. Agents reflexively monitor and police their own actions, from the point of view of the community. Moreover, this is a prerequisite of moral life. The capacity for 'taking the role of the other' and seeing the world in the way others do is integral to the 'mutual recognition' and 'categorical imperative' which Hegel ([1807] 1979) and Kant ([1788] 1975, [1785] 1995) respectively associate with the moral community (see also Habermas 1992; Honneth 1995). Morality, for both of these philosophers, involves individuals transcending their own particularity and accepting their place within a community as a part of that community, and this is exactly what taking the role of the other, particularly the generalized other, entails.

However, Mead does not understand conformity to social norms, nor indeed the validity of social norms themselves, in a 'culturally dopey' fashion. Norms, like any other aspect of tradition or culture, are the product of the generative praxes of the members of the community they regulate and shape, he argues. Specifically they are constructed through communicative processes of argument and debate. This entails both that they can and do change, and that they claim a legitimacy which can always, potentially, be contested. Blumer picks up this point in his writing, particularly his work on 'public opinion' and 'publics'. He emphasizes the inherent 'communicative' rationality of the process whereby norms are generated, debated and legitimated:

> . . . the very process of controversial discussion forces a certain amount of rational consideration and . . . the resulting collective opinion has a rational character. The fact that contentions have to be defended and justified and opposing contentions criticised and shown to be untenable, involves evaluation, weighing and judgement.
>
> (Blumer 1969: 93)

In other words, communication and argument impose a degree of rigour upon deliberations as they demand that agents respond to and/or anticipate the objections, alternatives and criticisms of their interlocuters, and, indeed, that they both seek out mutually agreeable premises upon which to construct their case and work logically from those premises. Such 'publics' form in diverse locations throughout the social formation, according to Blumer, and in relation to a wide range of concerns – indeed anywhere, potentially, where human agents have interests.

Mead (1967) adds to this that norms can only be deemed rational and legitimate insofar as they emerge out of a process of rational debate within a community, wherein all parties likely to be affected by them are included and, in the final instance, are persuaded of them. Arguing against Kant ([1788] 1975, [1785] 1995), who conceives of the formulation of moral law in monological terms, he argues that the claim to rationality and universality which any norm or moral law necessarily makes can only be accepted insofar as it has survived the test of critical dialogue. This argument, which is a precursor of Habermas's (1987, 1991, 1992) important work on 'discourse ethics' and 'communicative rationality', is a moral argument and should not be confused with any empirical claim that social norms are, in fact, the outcome of free and open argument. Mead and Blumer are both acutely aware that social norms, in practice, emerge out of situations of domination and conflict and may, as such, reflect the interests of dominant groups.

The second key element to come out of Mead's reflections on self-consciousness concerns the issue of identity or 'self'. The process whereby the I reflexively turns back upon itself, giving rise to a me, is constitutive of a sense of self or identity. Moreover, it is a sense which is built up through the life-course and particularly through interaction with others. Despite our capacity to turn back upon ourselves, Mead argues, we still remain very much our own blind spot. Like the eye, the I looks outwards onto the world and does not see itself. In our interactions with others, however, an image of our self is reflected back to us, affording us a basis for constructing an image of self. The way others address us and respond to us 'positions' us in a particular way and communicates to us, often tacitly and indirectly, how they view us. These communications are the basic experiences out of which we construct a sense of self or identity.

Selfhood is important, for Mead, for a multitude of reasons. What is most important for our purposes here is that the concept and evaluation of themselves that agents form, their sense of 'me', plays a crucial mediating role in shaping their specific projects and actions. An agent who views herself as 'weak', for example, may be less inclined to engage in those activities she imagines to involve 'strength' than an agent who deems herself 'strong'. The corollary of this, of course, is that changes in an individual's sense of self or identity may bring about changes in her behaviour.

Blumer, social unrest and elementary behaviour

These ideas regarding meaning, self, interaction, etc., form the basis of what Blumer (1986) labels 'symbolic interactionism'. He extends and uses them to develop an empirically engaged sociology. Our main concern is with the way he develops these ideas in terms of social movement analysis. His point of departure is the concept of 'collective behaviour'. All of symbolic interactionism is about 'collective behaviour', for Blumer, and all that sociology is interested in is collective behaviour. The social world is collective behaviour. He draws a distinction, however, between this generic sense of 'collective behaviour' and the sense usually associated with the study of social movements. Much of sociology is concerned with the established social order, he notes; with pre-existing social norms, values and institutions. Sociologists of social movements, by contrast, are interested in the manner in which such social orders give way or topple and are replaced or re-formed. They are concerned with those processes in social life where new forms of life and norms emerge:

> . . . sociology is interested in studying the social order and its constituents (customs, rules, institutions etc.) as they are; collective behaviour is concerned in studying the ways in which the social order comes into existence, in the sense of the emergence and solidification of new forms of collective behaviour.

> (Blumer 1969: 69)

His analysis of this process comes in three stages. First he discusses the condition of 'social unrest' and the various forms of 'elementary collective behaviour' it gives rise to. This, in effect, is an account of the way in which specific social orders begin to break down or become strained and thereby primed for change. Next he discusses a range of 'elementary collective groupings' which comprise the social order and out of which movements calling for change and resistance may emerge. Finally he discusses social movements. They emerge out of situations of social unrest, constituting a positive force for change. It is necessary, if we are to grasp Blumer's approach, for us to take each of these three stages of his analysis in turn. I will begin with 'social unrest'.

Social unrest

Following Mead, Blumer maintains that social action and interaction are ordinarily mediated and (socially) controlled by way of self-consciousness. Agents assume the role of the other towards themselves and thereby monitor and govern their own conduct. Moreover, as their capacity to do this is based upon an incorporation of the role of generalized and specific others, the way in which they monitor their own conduct is generally in accord with wider societal norms and values – albeit norms and values which are the product of human interaction and which can be remade by them. There is a double edge to this point. On one hand, Blumer emphasizes the conscious control that agents bring to bear upon their action and the 'distance' which this puts between them and both other people and their situation of action. Impulsive responses are largely kept under check. On the other hand, much of this happens habitually, without thought, and rests upon a bedrock of assumptions and norms which are taken for granted, again by force of habit. This can be sustained, according to Blumer, as long as interactions 'hang together' as all parties to them expect, that is, as long as things turn out as they are supposed to, everybody does what they are expected to and achievements, both mundane and extraordinary, are rewarded 'appropriately'. If these conditions are not met, however, situations become strained and the normal form of the social act and of social interaction loses the support it ordinarily finds within its environment. It becomes increasingly more difficult to plan and reflexively monitor (inter)actions since the environment of those (inter)actions has become unpredictable and confounds the usual expectations and routines. This gives rise to a (re-)emergence of more 'elementary' forms of social behaviour and interaction. In particular the aforementioned distance and self-consciousness in social relationships begins to break down, taking with it the social/self-control mechanism it entails. The normal 'rules of the game' cease to exert the same influence over conduct and the 'weight' of certain habits of thought and action is lifted.

Blumer maintains that the 'strains' which trigger this process are dependent upon subjective expectation and interpretation. Agents may live in objectively stressful, unjust or disadvantageous situations for any period of time, so long as they do not perceive their situation as such. Moreover, dissatisfaction can arise as much from a shift in expectations as from an objective decrease in standards of living. What is acceptable today may not be so tomorrow if expectations are raised. Whatever the source of strains, however, Blumer's key concern is that they give rise to social unrest. Behaviour, he argues, becomes dislocated and unstable. Emotions are heightened or excited. This may be manifest in different ways, from states of collective apathy and despair to states of aggression or enthusiasm, and these states may give rise to an equally varied range of projects, including, importantly, the formation of social movements which aim to change the status quo. We will consider social movements shortly. First, however, we consider the important behavioural shift which, in Blumer's view, is involved in social unrest: the emergence of 'elementary behaviour'.

Elementary behaviour

The three main forms of behaviour to which Blumer refers in this context are 'milling', 'collective excitement' and 'social contagion'. Each of these forms consists of the same basic ingredients, but each, as presented in the order above, is a more intense and 'speeded up' version of the one which precedes it. It is these elementary forms of collective behaviour which are the most likely features of Blumer's approach to enrage the critic of the collective behaviour approach. Their names invoke an image of irrational crowd behaviour. However, we should not take Blumer's unfortunate turns of phrase too literally. We need to look behind his labels to the important processes he is attempting to describe. What he is attempting to capture by these terms is a process whereby the privatization and individualization of selfhood, supported by a self-controlling self-consciousness, gives way to a more immediate form of social interaction and what he calls a 'rapport' between agents. He is attempting to capture the sense in which the inhibition which self-consciousness introduces into interaction gives way. Interlocutors become more responsive to one another and are drawn more deeply into the dynamic of interaction, such that they are more influenced by it:

> This may be viewed as a lowering of social resistance brought about by the fact that they suffer some loss of self-consciousness and, accordingly, of ability to interpret the activity of others. Self-consciousness is a means of barricading oneself against the influence of others, for with it the individual checks his immediate, natural responses and impulses, and makes judgements before acting.
>
> (Blumer 1969: 77)

With their interpretative defences down, interlocutors are more readily affected, in an immediate way, by the actions of others. Interaction speeds up and becomes more dynamic, unpredictable and creative. In addition an ever wider circle of agents are drawn into this, not least because it is difficult to maintain one's own inhibition and distance when others have lost theirs. This emotional and excited form of interaction exerts a powerful lure upon 'outsiders', drawing them in. It communicates at the level of basic gestural emotions which bypass the censor of reflective consciousness and the critical faculties which filter communicated ideas. Interactions are still primarily linguistic, of course, whatever other gestural significations they may entail, but the process of linguistic interaction is less reflectively managed, such that the course which an interaction may take is unpredictable for its participants and they find themselves saying and thinking things which they have never said or thought before.

These elementary forms of interaction are both degenerate and generative for Blumer. With the loss of some degree of self-consciousness goes the loss of some degree of social control and thus the grip of certain norms, roles and customs. Society's structure is thrown into flux. At the same time, however, these freed-up interactions remain ordered, albeit in a more basic sense, and are generative of new social forms and identities which may themselves 'sediment' into new traditions, norms, roles, etc. Elementary interactions, being freed of the inhibitions of self-consciousness and its controlling and conservative force, are creative and productive. As such they are precisely the preconditions for the emergence of various forms of collective behaviour. New dynamics and patterns emerge which are motors of social change.

Collective effervescence

The processes Blumer is describing bear a striking resemblance to those identified by Durkheim ([1912] 1915, [1924] 1974) in his various accounts of 'collective effervescence'. Human beings always live within groups or networks, Durkheim argues, but most of the time we enjoy a degree of distance from the group, to pursue our own private ends. Most action is social interaction and all interaction is normatively organized but interaction is not so intense, at least when compared with situations of collective effervescence. During these periods social interactions 'speed up' and become more intense. Individuals become less privatized in orientation and more focused upon collective activities, identities and goals.

Collective effervescence is most often associated, in the literature, with Durkheim's ([1912] 1915) account of the religious ceremonies of aboriginal cults, as presented in *The Elementary Forms of Religious Life*. As such it tends to be conceived of as a conservative process. The ceremonies of the cults function to regenerate the collective sentiments and identities which hold them together, their *esprit de corps*. Durkheim also uses this concept to make sense of the emergence of currents of social change, however, and he applies it to modern, secular contexts, including the French revolution (Durkheim [1912] 1915), the Reformation, the Renaissance and the birth of socialism (Durkheim [1924] 1974). If collective effervescence serves a conservative function, for Durkheim, this is only insofar as it has been preceded by an earlier more creative instance of effervescence which it effectively returns to. The creative moment is repeated and its 'products', the symbols and narratives of the group created by it, are celebrated.

The notion of collective effervescence is useful, in my view, as it refocuses our analytic gaze away from the intimations of crude crowd psychology that periodically surface in Blumer's account. Durkheim's examples, such as the Reformation, invoke an image of protracted periods of intellectual and social generation, far removed from a spot of 'crowd trouble'. Nevertheless, I suggest that Blumer and Durkheim are essentially attempting to capture the same thing in their accounts. Each is attempting to draw our attention to periods of time when certain of the rules of social life are either changed or suspended, giving rise to new and generative patterns of interaction which transform certain aspects of society or introduce currents of change into it. As we shall see, Blumer also shares Durkheim's sense of the importance of collective sentiments, rituals and symbols which are both created by and then conserved through these effervescent modes of action. It is Blumer, however, who explicitly ties these ideas into a theory of social movements.

Elementary groups

Having discussed elementary forms of collective behaviour, Blumer goes on to describe various elementary groupings within which such behaviours occur, specifically:

- a crowd (including casual, conventionalized, acting and expressive crowds);
- a mass;
- a public.

Crowds entail conditions where agents are in physically close and unobstructed proximity and where they are highly concentrated and dense. Agents may have relatively little to do with one another, as when commonly observing an event, such as street theatre (a casual crowd), or participating in an organized collective event, such as being spectators at a football match (a conventional crowd). By way of the elementary forms of behaviour, however, a crowd may become concerted in an effort to achieve certain ends (an acting crowd) or perhaps simply to enjoy and express themselves collectively (an expressive crowd). A mass, by contrast, is effectively a collective of individuals who each act as individuals but under the influence of a commonly shared reference point to which they have simultaneous access. The mass media, which beam the same message simultaneously into the houses of millions of individuated beings, provoking similar actions from those beings, is one example of this. The third group, 'a public', is a group who *come together*, having previously not been in interaction, to discuss an issue of common concern, over which they do not agree. It is a site of rational (in the aforementioned sense) argumentation and debate and conforms to what certain political philosophers refer to as a 'public sphere' (Arendt 1958; Habermas 1989a).

Social movements

Blumer is not entirely clear where social movements fit in this typology of collective groupings. However, he is clear that social movements emerge out of 'a condition of unrest' and that, in their initial stages of formation, they manifest many of the elements of elementary collective behaviour we have discussed. His major concern is with the manner in which these elementary forms of behaviour give rise to a durable and sustainable movement for change:

> In its beginning, a social movement is amorphous, poorly organised, and without form; the collective behaviour is on a primitive level that we have already discussed, and the mechanisms of interaction are the elementary spontaneous mechanisms of which we have spoken.
>
> (Blumer 1969: 99)

But, he continues,

> As a social movement develops, it takes on the character of a society. It acquires organisation and form, a body of customs and traditions, established leadership, an enduring division of labour, social rules and

social values – in short, a culture, a social organisation, and new scheme
of life.

(Blumer 1969: 99)

Most of Blumer's discussion of movements is devoted to an analysis of
what he calls 'specific social movements'. His account of these movements
is flanked, however, by a discussion of general social movements on one
side and expressive, revival and nationalist movements on the other. His
comments on these other movement forms are extremely brief but it would
be helpful to raise a couple of points regarding general movements before
we consider the more specific form.

There are seemingly two aspects to Blumer's definition of 'general social
movements'. On the one hand there is a generality to the concerns and
issues they raise. They are not focused upon any one issue in particular, but
rather upon a range of issues organized around a broad theme or set of
themes. Both the labour movement and the women's movement are examples which Blumer gives of what he means in this respect. Second, general movements lack any specific mechanisms of organization, coordination
or mobilization and, as a consequence, the activities one may identify with
them tend to be erratic and unevenly distributed across both time and
space. Indeed, at one extreme general social movements may be little more
than 'cultural drifts', that is, gradual and pervasive shifts in the way in
which members of a particular society or group make sense of their world
and the values and expectations they hold. What holds this movement
together and allows us to refer to it as a movement, Blumer contends, is the
presence of a 'literature' which communicates the ideas constitutive of the
movement and variously inspires and provokes a wider audience into some
change of behaviour – 'implanting suggestions, awakening hopes, and arous-
ing dissatisfaction . . . their example helps to develop sensitivities, arouse
hopes and break down resistances' (1969: 101). In this respect they are
akin to a public, although Blumer himself also compares them to a mass
who act individually in response to a common provocation. Such movements
form, he continues, 'in an informal, inconspicuous and largely subterranean fashion. Its media of interaction are primarily reading, conversations,
talks, discussions, and the perception of examples' (1969: 101).

The importance of these movements, as far as Blumer is concerned, is the
potential they generate. Insofar as they effect transformations in the way in
which people perceive, think, feel and act, and at the same time generate
sporadic forms of protest and conflict, they create the conditions out of
which more effective and specific social movements may develop.

Specific social movements and their mechanisms

Specific social movements are defined by the organization and focus that
general social movements lack and they tend, in many instances, to develop

out of general social movements. Some writers offer a staged account of the process of transition from general to specific, Blumer notes. However, he prefers to focus upon the *mechanisms* which effect a transition towards specific social movements. Rather than suggesting that movements necessarily move through fixed stages he prefers to identify those factors which, when present, lend the movement certain types of organization. The mechanisms he cites are: agitation, the development of an *esprit de corps*, development of morale, formation of an ideology, and the development of tactics. We need to look at each of these in turn.

Agitation

Agitation and the agents responsible for it, 'agitators', may be present at any stage in the development of a movement, Blumer notes, but it is particularly important at the early stages: 'For a movement to begin and gain impetus, it is necessary for people to be jarred loose from their customary ways of thinking and believing, and to have aroused within them new impulses and wishes. This is what agitation seeks to do' (1969: 104). In other words, old habits of thought need to be challenged and new ways of thinking and acting developed. How this is done will vary across situations. In some situations disadvantaged groups are unaware of their disadvantage, and agitators function both to point this out to them and then to steer the response which this generates. Agitators raise expectations or alter them, thereby knocking them out of line with the status quo and generating a strain which, in its turn, is the impetus for movement formation. In other situations feelings are already aroused, strains are manifest, but no clear way of channelling these feelings into a constructive and critical project has yet emerged. Agitators, in this context, give shape and direction to aroused feelings, channelling them in the direction of protest and movement formation.

Elementary behaviour is very important at this stage. Agitators generate the conditions which provoke elementary behaviour and/or seek to influence situations in this state of flux by leading agents in a particular direction. It should also be apparent, however, that by identifying agitators and their role, Blumer takes a considerable step away from the purely spontaneous view of movement formation that might otherwise follow from his account of elementary behaviour. Social unrest and the shift from unrest to movement formation do not 'just happen' for Blumer. They presuppose the activity of agitators. And, as such, they further presuppose the dispositions, skills and know-how which effectively constitute the agitator. Where agitators come from is never discussed by Blumer. Indeed, he does not elaborate in any detail upon this aspect of movement formation at all. But it is clearly important to his account and should be elaborated and examined in more detail.

Esprit de corps

Agitation is important to set the ball of movement formation rolling but the result would be somewhat sporadic and short-lived unless some element of solidarity is introduced. This takes the form of what Blumer calls the *esprit de corps*. The formation of an *esprit de corps* involves the members of an emergent group or movement incorporating a sense of that movement at the most basic bodily level of their agency: their basic repertoire of behaviours and sentiments. The 'role' of the group and its members is incorporated such that members each develop a new sense of their self and learn to experience the world from the 'point of view' of the group. This is less a matter of changes in reflectively held opinions and beliefs than in the basic dispositions and sensibilities that subtend, shape and give rise to reflective thought in the first place.

Elementary forms of behaviour are very important in this 'mechanism'. Change, at this bodily level, demands a loosening of the grip of the usual mechanisms of social control and 'reinforcement'. Blumer does suggest a number of specific activities which might further promote it, however. These include the formation of 'out-groups' (and, by definition, an in-group), informal forms of fellowship and association, including 'singing, dancing, picnics, joking, having fun', and various forms of ceremonial behaviour, including protests, meetings and the construction of collective symbols such as the logos and icons that many movement groups develop and become identified with. There are two important dimensions to what Blumer is describing here. First, there is a bodily and 'playful' dimension. Like Mead, Blumer is stressing that agents develop a feel for the movement by being actively involved in it and, in this way, incorporating it among their most fundamental repertoires of behaviour and basic sentiments. Through less inhibited forms of social interaction, which allow the sensuous basis of human association greater autonomy, the agent can develop a 'feel' for the movement and its goals. Second, there is a strong symbolic dimension; groups develop a visible way of marking out their identity (e.g. logos). This reinforces the bodily dimension because it invites 'outsiders' to treat the agent as a member of the group and thereby reinforces the feelings and role of membership which the agent has incorporated. Moreover, the symbol may become invested with a strong power for evoking the 'appropriate' emotion from a movement member, as flags and anthems do for a nationalist or patriot.

What Blumer offers in this account of the *esprit de corps* is an account of the very basic elements of what we might call the culture of a social movement and of the forms of selfhood and identification, collective and individual, that it entails. He is emphasizing the manner in which movement formation is coterminous with the formation of a new cultural form and with a process of resocialization in which members of a movement incorporate its cultural form at a basic level of corporeal–emotional orientation and self-identity. The model of both culture formation and socialization deployed in this context is the relatively sophisticated interactionist model developed by Mead (1967).

Development of morale

The basic feelings involved in an *esprit de corps* are further consolidated and reinforced through what Blumer calls 'morale'. He links this to the emergence of convictions regarding the rightness of the movement, its values and its mission. Much of his language is borrowed from the sociology of religion. He suggests that morale is constituted through the emergence of 'saints', 'heroes', 'martyrs', 'myths' and a sacred literature. We need not labour this religious imagery too strongly. The important point is that collective narratives emerge within a movement which give its members a sense of its (and thus their) identity, history and purpose. The group develops a collective self-image and identity, a collective 'me', by way of stories of the trials and tribulations of its past and present membership, or perhaps of the world as it was before 'the troubles' which the movement addresses. It simultaneously constitutes a sense of 'us' and of purpose and direction. The emergence of these various narratives constitutes a shift in the way in which specific types of situation will be defined and, combined with the emergence of a new *esprit de corps*, generates new forms of identity or 'me' for movement members. These changes, in turn, facilitate new forms of action, as agents perceive both their self and their situation in a new light. The narratives and identities referred to in this context are again central to what we can call the culture of the movement. In identifying the mechanisms which lend coherence and organization to movements and groups, Blumer is attempting to identify the cultural fabric which holds a movement together and binds its participants to it.

Formation of group ideology

Closely related to the development of morale is the formation of a group ideology, which will often assume both a scholarly and a popular form. This involves the discursive formulation of the beliefs of the group, its diagnosis of the situation it is addressing and its criticisms and remedies. It contains rhetorical tools of attack and defence which will mediate interactions with outsiders and outside ideas and objections. The point of such an ideology is to be persuasive. It must keep movement participants 'on side', despite the lure and persuasiveness of detractors. And wherever possible it must draw new recruits in. Once again this is a cultural constituent of the movement.

Tactics

Finally a movement must develop tactics. Blumer actually says least about this development, but he explains why. Tactics are and always will be both diverse and very closely tied into the situation of a movement and the dynamics of struggle. As such, while one must acknowledge their import-ance, indeed indispensability, there is little one can say at a general level about them, in his view.

Each of the mechanisms Blumer refers to is generated and constituted by way of interaction. These interactions operate at two levels: rational and pre-rational. They are rational in the 'communicative' sense discussed earlier. Tactics, rhetorical tools, agitation and narratives, even the name of a group and other symbolic resources, are all argued over, as any move-ment memoir will attest. Participants have different views and interpreta-tions and must, by way of argument, persuade each other of those views or strive to reach a workable compromise. Even as they make their rational case, however, those same members are involved in a process of commit-ting themselves, at the level of identity, embodied habits and feeling, to the movement that they are creating. It is common to want to separate these elements into cognitive or rational and emotional 'bits'. It is important not to. The mechanisms of movement formation are simultaneously rational and emotional, cognitive and embodied. Each element coexists in a whole: reasons shape feelings and feelings shape reasoning. In addition to this, we must be mindful to note that deliberations and actions based upon them generate a range of unintended consequences which, in turn, may sediment as aspects of movement culture. Movements create cultures in both intended and unintended ways.

The process as a whole

I have attempted, in Figure 2.1, to map out the process Blumer describes in the form of a diagram. From left to right we see a process whereby social order becomes strained, giving rise to elementary forms of behaviour which simultaneously break free of certain aspects of the old order and generate the various mechanisms of movement formation and movement culture we have referred to. The final product of this process is a stable and specific social movement which will seek pressure for change. We see from the diagram that Blumer's account of social movements is, in essence, an account of the way in which a space for change is generated by the loosening up of (internalized) mechanisms of social control, and of the manner in which social agents, when freed of these controls, are able to generate local and solidaristic cultures of resistance. As you read the diagram you should be aware that Blumer conceives of this process as contingent. That is to say, there is no necessity that, having arrived at one point on the chart, interacting agents will progress to the next. It is just as likely that the process will run aground. What Blumer is tracing is simply the steps which are likely to lead to the emergence of a recognizable and relatively stable social movement. It should also be noted that certain points

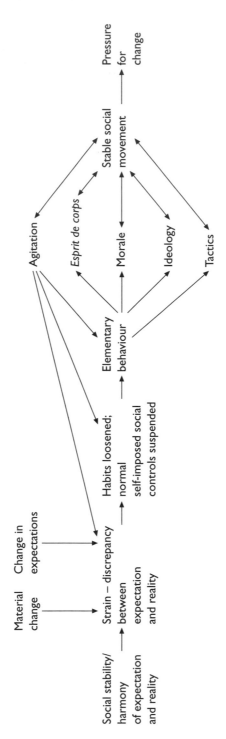

Figure 2.1 Blumer's model of movement formation

on the diagram, notably the arrows converging on 'strain', represent different possibilities rather than necessary prerequisites. Expectations can fall out of line with material reality either because of cultural shifts which alter them, or because material reality itself changes, or because of the work of agitators. It may be that each of these elements is involved but one alone may be sufficient.

Two further points regarding the diagram should be noted. First, note that the arrows connecting the mechanisms of movement formation (morale, etc.) with the movement itself run in two directions. This indicates that the mechanisms are necessary to the movement but also that the movement, *qua* interacting collective of agents, generates and regenerates those same mechanisms. Morale, *esprit de corps*, etc. aren't made once and for all. They must be constantly regenerated and sustained by movement members, within the context of the broader movement community itself. Movements must have some way of sustaining and reproducing their ideology, morale, *esprit de corps*, etc. Second, note that agitation potentially pitches in at a number of points in the diagram without seeming to be generated by the process itself. As such it stands out among the other mechanisms referred to by Blumer. This is appropriate because 'agitation' is, in effect, an outside influence which Blumer brings into his model, at a number of points, without adequate explanation or exploration.

Blumer assessed

I will begin my evaluation of Blumer by considering the weaknesses of his approach. These stem mostly from his almost exclusively social psychological focus. Although this focus is important it does not extend to a proper consideration of the structural conditions in which movement activity takes shape. I mean two things by this. First, Blumer pays no attention to the various factors in the environment of social agents which would either constrain or facilitate movement formation. He focuses upon what agents do with only a minimal consideration of the contexts in which they do it and the various forms of resources and power that can be mobilized both to support and to impede their actions. Related to this, he offers no reflection upon the systems or fields out of which struggles emerge (i.e. the systems or social contexts in which strains take shape), or those in which movement activists must conduct their struggles (i.e. the various 'arenas of struggle' in which movement members wage their wars). Having said this, it is important to note that his treatment of 'strains' is more sophisticated than the straw model of collective behaviour which, as I noted in the Introduction, has been criticized in the literature. Strain is not simply a matter of objective factors in the environment of agents, for Blumer, but rather arises out of an interaction of such conditions with the expectations and assumptions which those agents have about them; strain is a result of mismatch between expectations and reality.

Second, there is very little sense in his model of the manner in which agents are embedded or situated in social fields and structures. Blumer's agents are generic agents with generic statuses and ways of being-in-the-world. We need a stronger sense of the way in which agents are fitted into the social world, both in terms of the specific sites or fields of activity they are involved in and the various ways in which they embody forms of social distinction and inequality, such as gender and class. This is partly a matter of recognizing that different social groups have different resources for struggle available to them but it is equally a matter of recognizing that they may be differentially disposed towards specific types of protest and movement on account of their cultural backgrounds and different historical and biographical trajectories. Combining points one and two, we might say that Blumer is strong on 'agency' but very weak on 'structure'.

Finally, it is lamentable that Blumer does not discuss social networks in his account of elementary collective groupings. It is fairly clear that both he and Mead conceptualize human beings as nodes within social networks. After all, both take interaction, rather than action, as their basic unit of analysis. Indeed, both believe that the individual is an outcome of social interactions. And there can be no question that Blumer's movement activists are members of social groups, a far cry from the 'lonely misfits' of the collective behaviour caricature discussed in Chapter 1. And yet Blumer does not pull his background understanding of networks into the foreground of his discussion of movements. This is a wasted opportunity because, as we will see later, much work on social movements stresses the importance of social networks, and Blumer's theory, both specifically of social movements and more generally of symbolic interaction, could have a great deal to contribute in relation to this issue.

However, there is much of value in Blumer's work. In particular I want to highlight three important points. First, his discussion of *social unrest*, despite the problematic way in which it is expressed, is important because it serves to identify points in the history of a society, group or social space where the normal 'rules of the game' are partially suspended and social action and interaction follow a new and potentially innovative path. It links Durkheim's important observations on collective effervescence more directly to an account of social movements. This account may not apply to all social movements. Some social movement activity is more institutionalized and belongs, as we will see later, to an established and durable 'social movement sector'. Nevertheless, what is often so interesting about social movements is their creative and innovative impetus, the manner in which they shake loose of the habits of mind and action which hold the social world together, opening up a space for new ideas and calling hitherto unquestioned assumptions and practices into question. Very few theories of social movements attempt to engage with this process and it is to his credit, and our advantage, that Blumer does. Moreover, though his account is not without problems, his way of theorizing this is important.

At the risk of repetition, I want to specify and elaborate slightly upon what he says. In essence Blumer suggests that social unrest is caused by a 'shock' or tension which emerges when agents' expectations, habits and aspirations cease to 'fit' with the conditions in their environment, when they are 'jarred loose from their customary ways of thinking and believing'. This condition, which may come about either through the agency of agitators or as an effect of more gradual social changes, has the effect of lowering the habitual 'barricade' of self-conscious self-regulation which ordinarily keeps social action within the 'rules of the game' and inhibits social interaction, privatizing the agent. The agent is thus drawn more squarely into the public domain, where she engages in more open and free-ranging, less inhibited, forms of interaction. This, in turn, constitutes a generative and innovative dynamic. Out of these 'speeded-up' interactions new ideas and projects take shape. On this point, regarding the potential creativity of dialogical interaction, Blumer accords with a range of phenomenologically inspired writers, including Gadamer:

> The way one word follows another, with the conversation taking its own twists and reaching its own conclusion, may be conducted in some way, but the partners conversing are far less the leaders of it than the led. No one knows in advance what will 'come out' of a conversation.
>
> (Gadamer 1989: 383)

Out of such conversations and interactions, particularly when they are excited, new projects, plans and desires can take shape. For this to develop any further, however, other mechanisms of movement formation must fall into place.

This leads us to Blumer's second major contribution. He offers a highly suggestive account of the various elements involved in *movement cultures* and the respective functions they serve in organizing the movement and promoting solidarity. Contemporary work on movements is only now rediscovering the important role of movement cultures, identity and the affective bonds which integrate social agents within them. Thus we find a proliferation of works on 'movements and culture' or 'collective identity'. Blumer pointed this out many years ago and his account remains one of the clearest and most persuasive. In particular, in a move which is, again, very Durkheimian in flavour, his account situates movement culture firmly within the life of the group itself, noting, for example, how protests and meetings generate a deep and corporeal sense of movement belonging (an *esprit de corps*), and exploring the role of narratives and ideology in lending both coherence and defence mechanisms to the intersubjective world of the movement. We can undoubtedly improve upon Blumer's position in this respect, but he provides an extremely important point of departure.

Finally, Blumer's account is important because it emphasizes that *movements are made by the agents who are involved in them*. They are products of the creative actions of social agents. Blumer is not naive in his understanding of this. He recognizes that agents behave differently in movement contexts and periods of social unrest than during times of social stability and he attempts to theorize this. Furthermore, and importantly, he recognizes that by making social movements, agents effectively remake themselves, forging new identities and habits. In contrast to certain other accounts, however, including the one we will examine next, he does not succumb to a mechanistic or reductionist account of this transformation. Agents remain agents in Blumer's account.

Summary and conclusion

In this chapter I have discussed a version of the collective behaviour approach: that of Herbert Blumer. Within Blumer's work we have found a strong conception of social agency and a robust account of the interaction processes and mechanisms by way of which social agents construct social movements. We have also identified mechanisms which lend movements the solidarity and organization they need to survive. Blumer offers an interesting and promising account of movement cultures and conceptualizes clearly the role of identities, emotions and embodiment in the life of movements. On the negative side, however, he has relatively little to say about the societal environment in which movements and other forms of collective behaviour take shape.

Further reading

Blumer's key essay, 'Collective behaviour' (1969), is relatively accessible and not too long; Blumer himself provides a reasonable overview of the work of Mead, in his *Symbolic Interactionism* (1986). I find Joas's (1985) *G.H. Mead* much closer to the mark, however.

My own reflections on Mead can be found in *Intersubjectivity* (Crossley 1996, esp. 49–72), *The Social Body* (Crossley 2001a, esp. 144–50) and Crossley (2001c).

chapter three

Smelser's value-added approach

Blumer's account is only one of many ordinarily associated with the 'collective behaviour' approach, albeit one of the most persuasive and important. In this chapter I focus upon another, that of Neil Smelser (1962). Like Blumer's, Smelser's account is problematic in important respects and I intend to explore its problems. As with Blumer, however, there is also much of value in Smelser's work. Interestingly the strengths are very different to those I noted in Blumer, and it is for this reason that I have elected to examine both in the book. Smelser has an important contribution to make to modern movement theorizing which is complementary to but different from that of Blumer and it is my intention, in this chapter, to draw it out. In some instances this will involve me arguing that Smelser was wrong, but instructive. In particular I believe that his accounts of both social systems and emotions are poor, but I believe that they constitute a possible starting place for a reflection upon these issues, which have been lost in more recent theorizing. In other cases I will suggest that Smelser has a stronger grasp on specific issues than his critics. His value-added model of movement formation (see below) is the most obvious example of this and was my chief reason for devoting a chapter to him. I return to this model at a number points in the book and argue, in the final chapter, that, in reconstructed form, it is the best framework from which to approach movement analysis. I begin the chapter with a few brief paragraphs of necessary background information concerning Smelser's model, followed by a note on the differences between his model and the critics' caricature. This leads to a more detailed exposition of his model. Finally I offer an assessment and critique of the model.

Movements and systems

Smelser is concerned to explain social movements and other forms of collective behaviour as they take shape within social systems such as schools, factories and wider society itself. To this end he begins his theory with an account of the main components of such systems. Following Parsons (1951), he understands social systems as institutionalized patterns of interaction, characterized by four discrete and hierarchically arranged levels of integration (see Figure 3.1). It is easiest to approach this hierarchical model from the middle, with norms and organization. All interaction within social systems, Smelser argues, is oriented to social norms, that is, mutual expectations about appropriate forms of conduct which stipulate how agents should and should not behave. Many social systems have a set of formal and codified rules or laws but unwritten and informal rules can perform the same function, that is, the coordination and legitimation of specific patterns of (inter)action. Norms are not specific enough actually to account for and explain the particularities and dynamics of systems, in Smelser's view, however, so he adds a second layer to this, which he variously refers to as 'motivation' or 'organization'. This level includes the specific 'roles' that actors within any system might occupy, the hierarchies and interconnections between those roles, which organize them into a system, and the various arrangements of punishment and reward which motivate agents to act appropriately. For example, if we were interested in the medical system of a particular society we would not simply look at the formal rules of medical practice or its legal framework (its norms), but equally at the various interacting roles it involves (e.g. doctor, nurse, patient, etc.), the mechanisms by which those roles are coordinated and the various incentives and sanctions which encourage role conformity. Doctors, we might observe, are well paid and enjoy a high status but they can lose this if they deviate significantly from role or normative expectations; thus they have an incentive to conform.

'Above' norms, in this hierarchy of components, Smelser locates the values to which norms appeal. Laws or norms regarding racial and sexual discrimination, for example, are based upon the value of 'equality'. They function both to make that value more specific and concrete, and to turn it

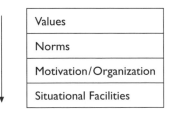

Figure 3.1 Smelser's hierarchy of system components

into specific guidelines for action. At the lower level, underneath 'organiza-tion', are what he calls 'situational facilities'. This refers to the various forms of competence and know-how which social agents draw upon in their interactions, which enable them to function within a role or organization.

The notion that these components are hierarchically arranged is based upon two considerations. First, that each is successively less abstract and more specific and concrete, as we move down the hierarchy. Norms, for example, are based upon general values which they translate into specific rules. But they themselves require more concrete forms of organization and motivation if they are to be realized. And these forms of organization, in turn, depend upon the very concrete skills and dispositions of interacting agents if they are to be successfully 'pulled off'. Second, it follows from this that elements at the lower end of the hierarchy can be altered, without necessitating change at the higher end, while change at the higher end will explicitly require changes at the lower end. If the values of society were to change, for example, this would necessitate a change in the norms (e.g. laws) which translate them into concrete rules. But this, in turn, would require changes in the forms of organization which support and enforce the norm, and consequently different skills and dispositions would be demanded of actors at the grassroots. A change in norms, by contrast, though it would still require changes in organization and dispositions, would not require a change in values. The same values can be realized through a whole variety of different types of norm or rule and the norm can only depart from values if the values upon which it is based are themselves changed. Similarly with motivation or organization: changes at this level would demand a change in dispositions but not in norms, since different forms of organization can implement the same norms and would only require a change in norms if already based upon a different system of norms.

Movements, strains and the value-added model

Smelser understands collective behaviour, which we have yet to define, as a response to problems or 'strains' within these systems, which aims to cor-rect them. In contrast to the collective behaviour caricature, which posits strain as a necessary, sufficient and immediate cause of protest, however, he qualifies this claim on three grounds. First, he argues that collective beha-viour and structural strain are not necessarily unusual or statistically devi-ant. If Smelser portrays social systems as smooth running and perfectly functioning this is only for the heuristic purpose of bringing to light the many ways in which real systems and societies fall short of that.

Second, like Blumer he argues that structural strain must be defined relat-ive to the subjective and intersubjective expectations of agents and groups. Whatever strains and problems may be manifest within a system are only effective in mobilizing action insofar as they depart from the expectations of those within it. A strain must also be a shock or affront:

> Before we can classify any event or situation as a source of strain, we must assess this event or situation with reference to cultural standards and personal expectations . . . [Strain] always expresses a relation between an event or situation and certain cultural and individual standards.
>
> (Smelser 1962: 51)

An interesting illustration of this is provided by Thompson's (1993) study of protest and collective action in eighteenth-century England. The lower classes were prepared to accept a range of hardships, Thompson notes, often quite devastating in their consequences, if those hardships were expected and deemed just. An informal code specifying just and unjust hardship existed. But they would tolerate no departure from their shared definitions of just hardship or, indeed, of reasonable and appropriate behaviour. A lord or seller who attempted to con or exploit them, beyond the bounds defined by their traditions, would be subject to immediate and often brutal attack. Thompson refers to this as the 'moral economy of the crowd'. Similar supporting evidence can be found in the work of Jasper (1997). He has shown, with respect to a number of case studies, the importance of 'moral shock' in precipitating social movement activity in the contemporary USA. What he means by 'moral shock' is precisely the effect generated by an experience which deviates from deeply held taken-for-granted assumptions about the world.

In making this point Smelser, like Blumer, departs from the caricature of the collective behaviour approach and places his theory beyond the remit of much of the empirical work which has been used to cast doubt upon it. His theory cannot be falsified by reference to studies which focus upon the relationship between protest and objective indicators of hardship because such studies take no account of expectations and (inter)subjective definitions. To test Smelser's theory we would have to investigate the lifeworld of the agents we are interested in: their expectations about and definitions of their world, their interests and priorities. This is exactly what Thompson and Jasper do, and their findings are supportive of the general thrust of Smelser's position, as outlined so far.

This is not the only or even the largest departure that Smelser makes from the cause–effect straw model, however. His third qualification is that structural strain is one of six factors which must combine, in 'value-added fashion', if collective behaviour is to follow. The notion of a 'value-added' model is one which Smelser borrows from economics. It identifies the manner in which the various stages of a production process contribute something different to it and thereby add value to the final product. Raw materials must be extracted, then melted down, next moulded, fitted together and finally painted. Each of these stages is necessary to the end result and failure at any one stage brings the process itself to a halt. So it is, Smelser argues, with collective behaviour. He outlines six factors which affect *both whether collective behaviour will occur and, if so, what sort of collective behaviour it will be.* I will explore some of these components in depth shortly, but first we require a brief overview of each:

1 *Structural conduciveness.* Social systems inhibit or facilitate and aid collective behaviour through the constraints and opportunities for action which they afford. Furthermore, the specific configuration of opportunities and constraints they involve shapes the types of collective behaviour which emerge.
2 *Structural strain.* Agents must experience the system as problematic and stressful in some way.
3 *Growth and spread of generalized belief.* Agents must 'diagnose' the problems they face and propose 'remedies'. If they do not, there will be no collective behaviour. What sort of collective behaviour emerges depends upon what sort of beliefs emerge.
4 *Precipitating factors.* That is, 'trigger events'. Whatever strains may be acting upon interaction situations they must be expressed in some form of concrete event or series of events if agents are to mobilize around them.
5 *Mobilization of participants for action.* This involves the emergence of communication networks and, in some cases, leaders and organizations. All action involves coordination and organization.
6 *Operation of social control.* Social control agencies, such as the police and media, can play a preventative role, smoothing over strains and problems before movements emerge, and their response to collective behaviour, when it does begin, can be a very important factor in determining what happens next. Repressive policing may be sufficient to quash an uprising, but if it is 'insufficiently repressive' it may have the opposite effect, causing moral outrage and mobilizing many more agents who might not otherwise have got involved. Similarly, the media can play a central role, 'amplifying' the process of movement formation by publicizing it (e.g. Crossley 1999b).

Each of these elements is analytic, for Smelser. The same concrete action or event may play more than one role. Sometimes police activities might simultaneously fulfil the role of strain, trigger and the operation of social control, for example. Moreover, the elements may emerge in any order and may each help to define the other. The emergence of a generalized set of beliefs or even a structural strain, for example, may generate a retrospective interpretation of a specific event, leading to that event becoming a 'trigger event' for mobilization. Similarly, a strain, even if subjectively experienced as such, may remain latent for many years until the other elements fall into place and a response emerges.

Type of collective behaviour	System element addressed

Value-oriented
social movement ─────────────────────→ Values

Norm-oriented
social movement ─────────────────────→ Norms

Hostile outburst ─────────────────────→ Organization

Craze ─┐
       ├──────────────────────────────→ Situational facilities
Panic ─┘

Figure 3.2 Smelser's types of collective behaviour and their relation to system elements

The interplay of these six factors does not simply determine whether collective behaviour occurs. As I noted above, it also determines what sort of collective behaviour will occur. Smelser outlines five basic types of collective behaviour (see Figure 3.2) which he relates to the four basic elements in his conception of the social system. His five basic types are:

1 *a panic*, which involves flight or an attempt to escape from a stressful situation;
2 *a craze*, in which actors become focused upon a very concrete 'solution' to their immediate situation;
3 *a hostile outburst*, in which a specific individual, group or institution is identified as the source of stress and is subject to assault or attack;
4 *a norm-oriented movement*, which seeks to alleviate stress by addressing and transforming the normative structure of the system in which it arises;
5 *a value-oriented movement*, which seeks to alleviate stress by questioning the very values upon which the system it occurs within is based.

Each type of collective behaviour seeks to address or resolve social strain at one specific level of the hierarchy, Smelser argues. Panics and crazes, for example, seek out solutions to strain at the level of situational facilities or immediate circumstances. In a panic agents seek to escape what they perceive to be the danger in their immediate circumstances: evacuating a burning building is one obvious example and rapidly selling devaluating shares is another. In a craze, by contrast, agents seek a very concrete and localized solution to a strain. The massive growth in the use of drugs such as Prozac or Ritalin to resolve stresses in domestic situations is one example of this. A hostile outburst, by contrast, focuses action 'one step up', on the motivational or organizational level. Agents no longer react to their immediate circumstances but rather focus upon the organizational features of their environment, including its various institutions and group divisions. Typically this involves the scapegoating of a particular individual or group. Finally, as should be clear, norm- and value-oriented movements seek to explain and address strain at the level of normative and value systems respectively.

The hierarchy of system elements figures again here. Any higher level behaviour may incorporate a lower level, but this does not work in the other direction. A norm-oriented movement may contain elements of panic and a hostile outburst within it, for example, and a hostile outburst may entail elements of a craze, but a norm-oriented movement cannot contain elements of a value-oriented movement without becoming one.

Which form of collective behaviour arises depends upon the interaction of all of the elements in the value-added process. In a particularly repressive society, for example, the development of norm- or value-oriented movements may simply not be 'structurally conducive', whatever other factors are at work. Repression prevents movement formation. This may mean that no collective behaviour occurs or that strains which might otherwise give rise to movements are expressed in other ways, such as panics or crazes. Smelser affords particular attention to strains and generalized beliefs in his account of the shaping of collective behaviour, however, and they merit a brief discussion.

Strain

Smelser's definition of structural strain is deliberately broad: '... an impairment of the relations among and consequently inadequate functioning of the components of action' (1962: 47). He wants a definition which incorporates all previous attempts to theorize strain, from theories of structural conflict to theories of anomie and alienation. Moreover, he identifies the potential for strain at each of the successive levels of his system hierarchy, with the usual proviso about lower levels being incorporated at higher levels, but not vice versa. At the situational level he focuses upon such things as ambiguities and technical failures which may induce strain; at the organization level, on such problems as mismatch between achievements and expected rewards; at the normative level on role strain and conflict; and at the top of the hierarchy he considers the possibility of a clash of values induced either by social change or contact between different societies or groups. Notwithstanding this, however, he argues that all types of strain will tend to manifest, in the first instance, at the lower levels. A clash of values, for example, first becomes apparent and causally effective at the concrete level of everyday interactions and the problems experienced therein. Moreover, he insists that 'Any type of structural strain may give rise to any type of collective behaviour' (1962: 66). The precise course of events, to reiterate, is determined by all factors in the value-added process.

Generalized belief

The type of belief that agents form and communicate between themselves, though itself shaped by other factors in the value-added process, has a strong effect upon the type of action which follows. A collective which forms the view that their problems are attributable to a particular out-group will, all other things being equal (they may not be), tend towards a hostile outbreak, while groups who form a normative critique will be more inclined towards a norm-oriented movement. This is an important point but the way Smelser develops it is problematic. His model is crudely psychodynamic. For example, a craze is said to be based upon a 'wish fulfilment' belief, which magically identifies a fetishized object with the power to resolve a specific problem or situation. Smelser apparently recognizes the objections which his sociological colleagues will raise to this use of psychology and is clear to distance himself from what he believes are its most problematic implications. He makes two defensive points. In the first instance he stresses that such psychological variables only come into play as a consequence of the sociological factors which trigger them and are then mediated, in their effects, by the broader sociological factors in the value-added process. His is not a psychological model of collective behaviour, he argues, but rather a sociological model which uses some psychological ideas. Second, he seeks to distance himself from the claim that his model is irrationalist:

> The definition we have presented does not, by itself, involve any assumptions that the persons involved in an episode are irrational, that they lose their critical faculties, that they experience psychological regression, that they revert to some animal state, or whatever.
>
> (1962: 11)

This argument is highly ambiguous, not least as Smelser flatly contradicts his point about critical faculties just a few sentences later, when he claims that certain social situations make agents more prone to 'suggestion', 'fantasy' and the whims of leaders. I will return to this later. For the moment, however, I want to consider a second problem with Smelser's theorization of 'generalized belief': namely, his argument that all generalized beliefs are inadequate. He expresses this, at numerous points in the *Theory of Collective Behaviour*, with the claim that collective behaviour 'short-circuits' a social system. What he means by this is unclear. However, his argument seems to be that a proper resolution of any problem of strain must necessarily address each of the aforementioned hierarchical elements of the social system and the relations between them (e.g. values, norms, motivation and situational facilties) but that any form of collective action, even those higher forms which incorporate lower forms within them, necessarily pitch in at one (primary) level only and, as such, fall short of a proper resolution of the problem. All generalized beliefs, it would seem, fall short of adequate analysis. In attempting to account for the 'crudeness, excess and eccentricity' of collective behaviour, for example, he argues:

> By short-circuiting from high-level to low-level components of social action, collective episodes by-pass many of the specifications, contingencies and controls that are required to make generalised components operative. This gives collective behaviour its clumsy or primitive character . . . Collective behaviour, then, is the action of the impatient. It contrasts with the processes of social readjustment that do not short-circuit the journey from generalised belief to specific situations.
>
> (1962: 73)

Collective behaviour may stimulate or trigger a more sophisticated and appropriate process of self-correction within the system, he continues, but it is not such a process in itself.

Smelser assessed

I will be offering my overall assessment of Smelser's position shortly. I want to focus upon this notion of short-circuiting first, however, because it is a major problem with his approach. We can concede that some forms of collective behaviour, such as scapegoating an out-group, may short-circuit a structural social problem by diverting attention from its complexity and true source. Indeed, any form of collective behaviour *could* be misguided and, as a consequence, *could* short-circuit a problem. In addition, we can concede that no collective action is going to be perfect, in either conception, execution or outcome, as nothing in life is. However, it is wrong to argue that *all* collective actions, of whatever form and at whatever level, *necessarily* short-circuit the system. The notion of short-circuiting implies that problems would be solved more satisfactorily were it not for these rather 'clumsy' efforts, but there is no reason to believe that this is so. Unless we are prepared to subscribe to a very strong version of systems theory, which posits a notion of self-correcting mechanisms within systems, we are forced to concede that collective behaviour is often the only way in which certain social strains are likely to be addressed. More to the point, it is not clear why generalized beliefs necessarily fail to provide an adequate diagnosis of a situation of strain or a realistic and appropriate solution. A hostile outburst against a corrupt elite whose actions cause hardship, for example, may be based on a perfectly adequate assessment of the problem and may prove just the right measure to bring that elite back into line. Similarly, there is no reason why a social movement might not have an extensive and elaborate analysis of a social strain which would equal all others. The critique of the ecology movement, for example, ranges from a discussion of the most mundane level of social practices (e.g. the use of detergents) through to questions of value and cosmology (e.g. in 'deep ecology'), taking in all manner of reflections on norms, laws and organizational forms along the way. No short-circuit there! The ecology movement, staffed and supported as it is by many distinguished scientists and philosophers, has an equal claim to rigour and validity to any other commentator, and a much superior claim to the average sociologist of collective behaviour. How can the sociologist deem the perspective of the environmentalist 'impatient' or 'magical'? What claim do we have to expertise on such matters?

This aspect of Smelser's model can be quite readily and easily dropped, without affecting much of the rest of it. I suggest that we do just that right now. Our 'Smelser' will have no truck with short-circuits.

Agents and emotions

I suggest that one of the reasons Smelser opts for the definition of collective action as a short-circuit is that he has an inadequate conception of the social actor. This conception focuses very heavily upon institutionalized forms of action. And it takes those institutions as given. Action follows an institutionalized pattern of norms and roles and the actor simply is one who follows such patterns. There is much that is of value in the way in which this conception is developed but it has the crucial flaw of being relatively paralysed in the face of actions, such as collective action, which break the institutional mould. Indeed, it cannot deal with any situation where the smooth running of interaction systems breaks down. How does one explain action in anomic situations, and where roles have broken down, if roles and norms are integral elements in one's model of agency? To take norms and roles away from his agent is like removing their limbs: it disables them. Smelser's solution, it would seem, is to resort to a relatively mechanistic psychology. When the social supports of action break down the agent regresses to a level of 'primary' psychological processes. This model feeds his short-circuit theory since it both reduces action down to a 'lower' level and evacuates any sense or reason from it. The formation of generalized beliefs becomes, in effect, a process of mechanical psychological reaction. We need a more sophisticated conception of action and agency which can account for both institutionalized and non-institutionalized action. And this necessarily entails that we rethink the whole notion of social systems to which his model of the agent belongs.

Having said this, there is something of value in Smelser's conception of the psychodynamics of collective action that we would do well to reformulate rather than completely abandon. He draws our attention to the emotionality of collective action and to what he identifies as the 'magical beliefs' *sometimes* involved in such actions. This contrasts sharply with later writers (see Chapters 4, 5 and 6) who explain collective action as a rational choice and who conceive rationality in terms which are both narrowly instrumental and preclusive of an affective element. We need to hold on to this emotional element, I suggest, but we need to do so in a manner which does not juxtapose it so sharply to rationality. There are two ways in which we can do this. First, by recognizing that some emotional states are, to all intents and purposes, rational, at least if we mean by 'rational' mutually understandable and 'persuasive' (see Crossley 1998c, 2000c). It is perfectly understandable that a person who is mistreated will become angry, for example, just as it is perfectly understandable that an individual who loses a loved one will become upset. We would not deem an individual who reacted in these ways irrational and would probably think it odd if they did not react in these ways. In narrowly instrumental terms such emotional reactions may not do anything to resolve the difficult situation which occasions them but it would be a very narrow definition of rationality indeed which suggests that they must in order to qualify as rational. They are rational because we can understand why a person would respond like that and can imagine that we and others would respond similarly in the same circumstances. It would be a different matter if they burst into fits of laughter *for no apparent reason*, of course, lacking a 'reason', that would be irrational.

Emotions can be rational in this sense because they are occasioned by specific aspects of our life and situation and because others, who perceive those occasioning circumstances, know that any reasonable person would act in the same way. This leads to my second point, which is that emotions can be discussed and argued over in a reasonable way (Crossley 1998c, 2000c). A person who acts angrily on the basis of a misreading of a situation may be talked out of their anger, for example, by another individual who can explain to them that they have misunderstood. Similarly, arguments over emotion might centre upon the appropriateness of their being expressed in particular ways or contexts. Interlocuters may persuade one another to save their anger for another time or perhaps to channel it in another way. This is an important point in relation to collective behaviour and social movements because these are precisely communicative situations where emotions will be discussed and formulated in particular ways.

I do not mean to deny that emotions can manifest a magical form of thinking, particularly when they emerge in situations where agents are relatively powerless or ill-equipped to act in such a way as to resolve the strains or problems they are experiencing. Sartre (1993) posits a highly plausible theory of emotion along just these lines (see also Crossley 1998c). He points out, for example, how such emotions as 'envy' magically transform those things we most desire into objects we hate and wish to destroy, and he even goes so far as to suggest that a swoon or feint can be a magical way of trying to escape from an overwhelming situation. What I am suggesting is that such phenomena are not as radically opposed to 'rationality' as we might at first believe, not least because emotions do not cease to belong to the human world of communicative interaction where they might be transformed or re-channelled through negotiation. In addition, I suggest that we can learn an important lesson from Sartre's treatment of 'emotional magic'. Following the basic tenets of phenomenological philosophy, he refuses to treat emotion, however magical, as a mechanical or meaningless reaction. It is a purposive and meaningful response to a situation, he argues, a way of apprehending and making sense of the world. This is a call to study emotion without downgrading it, as Smelser does. It requires us to focus upon the sense and intelligibility of our emotional responses.

This is not to say that emotional responses are always desirable or constructive. Hate movements are at least as prevalent as more constructive movements, probably more so. This is another reason why we need to hold on to a reconstructed version of Smelser's psychodynamics. Many movements can and do manifest strange beliefs and feelings. Hatred and prejudice are not uncommon. We need to be able to account for this and reconstructing Smelser may well be a start.

Agency, mobilization and belief

The problem of agency in Smelser's account reflects in his value-added model. The elements in this model, to reiterate, are:

1 structural conduciveness;
2 strain;
3 formation of generalized belief;
4 precipitating factors;
5 mobilization of participants;
6 operation of social control.

As I note below, I find this model persuasive on many levels. However, I am concerned that Smelser conflates two distinct types of factor. Strain, conduciveness, precipitating factors and operation of social control are all external to movements and the collectives who form them. Mobilization and the formation of generalized beliefs, by contrast, are what agents do in the process of constructing their movements and collective actions. They are not conditions which determine whether and how agents act but rather descriptions of the way in which agents act. This is particularly so if we drop Smelser's mechanistic perspective on the formation of generalized beliefs and recognize that new beliefs emerge by way of communication and interaction between agents. If we conflate these agentic elements in the process of movement formation with the more environmental factors, as Smelser does, treating all elements, in effect, as environmental factors, we inevitably ignore the role of active agency within movements.

It is important to add here that Smelser says very little with respect to the issue of mobilization. This is a problem for two reasons. First, given what I have just argued, it contributes to his tendency to erase agency from his account. Second, as we will see later, conditions for mobilization have proved to be a very important factor in movement analysis.

Systems and differentiation

Smelser's attempt to locate his theory of collective behaviour within a broader theory of social systems is important on three counts. First, it connects movement analysis to the broader concerns of sociology and social theory, and anchors it in an account of social stability and order. This is important because scientific rigour demands that our account of movement and change square with our broader conception of stability and order, and indeed with our broader theory of society. Second, it forces us to reflect upon the environment out of which movements emerge and the logic of the specific strains which give rise to them. We deepen our understanding of movements by reflecting upon the broader conflicts of interest and strains that they mobilize around and the systems within which those interests and strains emerge. Third, there is at least a tacit recognition in Smelser's account of the differentiation of society. He does not refer to *the* social system but rather to social *systems*, in the plural. This, in turn, is important for two interrelated reasons. First, it alerts us to the diverse range of contexts out of which movements emerge and the very different types of conditions which prevail within those contexts. If I wish to study 'mental health movements', for example, Smelser both alerts me to the need to examine the specific conditions of the 'mental health system' which may have given rise to those movements and offers me a model which I may use to conduct such an analysis. Given the value-added nature of Smelser's model this will involve looking at the strains, controls and conduciveness of the mental health system, which variously provoke, constrain and facilitate the possibility of movement development. This does not preclude an account of the bigger picture: e.g. strains and controls at the societal level. Smelser's model accounts for that too. Nevertheless, specific localized systems in a society may offer differing degrees of 'conduciveness', 'strain' and 'control' to those identified at the broader level and there can be little doubt that these will be of significance in relation to movement formation. The mental health system is a very good example of this since it has exercised a much tighter constraint over its members than is the case in most systems, and has generally been unconducive to movement mobilization until relatively recently, since its 'inmates' were kept under tight lock and key, with no access to the resources required for mobilization. Second, Smelser alerts us to the different sites of struggle within which movements wage their campaigns and the different conditions of struggle they encounter therein. Having emerged out of a diverse range of structural contexts (e.g. the economy, the family, psychiatry), movements fight their battles within different structural contexts (e.g. the political system, the media, the legal system), each of which offers them distinct possibilities and opportunities. A legal campaign, for example, must be fought in accordance with the legal 'game', using resources and making moves that are recognized in that game. But this is different from the media game, and what proves successful in one context will not be successful in another. Thus the media may prove conducive to one movement at one time, while the legal system is hopeless, but quite the opposite could be true for another movement. We need to be aware of this complex and differentiated field of struggle if we are to make sense of movements in the contemporary era.

However, there are problems with Smelser's conception of social structures. The first relates to the above-mentioned problems with his theory of agency. His systems are 'action systems' and any problems with his theory of agency are therefore problems with his theory of systems. Second, though his conception of systems is a far cry from the harmonious and smooth running systems suggested by his mentor, Parsons (1951), on account of his acknowledgement of strains, he tends to portray conflict as extrinsic to systems and views strain as an effect of imbalance. He fails to recognize the intrinsically conflictual nature of some social systems, that they entail exchange and competition over scarce resources and that their boundaries are very often moving because they are themselves a stake in such struggles. Notwithstanding his differences from Parsons, this stems from the functionalist basis of his model. Third, though he recognizes the horizontal differentiation of society into relatively autonomous systems, he has very little to say on the issue of vertical differentiation: that is, on inequality, domination and power. Again these differentiations are not extrinsic to social systems but constitutive elements in them, and it hardly needs to be said that they play an important role in the organization and motivation of collective behaviour. Finally, his model tends to portray movements as relatively short lived, failing to account for the durability and even institutionalization which some of them achieve. Some movements do rise and fall incredibly quickly but others achieve a degree of permanence, becoming part of the society from which they have emerged. They become 'systems', to borrow Smelser's terminology temporarily, in their own right. In addition, as some of the theories we will examine later have shown, some movements are aided and prompted by a relatively durable field or system of movement politics, staffed by professional movement entrepreneurs who move between struggles, shifting their resources and skills with them.

The value-added approach

Having catalogued the weaknesses of Smelser's approach, I want now to focus upon its strengths. Two have already been discussed. First, he puts a great emphasis upon the lifeworld of social agents in attempting to make sense of social strains and their effects, that is, he highlights agents' respective ways of making sense of and evaluating their situations, and their subjective 'interests'. Ordinary social members have different subjective interests to social analysts and different ways of making sense of the world. Consequently they will not always act and react to those events which social scientists think they ought. Second, he attempts to locate movements within the structural systems which give rise to them. He links movement emergence to strain, and strain, in turn, to the broader social systems which generate it.

There is a third key strength in Smelser's account, however: his value-added model. This model is important. It distances his account from the caricature of collective behaviour discussed in the Introduction and introduces many themes which have been centralized in more recent movement theories. More centrally, however, the very idea of a value-added model is important. Much of the history of movement analysis, after Smelser as well as before, has involved a search for the one key factor which triggers movements or protest, or perhaps the one key sequence of two or three factors. Analysts have staked their reputation on the centrality of 'networks', 'opportunities' or 'resources' and have damned the advocates of 'strains' or 'beliefs'. If this had resulted in a watertight predictive model then it would be perfectly justified, but it has not. Although a limited range of variables do, arguably, account for much movement activism, the way in which they fall into place differs across movements, and different variables have a different weight in different cases. Smelser's value-added model is the only model in the literature which does justice to this fact (see also Kerbo 1982; Kerbo and Shaffer 1986). Thus, even if it is necessary to modify Smelser's value-added model, or even to go beyond it completely, I suggest that we do need a value-added model of movement formation and that, given this, Smelser remains an invaluable resource and guide.

Smelser and Blumer

Smelser wrote his *Theory of Collective Behaviour* several years after Blumer completed his account, and he (Smelser) states his intention to transcend the problems of Blumer's account within his own. In certain respects he achieves this. Certainly he attends to the structural factors which Blumer ignores and affords us a much more useful framework for considering the contexts out of which movements emerge and in which they take shape. In many respects, however, Smelser only offers us an inversion of Blumer's account. He is stronger where Blumer is weak (structure) but weak where Blumer is strong, particularly in the question of agency. This might seem to suggest scope for a marriage of the two approaches. I urge caution in this respect. Both Blumer and Smelser have something important to contribute to social movement theory, in my view, but the problems in the approaches of each, not to mention their very different starting points, make marriage out of the question. We need an alternative framework altogether in which to 'reinvent' their respective contributions.

Notwithstanding this, one of the paradoxical effects of Smelser's attempt to supersede Blumer's account is that he effectively draws the strengths of the latter into relief, allowing us to recognize those aspects of Blumer's account which we may wish to reinvent within our own. Specifically, Smelser's deletion of agency and his reliance on a mechanistic and reductionist psychology in his account of the formation of generalized beliefs highlights the necessity for an account of movement formation, such as that of Blumer, which focuses upon the generative role of 'reasonable' human communication and interaction. Human agents collectively make social movements, albeit in circumstances that are not of their choosing. Their generalized beliefs arise out of their interactions and discussions, and these same discussions serve to frame and channel their immediate emotional reactions to situations. Relatedly, Smelser's one-sided focus upon the external factors which shape social movements begs the question, addressed by Blumer, of the internal shaping of the movements through the interactions of their participants and the broader effects of these interactions: i.e. the generation of an *esprit de corps*, morale, ideology and tactics. To reiterate, I do not propose putting the ideas of these two writers together, like pieces of a whole, but they do each have a contribution to make and the contrasts between their respective strengths and weaknesses at least serve to indicate to us the type of 'whole' we do wish to create.

Summary and conclusion

Whatever its weaknesses, and it has many, Smelser's model departs significantly from the straw model of the collective behaviour approach. It is much stronger. It makes some important points and even where it is problematic it raises important questions and issues. I will not reiterate a list of the various pros and cons of the model here. Suffice it to say that Smelser lays the foundation for a persuasive theory of movements through both his conception of a value-added model and his attempt to locate movement analysis within a broader understanding of social systems and the differentiation of societies, but that he does not adequately carry this through. Later in the book we will discuss theories which outstrip that of Smelser on many levels but I will insist throughout that his key insights regarding differentiation and value-added processes provide an important corrective to this later work, and I will make a case for their reintroduction into movement theory in my conclusion.

Further reading

See Chapters 1, 9 and 10 of Smelser's (1962) *Theory of Collective Behaviour*. Goodwin *et al.* (2000) give an interesting discussion of emotion in social movements. On 'moral shock' see Jasper's (1997) *The Art of Moral Protest* – especially Chapters 5 and 6.

chapter four

Rational actor theory

In the Introduction to this book I noted that the collective behaviour approaches have been criticized for their alleged 'irrationalism' and focus on emotion, and that much of the post-1970s work in movement analysis has adopted a model of agency rooted in rational actor theory (RAT). The evidence of Chapters 2 and 3 should have been sufficient to indicate that not all collective behaviour approaches conform to the 'irrationalist' stereotype and I hope that my critique of Smelser, in particular, indicated both that emotions can be rational, in a broad sense (see also Crossley 1998c), and that irrational or magical beliefs do play a role in *some* movements and cannot therefore be completely dismissed. In this chapter I shift my attention to the alternative, RAT, model. It is my contention that, whatever the problems of the collective behaviour models, RAT has many of its own and serves us no better. The model is important, however, because it has underpinned a great deal of social movement analysis and continues to do so. This alone merits the relatively lengthy discussion I devote to it. I begin with a basic exposition of the model. This is followed by an account of what RATs call the 'collective action problem', a problem much discussed in contemporary movement analysis. Finally, I offer a critique of RAT, indicating why I believe that it is poorly suited to the tasks of movement analysis.

RAT: a basic outline

The first key defining feature of RAT is its methodological individualism (Elster 1989; Laver 1997). Proponents argue that, for methodological purposes at least, we must regard the social world as decomposable into the actions of individuals and must explain whatever social phenomena we seek to explain in terms of those actions and individuals. This claim is very often made, at least in the sociological context, against the claims of functionalism. Functionalist analyses of the 'parts' of the social world, which seek to explain them by reference to their functions for the whole, it is argued, are either no explanation at all or else poor and wholly illogical explanations (Popper 1945; Homans 1961, 1973; Elster 1989; Hollis 1994). The functions of a 'part' of the social world are consequences of it and the sociologist is perfectly entitled to trace those consequences and to call them functions. Tracing the consequences of a particular action pattern does not amount to an explanation of that pattern, however, because explanation would require that the sociologist identify the cause of the pattern itself, and to identify the consequences of an action as the cause of that same action would be absurd. If we really want to explain the 'parts' of the social world, RAT argues, then we need to examine the constituent elements of that part, that is, the human of which actions it is composed. We need a theory of individual human behaviour.

The theory of human behaviour that RAT proposes focuses upon three elements: first, desire. Desire serves a dual function within RAT. On the one hand, it defines goals and interests for human agents and, insofar as it can be thwarted, costs and losses too. Actions and their consequences are profitable and/or costly to the extent that they bolster or drain the agent's stock of desired 'goods'. On the other hand, desires are structures of motivation which drive action. Human desires are diverse and can be social. We may desire to help others and we may desire ends which can only exist within the context of group living: e.g. political office. However, many RATs, such as Laver's (1997), argue that altruistic and social desires should be regarded as second order phenomena, reducible in the final instance to a more basic set of private, asocial and selfish desires. The greater the number of possible desires we start out with in our theory, Laver argues, the closer we get to the untenable and futile position of explaining any and every form of action by way of a desire specific to it. The answer to the question 'Why did x do y?' simply becomes 'Because x desired to do y', which is no explanation at all. If we maintain the notion of a few basic desires, by contrast, we are in a position to offer meaningful and revealing explanations of second order desires and the actions motivated by them. To explain why x did y we need also to explain why x desired to do y, and we preserve the possibility of answering this question meaningfully only if we maintain that the desire to do y is one of many second or third order desires which are premised upon a more fundamental set of basic desires. These basic desires are deemed asocial, selfish and private because RAT aims to maximize the possibility of explaining social phenomena and, as such, needs to presuppose as little with respect to these phenomena as possible. To explain social and public phenomena fully, it is argued, one must start with asocial and private building blocks (Laver 1997). A social theory which assumes the existence of social phenomena effectively presupposes that which it seeks to explain and is therefore condemned to superficiality, if not circularity.

The second element in the RAT model consists of the opportunities and constraints for action within the external environment of the agent, which variously raise and lower costs and profits. Any desired goal can be costly or profitable depending upon how easily and painlessly it can be obtained and thus opportunities and constraints are an important consideration. A desire for a drink is very 'cheaply' satisfied if I am located in a house with a water tap but could be much more 'expensive', in terms of effort, if I am located in a desert, 15 miles from the next oasis. I must balance my desire for water against my desire to avoid a 15-mile trek.

The third component of the RAT model is rationality, that is, the capacity of agents to identify courses of action which would enable them to maximize the realization of their desires and weigh up the relative costs and benefits of a particular course of action. Rationality, in this context, means something different from what it means for Blumer, and, as RAT proponent Michael Laver (1997) argues, it means something different from what we ordinarily mean by 'rationality' in everyday parlance. Rationality is strictly instrumental for RATs. Rational agents are said to find the most effective means for realizing their goals or interests, whatever their goals or ends may be. If people desire to feel pain, for example, then it would be perfectly rational, according to this definition, for them to subject themselves to a variety of forms of torture. There would be no question of whether the desire for pain is a rational desire or goal. In contrast to everyday understandings of rationality and the version we discussed earlier in this book, 'rationality', for RAT, is purely and simply a matter of linking means to ends and does not extend to cover the specific ends that agents pursue, the beliefs upon which they act or, indeed, the normative rightness of their way of acting. Neither does it involve dialogue or argument, as in Blumer. It is an individual calculation of profit.

This model is generally complicated by a number of further assumptions. First, it is assumed that agents have a 'portfolio' of what may sometimes be competing or conflicting desires. Second, it is assumed that they are capable of ranking these desires into an order of preferences and even perhaps attaching a quasi-numerical value to each preference, such that the costs and benefits of particular situations can be meaningfully and accurately ascertained. Finally, it is assumed that these desires and their rank order are relatively stable over time. These assumptions allow RAT to predict that agents may not always act so as to realize their 'top' desire, if doing so would cost too much in terms of other preferences or acting otherwise would lead to a greater overall yield in terms of the combined value of certain lower preferences. An avid environmentalist may elect to miss a particular demonstration, for example, even though demonstrating is her chief objective in life, if doing so would pose too many costs in terms of her other basic desires: e.g. the call to demonstrate might just be outweighed by the combined lure of Sunday lunch, the 'big match' on TV and the chance to catch up with friends.

Versions of RAT vary in the importance they attach to the subjective interpretations that agents make with respect to their situation and the information they have regarding it. The classic RAT model, used in economics, assumes that agents have full information about their circumstances and does not probe into matters of interpretation. When economists predict the consequences of a specific rise in interest rates, for example, they assume that all potentially affected parties are aware of this rise and will act so as to maximize the benefits it potentiates and minimize any costs. Even within economics, however, this presupposition has been questioned. Simon (1979, 1982), for example, has questioned whether agents act on full information about their circumstances and whether it would be rational for them to seek to achieve full information – given the costs of doing so. Agents typically have routines or habits of information gathering, he argues, which are good enough for all practical purposes and which, on balance, make the process of choice making cost-effective. Outside economics, within philosophy, the work of Karl Popper (1945) takes this point a step further. Popper argues that agents in different positions within the social world have differing degrees of access to various sorts of information. Furthermore, he makes the important point that agents do not act upon the opportunities and constraints within their environment but rather on what they understand and interpret to be the opportunities and constraints within their environment, such that an effective implementation of RAT must focus simultaneously upon objective factors in the environment of social agents and the (inter)subjective interpretations those actors form of that situation.

As we have discussed it hitherto, RAT sounds like a psychological theory, that is, a theory of human nature. Some RATs see it as exactly this and celebrate the fact (Homans 1961, 1973; Elster 1989). Psychology, they argue, is the master discipline within the social sciences and whatever laws or theories might be posited in other social sciences, such as sociology, economics or political science, are always reducible to the basic psychological laws of cost–benefit calculation. Notwithstanding this, however, there is another way to construe the theory which has been more popular among some RAT advocates (e.g. Popper 1945; Goldthorpe 1998). RAT offers a very minimal conception of the human agent, they argue. It suggests that the nature of agents is more or less homogeneous and does not change across either the short or long term. Human beings are just the same wherever and whenever one elects to study them. What does change, however, by virtue of the dynamics of interaction situations, is the set of circumstances which agents find themselves in. While human agents may not often change their priorities, at least not at the basic level, alterations in the social environment, brought about by the actions and interactions of others, may well alter the ratio of costs and benefits attached to specific courses of action, such that rational agents would be persuaded to change their behaviour. Moreover, within the context of the vast web of interactions which make up the social world and have done so historically, different agents will face different types of cost and opportunity, such that we might expect agents in those different situations to act differently. In this respect, in spite of its asocial and individualistic orientation, RAT directs our attention away from the domain of psychology and towards the structures of the social world. In seeking to explain a specific change in behaviour RAT will look for those changes in the environment of agents which has made that change less costly or more profitable. The RAT who seeks to explain a rise in crime figures, for example, will seek out those changes within society that have either increased the rewards or decreased the costs of criminal activity. They will not suppose that certain individuals have undergone a mental metamorphosis or have changed their basic values or goals. Similarly, if particular groups are more inclined towards particular types of crime, they will ask why the utilitarian calculus of costs and rewards favours that type of crime for that type of group but not other crimes or other groups. The social world, from this point of view, consists in a series of exchanges of 'goods', including time and energy, in which agents expend their various resources in order to gain further resources, always with the aim of maximizing 'profit' and minimizing 'costs' (see esp. Homans 1961). There is no society or community as such but rather only a mass of self-interested individuals whose relations to one another are strategic and oriented to self-gain.

For those RAT advocates who are more inclined towards empirical application there is an additional, methodological reason to maintain a more 'sociological' focus. Desires and interests, it is argued, are unobservable and for that reason nebulous and difficult to ascertain empirically. We can only infer their existence, indirectly, from the courses of action an individual takes over a range of different contexts. Many of the opportunities and constraints faced by social agents, by contrast, are open to observation and often measurement. Unemployment figures, for example, may be used as an index of opportunities for gainful employment, while an investigation of various legal changes and social policies provides a relatively clear picture of the basic rewards and punishments attached to specific courses of action at any one time. It is much easier, therefore, to approach the analysis of behaviour from this angle, and the opportunity for precision and rigour is much greater.

The 'realism' of the RAT model is an issue which has been discussed by many of its advocates. On one hand it seems to oversimplify the nature of human agency, ignoring a great many factors, and on the other it seems to attribute calculative properties to agents which have little phenomenological resonance and seem very far removed from the rather more vague manifestations of practical reason that we are aware of. In response to this many RATs have argued for the heuristic value of their approach, over any claims it may or may not have to realism. In effect, this amounts to suggesting that social action happens 'as if' RAT were true, even if we have reason to doubt it at the phenomenological level, and thus that RAT is our best bet it we desire a predictive approach to social science. Whether RAT can deliver on this predictive promise is an issue we will discuss later.

Collective action

The main issue regarding RAT, in this book, is the way it has been applied to the study of social movements. Much of this work of application centres upon what RATs call the collective action problem, a problem most famously associated with the work of Mancur Olson (1971). Olson begins his account of this problem by outlining a concept of 'public goods'. A public good is a good which can only be achieved for a population as a whole or not at all, that is, a good which individuals cannot consume individually or keep to themselves. Moreover, it generally entails some collective effort to achieve it. Many of the goals of social movements and campaign groups fall within this category. Environmental groups cannot win improvements to only their environment, for example, since the environment is something which we all share. Even if environmental policies affect different populations differently, an improvement in the environment is one which we all benefit from to some degree. Similarly, the suffragette campaign to win women the right to vote was a goal which all women stood to gain from, not just those brave souls who fought for their vote. This is a useful example because it draws out the implicit peculiarity of public goods which, in turn, raises the collective action problem. What characterizes public goods is that members of a given population stand to gain from them, whether or not they do anything to help to achieve them. A woman may join the suffragette movement and fight for her vote or she may do nothing but still get the vote anyway because others are fighting for it. She may, to use the jargon, take a 'free ride' on the back of the efforts of others without in any way suffering as a consequence. Similarly, I could join an environmental group and fight to save my environment or I could free ride on the backs of others, that is, spend my time striving for other goals that are important to me and still share equally in the benefits of the activities of those who have elected to fight. Moreover, as I know that my individual effort would contribute very little to the overall campaign of that group, I can reason that the specific improvements to my environment are not affected, either way, by my decision over whether to become involved.

This generates a real theoretical problem for RAT. If the benefits of an action are available to an agent without that agent having to incur any costs, in terms of time, money or effort, then it would be irrational for the agent to elect to pay the costs. This applies equally to all agents within a specific community, however, such that nobody should, in theory, have the motivation to pursue public goods. Consequently, one would predict that nobody would pursue such goods. The force of this problem derives from the fact that people do become involved in the pursuit of collective goals. And importantly, from our point of view, social movement activity is a key example of this. Most people do not join social movements or campaign groups, most of the time, but some people do. They fight to preserve the environment or to win rights for a broad collectivity, such as women or blacks, whether or not the vast majority do. Furthermore, history is replete with examples of mass political action which, by definition, have involved large groups of agents pursuing a specific shared objective, and much of social movements analysis is concerned with precisely these incidents.

The collective action problem is a problem for RAT, in Olson's view, however, not a problem with RAT: that is, it is a problem which RAT must address with its own specific toolbox of concepts. It must explain why, in spite of appearances, it is rational for social agents to engage in collective actions which pursue some form of collective good. His own attempt identifies three particular possibilities for resolving the problem. In the first instance, he points to *the size of the group involved*. If the group is small, he argues, then it can effectively enforce participation from all of its members. Expectations about appropriate conduct can be communicated. All members can be observed by all others, to check that they do what is required. And free riders can be punished. Participation is rational in this context or at least can be made so because the costs of free riding, in the form of punishment, can be made sufficiently high as to outweigh any possible benefits it may have. Moreover, the certainty of being found out for free riding negates any possible risk that the agent might otherwise be prepared to take. Trade unions or at least their local branches, particularly when located in tightly knit geographically concentrated communities, provide a good example of this. They can easily identify and punish free riding strike breakers.

Group size is of particular importance to Olson in this respect but it need not be. In a relatively complex society with a sophisticated technology of surveillance and social control, citizens can be coerced into public actions, such as the paying of taxation, in much the same way as he suggests for the small group. Furthermore, each tax paying individual, who genuinely values the benefits of public spending, would presumably be motivated towards ensuring that the state performed its duties of surveillance and control appropriately in this respect. That is, it might be rational, in light of the free rider problem and its ultimate consequence, namely, that no public goods are achieved, to authorize and buy into a scheme of collective control. This is not a far cry from Hobbes's ([1651] 1971) famous arguments about the *Leviathan* state, although he was talking about a monarchical system of government, with a number of peculiarities which arguably undermine the RAT argument (Laver 1997), while I am referring to a democratic state, funded and legitimated by a (self-interested) citizenry.

The second situation in which it may be rational to partake rather than free ride is when *one is sufficiently rich in whatever resources are required in the form of costs as to make payment cost-effective*, even if others do not do likewise. If I have a great deal of money, for example, the relative cost of a financial donation may be much smaller to me than to my poorer contemporaries. I lose a tiny fraction of my wealth by paying, and am to all intents and purposes completely unaffected, whereas they might be greatly affected by paying the same sum. This does not matter to me, of course, if the public good in question is not of much interest to me, but if it is and I know that nobody will pay for it if I do not, it may be worthwhile for me to pay. The cost–benefit ratio is different for me because cost is defined relative to resources and I am richer in resources.

The third situation, which is perhaps most important in our terms, entails the provision of what Olson terms '*selective incentives*'. A selective incentive is a reward, additional to a basic public good, which is achieved by the same action as that which secures a given public good, but which is only enjoyed by those who contribute directly to securing that public good. Any form of collective action, in other words, might produce two sorts of good: first, a public good which is shared by everyone, irrespective of whether they do anything to secure that good; second, an additional good which is enjoyed only by those who directly participate in securing the public good. These selective benefits provide the additional goods which make the cost–benefit ratio of participation worthwhile for those who work to satisfy the public good. A good example of this idea in practice involves the provision of small incentives for charitable giving. The promise of a 'Save the Whale' car sticker and monthly newsletter might be just the incentive individuals need to donate to Greenpeace, for example, given that they will benefit from the actions of the group whether they donate or not and can reason to themselves that whatever amount they contribute will not make an appreciable difference to the benefits Greenpeace actions are able to achieve in any case.

I will have more to say about the issue of selective incentives in the next chapter. For the moment, however, it must suffice to flag up two potentially problematic issues which stem from it. First, Laver (1997) has argued that this solution raises the question of *who provides selective incentives and what incentive or motivation they have to do so*. Who, for example, would be sufficiently interested in striving to achieve a public good that they would not only initiate a campaign to do so but would also arrange a series of secondary benefits in an effort to coax others into action? More to the point, why would anybody do that? If there are private advantages to be secured through the provision of public goods why would any rational individual elect to take up the role of an organiser who will distribute those advantages to others? Laver believes that there is no good reason for an individual to act in this way and thus questions the selective incentives argument. I am not greatly impressed by this objection. First, selective incentives can be graded within a movement or group, such that those most involved, including those who arrange selective benefits for others, benefit most from them. Many movement organizations, for example, have paid employees. Their incentive to do more than anybody else is that they get paid for what they do and one very clear incentive they have is to do whatever is necessary to maintain the efforts of volunteers, in order that their job is kept safe. This might well involve arranging inducement for unpaid volunteers. Second, there is no obvious reason to suppose that selective benefits will necessarily involve any additional action or production of goods. There may be aspects of movement participation which are sufficiently rewarding, in themselves, to reward those who take the trouble. The feelings of solidarity and purpose which belonging to a movement can afford may be more than enough benefit, for example, to outweigh whatever costs it also entails.

This does lead us to the second problem, however, which is more genuine in my view: the *potential slipperiness of the 'selective incentives' argument* and its overall damaging consequences for the RAT position. The collective action problem is solved at a stroke if we concede that participation in collective action is, in some way, intrinsically satisfying. Our solution becomes even better if we are prepared to say that some people find it more satisfying than others – since that also helps to explain why some people become more involved than others. However, whether or not it is true that collective action is or can be intrinsically satisfying, and sufficiently so to motivate some to engage in it, arguing this would go very much against the grain of the RAT approach. As I noted earlier, any action can be 'explained' by the claim that agents find it sufficiently satisfying or rewarding as to be motivated to engage in it, but this is ultimately unsatisfying for RAT because it takes all the steam out of their explanatory schema, reducing it to the truism that agents generally do whatever it is that they want to do. The selective incentives argument, in other words, looks like the first step on a slippery slope to the banal argument that agents engage in collective action because they enjoy it and therefore want to.

Other ways out of the collective action problem have been proposed (see Laver 1997). These need not concern us here. We have covered sufficient ground to grasp the foundations of the movement theories we will consider in the next two chapters. For the moment it is important to turn to consider some of the basic problems of RAT.

Evaluating RAT

RAT has the potential to present a fascinating thought experiment to social science and its more coherent exponents are able to mount a formidable challenge to many of the deep-seated assumptions of our craft. Furthermore, RAT posits some fairly sensible points about the explanation of behaviour. In particular the claim that changes in human behaviour are often best explained by a changing balance of costs/benefits or opportunities/constraints within the social environment is an instructive one. However, this basic insight does not necessitate all the individualist and asocial baggage which RAT frames it with. Many theories can and do operate, at least tacitly, with such a conception. Durkheim, for example, though critical of utilitarian models of agency such as that of RAT, clearly admits both that much action is utilitarian in orientation and that systems of duty and norms, which he gives more weight to in his account, are most likely to be adhered to when agents have an additional (to duty) incentive for adhering to them (Durkheim [1924] 1974). Human agents are constantly torn between their particular interests and the universal norms of the social world, he argues; but he insists that we can only begin to make sense of this duplex state if we move beyond the naive one-sidedness of Utilitarianism and, by implication, of RAT. Similarly with Mead and Blumer: the largest part of their work is devoted to establishing, against behaviourism, a purposive model of human action, and this model necessarily entails that agents orient to the costs, opportunities and potential profits which their environment affords them. But this is not all that agents orient to for these theorists of collective behaviour. Their socialization, which involves an incorporation of the perspective of both specific and generalized others, draws them out of their particularity such that they orient to universal (or at least generalized) moral expectations, duties and norms. Like Durkheim's agents they find themselves occasionally torn between their particular interests and the demands of moral law. We do not need RAT, therefore, if all we are to take from it is the commonsensical observation that social actors will, all things being equal, act purposively in the pursuit of their own interests. More importantly, it is my contention that the asocial and individualistic baggage which RAT attaches to this basic observation, and which constitutes the real difference between their model and that of others who propose a broadly rational or purposive conception of agency, is deeply problematic. I have arranged my reasons for suggesting this under seven broad headings: sociality, embeddedness, moral theory, rationality, subjectivity, preference and empirical value.

Sociality

As just stated, we can find the basic notion that social agents pursue goals in purposive ways in the work of Blumer, Mead, Durkheim and most other sociologists. Consequently we might equally well attempt to explain and predict action, from the point of view of these theories, by reference to changes in cost/benefit ratios within the social environment of agents. RAT requires us to go one step further than this, however, by assuming a position of methodological individualism and adopting a notion of social agents as basically selfish and asocial. This is one step too far in my view. It is both unnecessary and unhelpful. Methodological individualism, for example, flies in the face of the basic empirical fact that biological individuals become social agents by way of a process of socialization, which involves them 'incorporating' or 'internalizing' structures which are irreducibly social. Many agentic capacities presuppose language use, for example, and language is, both in principle and practice, a social structure. There can be no private language (Wittgenstein 1953) and there can be no social agent without language (Mead 1967). Similarly, the strategic orientation that RATs attribute to agents presupposes an empathic capacity which is derived, in part, from interaction with others, as Mead's (1967) notion of 'taking the role of the other' suggests (see Chapter 2 and Crossley 1996). To act strategically in relation to others one must be capable of second guessing their probable reactions to one's own actions, and one does this by adopting their role, a skill which one acquires through interaction with and imitation of them. By the same token, much of what has value for human beings, including money and status, only has value by virtue of the collective agreement of the group and, in some cases, can only be valuable for individuals insofar as they assume the perspective of the group. The esteem which others bestow, by definition, upon high-status goods, can only be of value to the agent insofar as she experiences that esteem, and this presupposes an intersubjective orientation to the perspective of the group.

What these points amount to is a claim that the social theories I discussed earlier in this book actually provide a better framework for making sense of the notion of purposive, cost–benefit behaviour, both because RAT makes some untenable assumptions and, more positively, because theories which assume a social or intersubjective position are better placed to explain many of the basic empirical attributes of social agents. This is not simply a matter of making the cost–benefit model work better, however. RAT is limited to an account of cost–benefit behaviour where, in the other theories, this is one aspect in a much broader and more complex approach to social life. We could say a great deal in this context but it must suffice to make two points. First, Durkheim and Mead, in particular, add much complexity to the basic utilitarian model of agency by drawing our attention to the competing and sometimes conflicting claims which private desires and public duties or norms can make upon an agent. Utility is only one consideration in their theory of agency. Second, as we saw in Chapter 2, Mead in particular draws out the central importance of identity to both the constitution of the agent and the steering of action. Again, he shows that there is more to agency than utility.

This is not just a matter of theory in general. It concerns the theorization of social movements. The collective action problem posed by RAT is useful and interesting. Even if one is not wholly convinced of its premises it would be foolhardy to deny that it points to a very real issue. Moreover, reflection upon this issue or problem can serve a useful heuristic purpose for those of us who wish to research and theorize about social movements. We should be asking ourselves how movements which serve a common public good manage to enlist supporters. And we might extend this further by asking how and why such movements as animal rights movements, which advocate entirely on the behalf of others (in this case other species) and seemingly do not stand to benefit at all from the goals they pursue, nevertheless manage to secure devoted recruits. Thinking along with RAT in such cases, providing we do not succumb too readily to simple-minded cynicism, may serve a useful function in opening up important and researchable questions. Notwithstanding this, however, it is only too obvious that many aspects of social movement activity fall outside the remit of the collective action problem and of RAT itself. Identity, for example is an issue even in those movements which are not explicitly 'identity movements': e.g. labour movements are concerned with working-class consciousness and black civil rights movements with black pride and identity. More to the point, 'identity' is an issue which social movement analysts might quite legitimately wish to explore. But it is an issue which RAT overlooks both in its minimal conception of the actor and its minimal construction of the question of social movements around the collective action problem. In this respect RAT is overly restrictive in the questions it allows us to ask and answer.

Embeddedness

A further and related problem with RAT is that it operates with a generic conception of the agent, failing to appreciate fully the extent to which agents are embedded in the social structure. More sophisticated RATs recognize that social agents occupy different spaces in a social order which is both horizontally and vertically differentiated. But they fail to recognize the extent to which occupation of those differential social locations gives rise to a different range of agentic dispositions. They have little conception, for example, of class cultures or of gender or ethnic variations in cultural forms of being-in-the-world (Savage 2000). This is of importance in relation to social movement analysis for a range of reasons. In particular, as we will note later, some social groups, particularly the educated middle classes, are considerably more likely to participate in and contribute to movement causes that they do not stand to benefit directly from (Bagguley 1992, 1995a; Rootes 1995). Moreover, this is seemingly a reflection of their group culture or 'habitus' (see Chapter 9) and not simply a response to structural location or shifts in resources. Indeed, it defies the logic of RAT (see Chapter 5).

Moral theory

RAT is an analytic and explanatory theory rather than a normative theory. It aims to predict and explain how things actually happen in the world rather than stipulating what ought to happen. These distinctions are important and analytically solid. Notwithstanding this, however, explanatory and normative theories do overlap. Both of the two main moral theories of modern philosophy, Utilitarianism and Kantian deontological ethics, for example, explicitly rest upon a particular theory of the nature of social agents. And as Parsons (1968) famously shows, the very birth of sociology, in the work of Durkheim and Weber, was premised upon a critique of the Utilitarian conception in favour of a more deontological view. To spell this out briefly and somewhat crudely, the Utilitarians believed that human beings are motivated by the pursuit of pleasure and the avoidance of pain and that the only proper definition of the moral 'good', therefore, could be that which maximizes pleasure and minimizes pain for the largest number of people. Kant, by contrast, defined morality in terms of an overcoming of particular wants or pleasures in terms of a universal standard. A potential course of action is 'right', he argues, if we can reasonably wish for all people in the same situation to act in that way. This introduces notions of shared norms, duty and a 'sense of duty' into moral theory, and it is this that appealed to the early sociologists in their work. They believed that social order is impossible to achieve in a situation in which all individuals privately pursue their selfish ends. Such a situation could only result in chaos and fragmentation, much as Hobbes ([1651] 1971) conveys in his image of the 'war of all against all'. Society as we know it, they argued, presupposes universalized (that is, throughout society) normative frameworks and systems of duty or obligation, which require agents, on some occasions at least, to subordinate their own private pleasures to the good of the collective. It is for this reason that many sociological theories, including those of both Mead and Durkheim, whom we have discussed, identify a tension or division within social agents between utilitarian wants and social obligations and duties.

These moral issues are of relevance in relation to the analysis of social movements because the action of movements is very often focused upon the legitimacy of norms, duties and obligations. Many movements, particularly the so-called 'new social movements', are moral movements. They embody the emergence of a new ethos, in Weber's ([1956] 1978) sense of the term, that is, a new ethical orientation towards, for example, animals, the environment or simply the living of everyday life, and a new conception of what 'the good life' would be. We need a perspective which can connect with these issues. One of my concerns about RAT is that it cannot. It is a species of Utilitarianism and issues of duty, norms and justice are difficult to conceive from this position. Agents act for profit (utility) according to RAT, not according to principles or duty. In this respect RAT is incapable of adequately making sense of a very large aspect of movement activity (see also Jasper 1997).

Rationality

Further problems stem from RAT's conception of rationality. Why should we collude with RAT in supposing that human rationality is reducible to an instrumental disposition for linking means to ends and weighing up costs and benefits, when the evidence of our everyday experience, not to mention social movement activity, points to a much wider conception? The moral arguments raised by social movements, from the labour movements and suffragettes through black civil rights and anti-apartheid movements to contemporary concerns with the environment and animal rights, all demonstrate a quite different form or use of rationality. Movements are communicatively rational, in Blumer's sense, or at least they can be so. Their rationality manifests itself in the persuasiveness of the arguments they are able to level in defence of their cause and the force which those arguments are able to exert as a consequence. They reveal a reflexive rationality within the social world which enables the members of that world to turn back upon it and subject it to critical analysis and evaluation. To ignore this, as RAT does, is to ignore some of the most important and interesting aspects of the activity of social movements. Furthermore, it is to fail to take seriously the moral force and claim of these movements.

We encounter an interesting paradox here. Part of the appeal of RAT, for some movement analysts, is that it restores rationality and thus dignity to the agent, avoiding the irrational and derisory picture, which, it is alleged, is painted by the collective behaviour approach. My exposition of Blumer gives ample reason to believe that this caricature of collective behaviour is wholly inappropriate. More to the point, however, we can see that in its own way the RAT model is equally derisory. It ignores and must ignore the rational–moral force of the arguments raised by social movement activists, since it has no means by which to address or understand such arguments. And in the final instance it must reduce whatever claims are posited within the movement context to the narrow self-interests of movement participants.

I do not mean to deny that movements can and do reason in instrumentally or strategically rational ways, nor that individuals, including movement participants, are sometimes devious and selfish. But to suggest that this is all that human rationality consists of and that human beings are incapable of either recognizing others or struggling to overcome their own utilitarian motivations is, in my view, narrow, false and analytically unhelpful (see also Fereee 1992; Jasper 1997).

Subjectivity

It is not simply the conception of rationality that is flawed within RAT. A capacity for instrumental reasoning is by no means a self-sufficient basis for agency. To make even a basic choice about action agents must have:

- preferences, desires or goals which make a choice meaningful and not simply arbitrary;
- a means of gathering further information about the world, should further information be required;
- an understanding or interpretation of their situation and the various obstacles and opportunities it poses, such that action can be reasonably oriented to its environment and costs and benefits calculated;
- a means of deliberation for deciding between possible alternatives.

Given that these are basic prerequisites for choice, they cannot, in the final instance, be explained as an outcome of choice. They constitute the unchosen basis of choice. As such they each pose a number of problems for RAT. I consider the issue of preference separately under my next heading. In the meantime I will briefly consider the problems posed by the other three.

The issue of *information gathering* was discussed above in connection with Simon's (1979, 1982) work. He rightly challenges the assumption of 'full information', I noted, and suggests that agents generally have basic habits or routines of information gathering which are 'good enough' for all practical purposes. This complicates the RAT model because it forces us to consider possible sociological variations in information seeking practices, thereby introducing the possibility that choice is affected by unchosen social influences. The agent who, by force of habit, 'knows where to look' for specific sorts of information about certain situations will act differently in those situations from the one who does not. And knowing where to look is a function of prior experience, which is inevitably shaped by one's location in a social structure. Individuals raised in a 'share dealing' family, for example, are more likely to know where to look to find out more about good opportunities for investment. They will have habits of information seeking better suited to this pursuit. Similarly, agents raised in differently politicized contexts will acquire different habits of political information seeking.

This already shades into the issue of *understanding and interpretation*. Access to information is never simply a matter of brute data but also of the active processes by which the agent reads and makes sense of data, a process which could run in very different directions for different agents. This may be a matter of competence. The financial pages of my newspaper are of little value to me in my economic decision making if I have never been taught how to decipher their various tables. Similarly, Japanese newspapers inform me of nothing because I do not read Japanese and the basic meteorological 'signs' of an impending storm pass me by because I do not know how to read them either. In all these cases something unequivocal may be 'communicated' but not to me because I lack the necessary schemas of understanding to make sense of them. Information only informs those who are predisposed to be informed by it and it thereby only has (relatively) predictable effects upon that group. In addition, even competent and appropriately skilled agents may disagree in their reading of a specific situation on account of differences in their interests and the various accumulated typifications and prejudgements or prejudices they bring to that situation. Highly competent political analysts often read political situations differently, for example, and deduce widely varying predictions upon this basis. And if their interpretations form the basis of actions then these too will be different. Not that this is a strictly individual matter. My interests and schemas of interpretation are a function of my accumulated social experiences and while nobody has quite the same background as I do, the broad conditions of my formative experiences are by no means unique and were scarcely undergone in isolation. Interpretative schemas, in at least some instances, have a social distribution. They emerge in group contexts such as status groups, communities or classes.

As I noted above, some RATs, such as Popper (1945), recognize this. They do not offer any suitable means for analysing these processes of interpretation, however, thus generating a major stumbling block for their own recommendations. Moreover, the question of interpretation is just the sort of Pandora's box that RATs want to keep a lid on. Once this issue is raised the simple and parsimonious model they want to use is shot through with complexities and complications, and the hope of preserving an asocial and individual conception of agency drops over to the further side of futility.

In light of this RATs may elect to ignore the issue of interpretation, to pretend, for argument's sake, that agents respond to objective conditions in the social world, as they are, or perhaps rather to assume that interpretations do not vary so significantly as to constitute a major obstacle. This latter point may be true to some extent, but then we have to ask both what the greater good is that motivates us to ignore interpretative processes, however sticky a datum they prove to be, and whether electing to do so can ever be anything other than a temporary stage in a broader and more interpretative approach. There is no reason to bracket out issues of interpretation, except perhaps as a temporary stage in a wider analytic strategy, unless we have a specific desire to 'save the RAT' and that is no reason at all! Furthermore, within the movements context in particular we are forced to confront the important objection that one of the defining features of movements, very often, is that they bring a new interpretation to a particular situation and/or clash with established interpretations, such that interpretation and its modalities are an important and non-bracketable feature of the phenomenon we are supposed to be investigating. What makes the animal rights movement if not a different way of perceiving animals? And what sense could we possibly hope to make of the emergence of that movement if we were not prepared to consider the nature and emergence of that particular perspective (see Jasper and Nelkin 1992)? I do not intend to suggest by this that movement analysis should be or could be dissolved into hermeneutics, nor that it may not sometimes be possible and preferable to treat the interpretative aspect of a movement's action as relatively unproblematic. But without the willingness and the tools to address the problem of interpretation we are very poorly equipped to make sense of social movements. RAT has neither.

The final precondition of choice which I have listed above is access to a *technique of deliberation*. This issue is raised in an important critique of the RAT approach by Hindess (1988). He observes that decision making, in practice, depends upon a specific technique of decision making and that, again in practice, different techniques are evident. Extreme examples include the oracle magic studied by Evans-Pritchard (1976) in his much cited study of the Azande; astrological consultation, such as famously guided Ronald Reagan through some of his more pressing dilemmas as American president; and the roll of a dice or toss of a coin as depicted by Luke Rhinehart in his novel, *The Diceman*. Less extreme examples would be the different techniques which various organizations, including movement organizations, use to arrive at decisions for courses of action. The current British Labour Party, for example, prides itself on balloting its members on key decisions so as to let them 'decide' important issues and policy directions for the party, but it has lurched from one crisis to the next over the specific methods of balloting it has used. As with individual methods of 'weighing up the odds', different techniques generate different results and therefore suggest different courses of action. RAT, Hindess notes, ignores this. It assumes that decision making is an unproblematic process of enumerating and calculating odds and cost/benefit ratios. And it therefore ignores a crucial determinate of choice and action. As a consequence, he continues, it reduces its chances of effectively predicting the course of action in any given situation. Agents simply will arrive at different courses of action if they use different techniques of deliberation.

As with the other points mentioned above, this indicates an element of agency which is potentially open to social determination and differentiation in a way that is quite strongly at odds with the asocial assumptions of RAT. We acquire schemas of deliberation as surely as any form of competence and like other dispositions such schemas may therefore be expected to follow a social distribution. The Azande are more likely to be guided by a sacred oracle in their action than a western European, and only modern economic agents, as Weber ([1956] 1978) reveals, will use double entry bookkeeping to take stock of their position.

Even the notion of deliberation itself is problematic, however. It paints an overly reflective picture of action. Individual agents do not deliberate over their every action, not least because there is not always time and because social situations are unpredictable to a point whereby they defy exact planning. Like players in sport, social agents have a practical feel for their fields of action, rooted in experience and competence, and they must trust to this feel if they are to act competently in those fields (Bourdieu 1992a; Crossley 2001a, b). This is nowhere more pertinent than in the field of protest and social movements where social agents must respond to new and novel events as they unfold, acting strategically without always having the time to form detailed reflective strategies.

Preference

Similar problems arise in relation to the issue of preference or desire. Some RATs choose to ignore this aspect of agency on account of its rather nebulous character. Others are concerned to offer reductive and asocial explanations of the origins of whatever apparently pro-social goals or desires they can identify. Neither strategy is particularly satisfying. We cannot elect to ignore desires or take them for granted, particularly in social movement analyses, for the same reason that we cannot generally ignore interpretations: what is often very interesting about social movements is the formulation of preferences or interests that they bring into being. This is most obvious in relation to such movements as environmentalism and animal rights. When and how did social agents acquire a preference for saving the environment or other species? When and how was this interest formulated? We need to explore these questions, not least because they are fundamental to the question of how many movements have emerged. If we do elect to study these issues, however, it must be in a historical way. The 'just so' stories that RAT is liable to concoct about the base motivations of even the most altruistic of sentiments really serve little purpose. Suppose, for example, that the desire to save whales serves a selfish end. Does knowing this fact help us to predict how whale savers will act? It does not. The best cue we have to predicting the way in which they will act is the fact that they claim to want to save whales and are therefore likely to act in whatever ways will promote this end – although there are other considerations of course. If we are really interested in the origin of this sentiment we would do better to analyse the conditions of its historical emergence and reproduction within specific societies rather than second-guessing the 'true' or 'underlying' motivations which give rise to it.

This point touches upon one final problem with RAT: its illusion of depth. RATs aim to explain all human behaviour in terms of a few basic, selfish desires. Their argument, to reiterate, is that we can postulate a desire or preference to correspond with each and every sort of behaviour in which human beings engage, but that doing so reduces the process of explanation to a superficial tautology. Hence they aim to reduce all preferences to a few basic desires. In my view this strategy is no better. If all actions are explained in terms of a very narrow range of possible desires the results are no more illuminating than if a vast range of desires are invoked. As in the caricature of Freudian explanations, we know that sooner or later the analysis will boil down, by however obscure a path, to the one basic motivation that is alleged to underlie everything. The problem here, more specifically, is that it becomes increasingly difficult to explain why agents act in different ways if we assume that their basic motivations are the same. Why does John pursue his selfish desire by fighting for animal rights when Jane pursues hers by buying an expensive mink coat? More to the point, what possible purpose is served by explaining John's animal rights activism in terms of a basic selfish desire if the same desire makes Jane behave so differently? Boiling actions down to a few basic desires is just as unhelpful and banal as multiplying them up so as to identify one for each and every form of behaviour.

If we wish to understand preferences, I suggest, we should adopt a double strategy. First, to understand why specific agents develop specific preferences we must attend to their biographies and, particularly, to those events which have seemingly shaped their preferences. Insofar as this might point to experiences which are more common among certain social groups, it could pan out into a broader historical account. Second, at a broader level, we should seek to explore the history of specific preferences in general, that is, the manner in which specific types of preference (such as the preference for animal welfare) have emerged and spread within our societies. To some extent the decision of the individual to advocate for specific social causes is an effect of the pre-existence of those causes as possible avenues for action and the individual preference cannot therefore be explained independently of the broader social history of that preference.

Empirical value

RAT might be forgiven any of these omissions or problems if, in practice, it was able to provide strong and reliable empirical predictions about social and political behaviour. This, after all, is the rationale for RAT, given that even its proponents acknowledge its lack of realism. It is, they argue, a heuristically useful and parsimonious model. Unfortunately, however, empirical tests have not proved favourable. Agents do not often act as RAT predicts that they will (Green and Shapiro 1994). Laver (1997) has attempted to defend RAT against this charge. He concedes that the empirical contributions of RAT are 'few and far between' and that what applications there have been are 'decidedly unimpressive'. But he sees a virtue in this:

> This is that it does tend to be a rigorous theory, generating well speci-fied propositions that with the appropriate evidence can be determined as being either true or false, in a discipline [political science] in which much of the other theorising is imprecise, casual, ad hoc and therefore much easier to find some sort of generalised empirical support for.
>
> . . . The bottom line for our purposes is that rational choice models do as well empirically, as most other *rigorous and well specified* models in political science, when it comes to the business of empirical evaluation.
>
> (Laver 1997: 14–15, his emphasis)

I have some sympathy with this retort. It is very easy to find support for vague claims and the Popperian values of clarity and falsifiability are important. However, my sympathy is not too great. Theoretical models in the social sciences often fail to formulate clear and testable propositions, in Laver's sense, because they suggest that the actual course of events in any social situation is subject to too many conditions and complications to admit of straightforward prediction: e.g. matters of interpretation which cannot be predicted with sufficient accuracy in advance. RAT suggests it can do better than this. It suggests that it is possible to predict social action on the basis of a few simple propositions. But it has so far failed to do so. It has failed by the criteria which it has set for itself and which it has used, theoretically, to sidestep obvious objections about its oversimplification of the nature of agency and the social world. The question therefore inevitably emerges as to whether it might not make more sense to admit that a more complex model of the agent is required, even if this might reduce the pro-spect of our formulating straightforwardly falsifiable claims. I suggest that it would.

On a positive note

I do not want to conclude this chapter on a purely negative note. There are two positive points that need to be drawn out of the discussion of this chapter. First, to reiterate my earlier point, however one-sided and prob-lematic RAT may be it remains a useful intellectual tool. It obscures some issues and oversimplifies others but it can provide a useful first step for addressing such issues as movement formation and participation. It is an instructive foil which we may bring into dialogue with more complex positions. Furthermore, as I have also noted, many theories subscribe to the basic assumptions of the model, even if they do not take them to extremes. This is another reason why it may work as a point of departure. Second, the criticisms I have made of rational choice should be viewed as critical tests that we can use to construct a more persuasive account of movement formation. We need a model of agency which can deal with the problems that RAT cannot. The interactionist model of Mead and Blumer, discussed in Chapter 2, goes some of the way towards meeting this critical test. I will be suggesting in the final chapter that there is a better alternative, however. With this said we can turn to examining some of those models which have used the RAT model.

Summary and conclusion

The latter part of this chapter has listed a considerable number of problems with RAT. These are genuine problems and, insofar as they are carried over into social movement theories informed by RAT, we need to be alert to them. Notwithstanding this, however, we need also to recognize the value of RAT, and not simply in its role as thought-provoking adversary. The collective action problem raised by RAT poses important issues for movement theory, even if we do not wholly accept its premises. Moreover, in moving the language of opportunities, costs and restraints to the centre of our theoretical frame, even if those issues are tacitly presupposed in other theories we have examined, RAT performs an important function. It alerts us to a range of concerns that are, at best, only poorly accounted for in the collective behaviour approach.

Further reading

For a good basic introduction to RAT, which is more sophisticated than many, see Elster's (1989) *Nuts and Bolts for the Social Sciences*. A good review of the variations of the theory and their respective degrees of relevance to sociology can be found in Goldthorpe's (1998) article, 'Rational actor theory for sociology'.

chapter five

Resources, networks and organizations

Although it has been important in social movement analysis, RAT cannot be regarded as an independent perspective on movement formation in its own right. Its influence has been felt through other perspectives which have incorporated, to varying degrees, its basic assumptions and models. In this chapter I focus on the first of two such approaches: 'resource mobilization' (RM). In the first section I discuss what I call the basic position of RM. This section will focus particularly upon the theoretical formulations of Oberschall (1973) and upon an empirical study of a farm workers' protest in the USA by Jenkins and Perrow (1977). In the second section I consider a slightly more elaborate RM model developed by McCarthy, Zald and Ash (McCarthy and Zald 1977; Zald and Ash 1966). This model introduces many of the central concepts usually associated with RM and offers a very interesting account of how movements work. Finally, I discuss what I call the 'network argument'. This is an RM argument which has been appropriated by other theoretical camps, beyond RM, and my account follows this path of migration. I begin with an RM version of the network argument but then devote my discussion to the more general emphasis on networks in movement theory.

The basic position

There can be little doubt that the main pioneers of RM were all greatly impressed by Olson's collective action problem and the RAT model which underlay it. All the key foundational texts of the approach make some reference to Olson and many make quite explicit reference, albeit under different names, to RAT (e.g. Oberschall 1973; Tilly 1978; Jenkins 1983). It is also apparent, however, that most felt free to pick up certain aspects of RAT which were useful, without buying into the model lock, stock and barrel. Of all RM theorists Oberschall (1973) is most explicit regarding both his appropriation of the work of Olson and those aspects of it which, he believes, require modification. He accepts Olson's basic model of the actor. There is no reason to 'relax the assumption of rational, self-interested behaviour postulated by Olson', he argues. Some sociologists believe that there is because, following Olson's formulation of the collective action problem, they assume that it would not be rational for a self-interested actor to become involved in a collective struggle. Against this, however, Oberschall invokes Olson's notion of 'selective incentives', which, he argues, are more than sufficient to draw a rational actor into a collective struggle:

> Olson's theory in no way implies that individual goods and selective incentives are not also present in group formation, and it is precisely individual goods and selective incentives that can account for the emergence of leaders and activists . . .
>
> (Oberschall 1973: 116)

This statement draws a distinction between leaders of movements and rank and file activists. In the case of the rank and file, Oberschall argues, incentives are often provided or mobilized by leaders. Leaders can reward with praise or valued goods, for example, and can, under certain circumstances, punish the inactive. But there are many naturally occurring incentives to motivate leaders too. One that Oberschall particularly emphasizes is the promise of status and political office, a reward which is all the more tempting if the talented and highly motivated members of an oppressed social group have no other route out of their disadvantaged situation. There are few rewards for the talented and motivated members of an oppressed group, he argues, particularly if that group is restricted to menial forms of work. But community and political leadership, with the status and recognition it affords, can serve in just this way. Furthermore, such individuals may find that it becomes increasingly costly not to mobilize their community if their elevated or prominent profile in the community marks them out for hostile treatment from external elites. The more talented and motivated can often become the most persecuted in an oppressed group and thus those with the least to lose and the most to gain from mobilization.

Reference to costs and rewards brings to light the processes of resource exchange and mobilization that are involved in movement politics. This applies, as we have seen, to interactions between leaders and the rank and file. The actions of each are determined by the various exchanges between them and what each is able and willing to give to the other; the rank and file bestow recognition upon their leaders and leaders mobilize the rank and file with whatever 'rewards' this elevated position puts at their disposal. It has a wider and more general application too, however. In order to mobilize politically, agents and groups require the resources to do so and they must mobilize those resources, that is, use them and put them into effect. By resources Oberschall means '. . . anything from material resources – jobs, incomes, savings, and the right to material goods and services – to nonmaterial resources – authority, moral commitment, trust, friendship, skills, habits of industry . . .' (Oberschall 1973: 28), and he adds:

> In ordinary everyday activity, at work, in family life, and in politics, people manage their resources in complex ways: they exchange some resources for other resources; they make up resource deficits by bor- rowing resources; they recall their earlier investments. Resources are constantly being created, consumed, transferred, assembled and reallo- cated, exchanged, and even lost.
>
> (Oberschall 1973: 28)

Political mobilization is, in this respect, much like any other branch of social life. It is motivated, coordinated and facilitated by shifts in resources.

Oberschall uses this insight to add to Olson's model in two important respects. First, he notes that it provides us with a means of examining the relationship between broad structural shifts in society and the various forms of political mobilization which sometimes accompany it. Olson's theory does not examine the effect of shifts in political or economic life, Oberschall observes, but the well-documented effect of such shifts quite clearly bears out his position if this fundamental observation about resources is kept firmly in sight. It is often noted, for example, that uprisings and revolutions occur at times of political liberalization, rather than of increased repres- sion, or at times of economic upturn rather than depression. This is difficult to explain from the point of view of a theory which focuses upon griev- ances as the chief cause of revolt. From Olson's point of view, however, it makes perfect sense. The lifting of certain forms of political repression, for example, makes organization and mobilization less costly and thus shifts the utilitarian balance in favour of action. And similarly with economic upturn: 'In difficult times, people are too busy just making a living and are consuming all of their resources, but, in more prosperous times, they have a small surplus of time, energy, and material resources that they are able to 'invest' in protest organisation and behaviour' (Oberschall 1973: 115). Thus, we need to factor this notion of structural changes which affect the costs and benefits of activism into our model.

Second, Oberschall argues that mobilization can be effected through an importation of 'external' resources. The collective action problem is focused upon a community which must act alone, he observes. In real life, however, oppressed communities or groups are often helped by other, better resourced communities or groups who form alliances with them and supply them with resources for mobilization which they might other- wise lack. Indeed, he even goes so far as to suggest that the protests and movements of relatively powerless groups are often facilitated and triggered by an injection of resources and support from external elites. Powerless groups, he argues, are often precisely what their name suggests, 'powerless'. It is only when more powerful groups come to their aid that the resource base necessary for effective protest falls into place. A number of RM theorists have sought to support this point empirically, including Oberschall himself. As it is an important aspect of RM theory I will offer an extended discussion of one important supporting study: Jenkins and Perrow's (1977) study of the insurgency of US farm workers in the late 1960s.

The farm workers' struggle

Jenkins and Perrow focus their study on the protest behaviour of farm workers in the USA between 1946 and 1972. They are particularly interested in the activism of the farm workers in the late 1960s, which formed part of the wider activism of that period, but they set this within the longer historical context, not least because this provides them with a comparative perspective from which to infer the active ingredients responsible for the specific characteristics of the later period. They divide the time series they analyse into three periods: 1946–55, 1956–64, and 1965–72. In the first period, they note, there was a brief attempt by the Farm Labor Union to mobilize workers to improve their conditions of work, chiefly by way of strikes. This action was short-lived, however, and relatively unsuccessful. Strike actions were thwarted by strike-breaking labour and the efforts to prevent this strike-breaking activity were challenged by elites at both the local and national level. Perhaps as a consequence of this, the second period (1956–64) was a much quieter time, at least for the farm workers themselves. This was a time of wider political change in the USA, however, much of which was favourable to farm workers. Conflicts between elite groups and the activism of liberal pressure groups functioned to remove many of the factors that had prevented the earlier farm strikes from being successful and generated an atmosphere more favourable to the plight of the farm workers. Jenkins and Perrow attribute this, in turn, to a rise in economic prosperity: 'The activism of several key liberal organisations depended, in turn, upon broad economic trends, especially the growth of middle-class disposable income that might be invested in worthy causes (Jenkins and Perrow 1977: 263). This then set the scene for the final period (1965–72), which involved a return to activism. Protest activity reached new peaks of intensity during this period and was sustained throughout. Furthermore, it was successful in bringing about desired improvements in farm workers' conditions of employment. Strike activity intensified and in this case attempted strike breaking was not generally upheld. Moreover, a general boycott of the fruits of 'scab labour' was successfully implemented and proved effective in forcing the hand of more recalcitrant elites.

In their attempt to explain this pattern of activism, Jenkins and Perrow counterpose their argument, which focuses upon resources, with a straw model of the collective behaviour approach, focused upon 'grievances' and strain. Though they lack the evidence they conjecture that the degree of strain that farm workers were under and the grievances consequently experienced were constant throughout the period they studied. There is no reason to think otherwise, they maintain. Consequently grievances and strains cannot explain the pattern. One cannot explain variation by reference to a constant factor. Resources for struggle, by contrast, did vary during this period, and they varied in just the way one would predict to explain the pattern of struggle their survey discovered. The initial protests of the farm workers, during the 1940s, were aided by a small influx of resources from outside elites. But these resources were too small and insufficiently constant to enable a major action. In the late 1960s, by contrast, liberals and some elites had developed a sympathy for the farm workers' plight and were in a position to inject resources into that domain, with the net outcome of increased and more successful insurgency. They offered organizational help, as well as money, but more particularly they organized and supported a boycott on strike-breaking produce. This shift in sympathy and resource allocation began to take place in the second period, but its consequences are what largely make up the third. An injection of resources from outside both made political insurgency possible and increased its chances of success.

What Jenkins and Perrow are arguing, at one level, is that farm workers, who are a relatively powerless and resource-poor group, were not able to organize themselves effectively without an inflow of resources. These workers needed help before they could mount an effective campaign. The case is taken further than this, however. What Jenkins and Perrow describe is a situation in which liberal elites took over the struggle of the farm workers:

> The effectiveness of the boycott depended little upon the resources of mobilised farm workers; instead, they became a political symbol. It was the massive outpouring of support, especially from liberals and organised labor, that made the boycott effective and, thereby, forced the growers to the bargaining table.
>
> (Jenkins and Perrow 1977: 264)

and

> Marches, symbolic arrests of clergy, and public speeches captured public attention; contributions of labour unions, theatre showings and 'radical chic' cocktail parties with products to '*La Causa*' supplemented the budget provided by sponsors and membership dues.
>
> (Jenkins and Perrow 1977: 264)

I will return to this argument later. For the moment, however, it must suffice to offer two brief observations. In the first instance it presupposes the existence of a liberal left elite who, when they have excess resources, in the form of time or money, etc., are both willing and able to inject them into good causes. This is a common assumption in some RM work and it raises interesting questions which we will discuss at the end of this chapter. Second, the argument suggests that protests by oppressed and powerless groups may often need to be 'patronized' by middle-class elites if they are to succeed. Struggles 'from below' are determined by preferences 'from above'. Another way of putting this might be to say that we should not be misled by the success of certain movements into believing that the power structure of western democracies is more open and power more dispersed than it actually is. Struggles against the establishment may succeed because some members of that establishment wish them to.

Criticism of the basic position

There is much to commend in this basic position but also much to criticize. I will return to many of the faults of the position later in the paper, when we have explored RM a little more deeply. However, it would be useful to examine some of the criticisms which have been directed against this very specific argument about elite patronization. McAdam (1982) has been a very vocal and insightful critic. His critique has two basic aspects. First, he offers a theoretical objection. RM theory is based upon an elite model of power, he notes. It suggests that political power is concentrated in the hands of a minority. This is an improvement upon pluralist models of power, which suggest that power is equally distributed throughout the polity. From the pluralist position, which takes no account of the exclusion of certain groups from the political and power centres of society, the adoption of extra-institutional forms of protest by such groups inevitably appears excessive, unnecessary and therefore irrational (see also Piven and Cloward 1979). Elite theory takes an important step in remedying this by highlighting the concentrated nature of power and related processes of political exclusion. It is perfectly rational for an excluded group to adopt extra-institutional tactics of struggle, from the point of view of elite theory, because there are really no other channels open to them.

Notwithstanding this, McAdam is critical of elite theory, and more particularly of RM theory, for failing to identify the latent power of excluded groups. Adopting what he dubs a more 'Marxist' approach, McAdam argues that excluded groups are often in a structural position to generate a considerable amount of power and leverage, albeit by extra-institutional means, if they are sufficiently well organized and they realize their own (potential) power. This criticism raises issues to do with organization, networks and cognition which I deal with later in this chapter and in the next. For the moment suffice it to say that the implication of McAdam's position is that excluded and apparently powerless groups are not actually as powerless as they may seem and are not, for this reason, dependent upon elite groups for patronage and resource mobilization. They have the potential to do it on their own.

This theoretical argument is supported empirically by McAdam by reference to black insurgency and the rise of the civil rights movement in the USA between the forties and the late sixties. An injection of external resources was not necessary to initiate this movement. External resources did flow into it but only after it had gathered momentum and achieved a few victories. Successful movement mobilization led to resource mobilization, not vice versa. Furthermore, McAdam notes that the effect of this resourcing was not entirely beneficial. It tended in certain circumstances to inhibit the movement. Some radical groups became dependent upon the elites who patronized them and these elites, who were opposed to more radical sentiments and tactics, thereby acquired the leverage to steer these groups in a less radical direction. Radicals were 'encouraged' and 'persuaded' to tone down their speeches and demands, for example (see also Piven and Cloward 1979).

These criticisms are important. They falsify any claim which RM theorists might make to the universal application of their theory of external sponsorship. However, McAdam's observations do not warrant a claim that things never happen as the RM theorists suggest. Whether or not excluded groups enjoy a latent structural power it might still be the case, in some instances, that struggle is triggered by an injection of external resources – although elites, assuming they are not Blumer's (1969) 'agitators', can only pump resources into causes which already exist and, in this respect, there must be some semblance of struggle in process before they become involved. Furthermore, the degree to which patronizing elites interfere in the organization of the struggles they patronize is assumedly subject to variation between struggles and across time. McAdam's critique shows that events do not necessarily unfold as the RM theory suggests but not that they never unfold in that way or that they always unfold in a different way.

There is another problem with this theory of elite sponsorship, however. It sits very unhappily with Obershall's aforementioned claim that there is no reason to 'relax the assumption of rational self-interested behaviour postulated by Olson' (1973: 116). From Olson's point of view it is odd enough that any agent would pursue a collective good that they stand to benefit directly from but RM theory, while claiming to stick tightly to Olson, is proposing that a liberal grouping within the middle class are prepared to pump resources of time, energy and money into struggles from which they have nothing to gain directly. I am not questioning that these elites exist or that they sometimes do what the RM theorists say that they do. There is much empirical evidence to suggest that they do just this. But it is not at all clear how this observation squares with the basic theoretical assumption that agents act in self-interested ways. It may be argued here that McAdam has answered our query for us. The reason that liberal elites sponsor struggles, it might be argued, is that they are not quite so liberal as they appear. They sponsor struggles because that is the best way of taming those struggles, so as to preserve the status quo. Moreover, it could be that by promoting certain sorts of struggle they can rally others into an attack upon their own chief competitors within the 'field of power'. However, this type of response will only go so far. It is entirely plausible that threatened elites might willingly embrace insurgent groups as a way of containing potential struggle and lessening the prospect of major social changes which might threaten their privileged position. It is commonly suggested, for example, that British liberals took the first steps towards a welfare state in the UK as a way of pre-empting what appeared to be a brewing revolutionary fervour. They championed the workers' movement in order to save themselves from it (Gough 1979). However, much evidence points to the over-representation of the liberal middle classes in struggles which could not be interpreted in this way. Many studies of the so-called new social movements, such as environmentalism and pacifism, for example, reveal a considerable over-representation by the educated middle class (for an overview see Rootes 1995; Byrne 1997; Crossley 2000a). I will return to this point later. For the moment it must suffice to say that middle-class liberals are a spanner in the RM works.

Finally, we must question the apparent desire of the RM theorists to dispense with the matter of grievances. Two points are particularly pertinent here. First, a focus upon grievances is necessary if we are to maintain a sense of both the intelligibility and the normativity of struggles or movements. Grievances may do little to explain the timing of a movement's emergence but without a grasp upon these grievances we would find it very difficult to make any sense of what the movement was attempting to do or of the moral nature of their actions. The strains experienced by the farm workers in Jenkins and Perrow's study may not explain the timing of protests and movements studied, and thus might not be regarded as their cause, but they were, nevertheless, their reason. Second, though it may have been the case, in this example, that the grievances experienced by the farmers remained constant – Jenkins and Perrow only assert this so we do not know – this is not always the case. Societies change, sometimes quite dramatically and structurally, and as they do so too do the strains and grievances which they generate. New strains and grievances are constantly emerging and a mode of analysis which ignores them is very likely to miss this crucial point.

Mapping the terrain: SMOs, SMIs and the SMS

The work of Jenkins, Perrow and Oberschall operates with a conceptually very minimal model of resource mobilization and tends to focus upon specific cases of insurgency rather than positing a broader model of the movements field. This is common in the literature on RM but there is an important exception in the work of McCarthy and Zald (1977). McCarthy and Zald share many of the assumptions of the RM theorists we have discussed. They develop an extensive conceptual framework with which to formalize these assumptions, however, and they develop a general model of the movements field. My exposition of McCarthy and Zald, like their paper itself, reads like a list of definitions. I hope it will be apparent, however, that there is an important and quite interesting model of movement activity beneath this 'list'.

The first concept McCarthy and Zald define is '*social movement*' itself. Their definition is interestingly minimal: '. . . a set of opinions and beliefs in a population which represents preferences for changing some elements of the social structure and/or reward distribution of a society' (McCarthy and Zald 1977; 1217–18). For any movement, thus defined, they add, we may also find a counter-movement that consists of preferences or beliefs which oppose that of a movement. Counter-movements are by no means always to be found but they are common. We have both pro-choice and anti-abortion movements, for example; fascist and anti-fascist movements; pro- and anti-hunting lobbies. The minimalism of this definition of a movement is clearly going to limit what McCarthy and Zald can do with it. There is no reference, for example, to solidarity or organization. Indeed, McCarthy and Zald's 'movements' are akin to what Blumer (1969) refers to as 'masses', that is, collections of distinct individuals who share a similar inclination and point of reference but do not interact (see Chapter 3). The most important point to grasp about this definition, however, is the economic analogy which it trades upon. A movement, *qua* set of preferences within a population, is akin to what economists refer to as 'demand'. McCarthy and Zald are effectively arguing that a preference or demand for certain types of social change may build up within society, just as a preference or demand for colour televisions may build up. And they are labelling this demand, in the former case, a 'social movement'. A counter-movement is a competing demand for something contrary to the first demand.

The reason that McCarthy and Zald do not include organization within their definition of social movements is that they have a separate concept, 'social movement organization' (SMO), which covers this. SMOs may be formal organizations, such as Greenpeace, Friends of the Earth, the African National Congress or a trade union. Many accounts of SMOs broaden their scope further than this, however, to include communes and other movement experiments, terrorist cells, conferences, and looser networks of association and interaction (see Zald and Ash 1966; Loftland 1985; McAdam *et al.* 1988; Crossley 1999b). SMOs, McCarthy and Zald contend, are akin to those businesses or entrepreneurial units which are found in economic life and which respond to economic demand. They emerge in response to demand, or perhaps in some cases pump prime to create demand, which they then seek to satisfy. They are, in effect, the supply side of the supply and demand equation. The reason why they are prepared to stimulate and meet demand, as in the economy, is that 'consumers' are generally willing to pay for that which they demand: often in money but also in other forms of reward such as status, admiration and a variety of forms of payment in kind. If the public desires a reduction in animal cruelty, for example, then they are prepared to bestow some form of reward on those SMOs, whether the World Wildlife Fund or a more radical group, who are prepared to campaign to bring that change about. There are 'selective incentives' to be gained by pursuing public goods.

In itself this provides an interesting solution to Olson's collective action problem and one which very much conforms to the economistic logic which informs his framing of it. Social and political problems are solved, for McCarthy and Zald, like any other problem: through the initiative of quick-witted entrepreneurs who spot a market niche and move swiftly into it in order that they might secure whatever profits await the market leader. This picture is complicated, however, by the introduction of two further concepts: social movement industry (SMI) and social movement sector (SMS). These two concepts indicate, first, that any one cause may attract more than one SMO and that SMOs may therefore be forced to compete with one another to supply the basic demand. Second, they indicate that this competition itself forms part of a wider constellation of struggles over precious resources and the meeting of public demands. An SMI is the specific constellation of SMOs which form around a particular issue. We may refer, for example, to the environmental industry, in which such groups as Greenpeace, Friends of the Earth, Earth First! and Reclaim the Streets compete for market dominance. This industry is itself only one among many, however. It must compete with the peace industry, the feminist industry, the animal rights industry and many others. Moreover, all such movement industries, which collectively comprise the social movement sector (SMS), must compete with whatever other demands make a claim upon public resources, including straightforward economic demands in the narrow sense of that term. People will be less likely to donate to an SMO if they need the money to feed themselves and experience that demand as greater than the desire for, for example, nuclear disarmament. The SMS must therefore compete with the public, private and voluntary sectors for available societal resources.

In addition to this mapping of the organizational structure of the 'supply' side of the equation, McCarthy and Zald offer a similar map of the 'demand' side. The first distinction they draw is between adherents, who believe in the goals of the movement, and non-adherents, who do not. One aim of SMOs is to draw as many individuals and organizations into the adherents' camp as is possible. The SMOs servicing the disabilities movement, for example, must attempt to persuade as many individuals as is possible to accept or adhere to its claims, and they may be forced to compete with each other and with other movements in doing so.

Some adherents are also 'constituents'. They directly contribute resources to the movement. And as with the line between adherents and non-adherents, one of the chief objectives of SMOs is to draw as many adherents into the constituent camp as possible. The disability SMOs will welcome favourable attitudes among the populace, for example, but they would undoubtedly prefer it if those attitudes translated into cash donations and volunteer efforts.

The reason that some constituents are willing to put their resources into an SMO, McCarthy and Zald argue, is that they stand to benefit directly from the activities of that SMO or perhaps rather from the broad objectives of the movement itself. They are potential 'beneficiaries'. Disabled individuals who participate in one of the SMOs in the disability SMI, for example, investing their own time, energy and money into it, might do so in part because of the personal gains they stand to make if the movement is successful: e.g. increased life opportunities and social recognition. Selective benefits may be involved too, of course, and may be necessary to induce some to take up an activist role to fight for the benefit of the many. As this point reminds us, however, not all potential beneficiaries will necessarily become constituents. There will always be free riders. And the converse is also true. Not all constituents are potential beneficiaries. Some constituents are what McCarthy and Zald refer to as 'conscience constituents'. They may benefit from some selective benefits and this may go some way to explaining their participation. As the name suggests, however, this group, as McCarthy and Zald conceive of them, act on the basis of conscience. They have the resources to give to movements, or at least sometimes they do, and they are sufficiently well disposed towards 'good causes' that they are inclined to donate at least some of their surplus resources to those causes. The spectre of the liberal middle classes once again emerges here. Like Jenkins and Perrow (1977), McCarthy and Zald are suggesting that movements, even and perhaps especially movements of powerless groups, depend upon the resources and support of more powerful, richer (in various resources) but also sympathetically disposed groups.

Having mapped out this conceptual territory, McCarthy and Zald proceed to outline a range of hypotheses which might be deduced from their model and which, they suggest, are supported by the existing literature and research on social movements. There are too many of these hypotheses for us to deal with individually or in detail but it is important to get a general sense of their tenor. This will give us a sense of how the model works in practice. The first few hypotheses deal with the basic issue of levels of resources within the societal pool and among conscience constituents in particular. McCarthy and Zald argue that an increase in resources in society in general will lead to an increase in resources available to SMOs, which will in turn lead both to an increase in activism and an increase in the number of SMOs and even SMIs within the SMS. In times of affluence we can expect more activism because SMOs will have more of the resources required to mobilize it, but we can also expect a general increase in SMOs because the incentive is there for potential political entrepreneurs to try their luck. It is important to add here that resource levels in society and the SMS respectively do not grow symmetrically. Resources for activism are a luxury. Constituents, and particularly conscience constituents, whose relationship to the cause of a movement is less personal, will only give when they have the surplus resources to give and when other 'more urgent' calls are not being made upon them. A growth in prosperity may have no discernible effect on the SMS, therefore, if it does not succeed in lifting constituents into a sufficiently affluent position. But by the same token, once that threshold is crossed the SMS can expect disproportionate gains from a growth in prosperity, since all that is gained falls into the surplus category.

A second series of hypotheses, again argued to be both sound and supported empirically, concern the nature of the organizational form of SMOs. At a general level McCarthy and Zald make the claim that all SMOs, having been formed, will tend to become preoccupied with their own survival. Whatever movement they have emerged to service and whatever demands that movement makes, the SMO has basic prerequisites of survival and flourishing with the mere fact of being born. If it fails to attend to those requirements it will perish and will be of little value to the movement, except perhaps as a symbolic martyr to the cause. This means that SMOs generally become preoccupied with securing resources. More specifically, McCarthy and Zald argue that certain SMOs will be more dependent upon isolated constituents (i.e. have few local forms of organization and networking that encourage constituents to get involved) and that this will tend to make them less stable because support for them, in general, will be less stable. Conversely, SMOs which draw constituents in, through local groups and activities, should be more stable at the basic resource level. Having said that, affording a greater number of constituents a greater role within the SMO, particularly when that involves mixing conscience constituents and beneficiaries, can be a recipe for conflict and tension. Too many competing ideas and interests is an organizational nightmare which may detract from the basic purpose of the SMO. Finally, as with economic firms, McCarthy and Zald predict that the older SMOs will be more likely to weather the ups and downs of industry and sector fortune than the newer SMOs which perhaps emerge largely as a function of a growth in resource surplus. These older SMOs, to put it crudely, have a stronger market position which makes them less vulnerable to downturns in support.

The final point which we will take from McCarthy and Zald concerns 'advertising' and the media. I will be returning to this issue at a number of points later in the book. For the moment, however, suffice it to say that great emphasis is put upon the role of advertising. SMIs and the SMS are highly competitive and the SMS itself must compete with other social sectors, such as entertainment, the voluntary sector and even the public and private sectors. Consequently SMOs must construct a public profile and win support. In a world of mass communication this necessitates involvement in the media. SMOs must advertise!

McCarthy and Zald assessed

There is much to commend the model that McCarthy and Zald put forward. They identify and map a structured field of social movement activism. Moreover, in doing so they draw our attention to many of the more stable aspects of movement life, which outlive the comings and goings of specific SMOs and perhaps even whole movements themselves. There are problems with the model, however. The point of departure for my critique is the concept of 'conscience constituents'. This concept, like Jenkins and Perrow's concept of middle-class liberals, does not square with the RAT model of the agent that McCarthy and Zald advocate, nor with the more general economic model of activism that they seek to develop (see also Cohen 1985). Acting out of conscience is not 'economical', in either a literal or a metaphorical sense, and is not what RAT would predict. Economically rational actors act so as to maximize their own material benefits; conscience constituents, by contrast, act out of conscience. They join an animal welfare group or donate money to a specific campaign because their conscience 'tells them to'. A convinced RAT advocate may respond to this by arguing that agents pursue their own interests in salving their conscience, since a nagging conscience is unpleasant to experience. Or they may argue that altruistic acts are an attempt to procure group approval and status. This may be so but it does not really help the RAT argument to any great extent. It draws the RAT very close to a circular definition of 'self-interest' which encompasses any and all motivations, thus undermining the alleged parsimony and predictive value of the position. More seriously, however, by introducing the possibility of symbolic and moral rewards into the equation it draws the RAT position far from its basic model. It suggests, for example, that social agents feel the moral pressure of the group to which they belong and feel that pressure so profoundly that they are moved to act, even against their own material interests. I have no objection to this claim, as such. It is a perfectly good argument which one will find in Durkheim, Mead, Blumer and many others. But it is a claim which sits much more happily with the social ontology and theory of agency that one finds in the work of these writers than that of RAT. Indeed, it does not really fit with the RAT model at all.

This same argument applies to many SMOs. The lure of large material rewards could only really apply to very big, already established and formalized SMOs. These organizations do have the means to reward involvement

Many of the direct action networks that are common in contemporary protest offer no such rewards to their members, however; nor do they chase such rewards or have the economically rational constitution which would allow them to be responsive to market opportunities. Furthermore, even though these campaigns can generate a great deal of publicity and that publicity can, in a few cases, focus upon individuals (e.g. in the UK the famed 'eco-warrior', 'Swampy', achieved national celebrity status for a couple of months, on account of his endurance in underground protest tunnels), the symbolic rewards bestowed upon the individual involved in direct action are relatively small – not least because direct action is often illegal, such that participants are sometimes anonymous, and because direct action groups very often oppose the leadership structures and 'star systems' which allow members to secure celebrity from their actions. I do not mean to suggest by this that there are no personal rewards for those who partake in these sorts of projects or that their activities are pure and disinterested acts of self-sacrifice. What I would suggest, however, is that, at least in cases like those of direct action networks, we must look to the internal life of the group or network itself for the rewards and punishments which steer the actions of its members. We must seek to understand the symbolic reality which they have constructed for themselves (on symbolic realities see Merleau-Ponty 1965; Mead 1967; Crossley 2001a) and the 'games' in which their members are involved. To do this, however, requires that we break with the atomized and asocial model of agency posited in RAT. It requires that we see the agents involved as members of a group, who identify with the group and who feel its games and its symbolic reality within their bones. It requires that we break with the methodological individualism of RAT and seek to explore the nature of the group's symbolic reality. To seek to understand or explain the behaviour of a 'Swampy', 'Fungus' or 'Muppet Dave' without grasping the symbolic world which the radical ecology movement has created for itself, with its various forms of reward, goal and punishment, is akin to trying to explain the behaviour of a football player independently of any account of the game of football as a structured form of social reality: futile.

My reference to the game-like structure of movement activity is not intended to demean it or detract from its seriousness in any respect. People can suffer a range of grave consequences from their involvement in direct action, including death, and many are quite clearly devoted to their cause. It is not a game in that sense. What I am attempting to draw out, however, is the sense in which a movement culture can arise which motivates its members by offering rewards and punishments of various sorts, and yet which transcends those members *qua* individuals and which grounds their actions.

The concept of a social movement that McCarthy and Zald put forward is similarly problematic. Social movements, in their view, express a preference which, in turn, manifests itself as a 'demand' which is met by SMOs. As is the case with RAT, this begs the question of where such preferences arise from. In some cases this may not really be a question. The preference for more money or better working conditions among a poorly paid group is easily explained in terms of the Utilitarian model of the actor and basic survival instincts. Similarly with the demand for freedom by enslaved groups. Not all preferences are so easily dealt with, however. Some preferences express the interests of other human groups or even animal species; anti-fox hunting campaigns in the UK, for example, are seemingly in the interest of the fox. Other preferences, by contrast, are highly contentious. In the USA, for example, pro- and anti-abortion campaigners argue for radically opposed preferences. Such disagreements prevent us from assuming that the campaign of either side expresses a 'natural' preference or interest – otherwise there would be no disagreement. Indeed, even in cases like environmentalism and anti-nuclear campaigns, where one might believe that our instinct for survival generates some sort of basis for a preference, it is clear that preferences have a social distribution, that is to say, different social groups are differently disposed with respect to the degree of support they show for such issues. The origin and distribution of these preferences constitutes an important sociological question which RM theory ignores and is ill-equipped to answer. Moreover, this is a question which goes to the heart of the matter of movement formation itself. In response to a question regarding the origin of the animal rights movement, for example, it would simply be no answer at all to argue that animal rights SMOs developed in response to the growing preference for caring for the interests of animals. The question of the origin of the animal rights movement is precisely a question about the origin of the sentiments and preferences favouring animal protection. This is not to deny that, having accounted for the emergence of this preference, we may then look to McCarthy and Zald's model for a further stage of explanation, concerning the translation of preferences into campaigns; but this could only ever be a second stage and must necessarily presuppose the initial stage of preference formation.

A final area of critique which we must address concerns the question of organization, or perhaps rather organizations, in the formal sense. Our question is as to whether relatively formal organizations, such as RM theory tends to identify, are a necessary prerequisite of effective political struggle, or a conservative impediment. This debate stretches much wider than the confines of RM theory. Long before RM had been conceived, for example, Robert Michels (1949) was warning of the dangers of formal organization for political struggles. Organizations, he argued, tend inevitably towards oligarchy. The demands of organization and specialization tend to cut the ruling elite off from the rank and file. Moreover, the organization, or more precisely its survival, becomes an end in itself, to the detriment of the wider demands of the movement. And from the opposite end of the scale, long after the heyday of RM, in a book very critical of it, Doug McAdam (1982) sought to identify the virtues of the formal organizations which grew out of the black civil rights movement. The success of the civil rights movement, he argues, was largely attributable to the organization provided, first, by the churches and colleges and second, by the major SMOs who succeeded them. Even the competition between the main SMOs was positive for the movement because of the vitality, dynamism and innovation it generated. By the same token, the loss of this organization was a key factor explaining the eventual demise of the movement:

> Without the 'conscious planning or centralised direction' needed to link together the growing collection of autonomous protest units, the black movement had, by the decade's end, become a largely impotent political force at the national level. Lacking the strong centralised or-ganisational vehicles required to sustain the disruptive campaigns that earlier had supported federal action, the movement was increasingly confined to limited efforts at the local level.
>
> (McAdam 1982: 186)

Within contemporary debates, particularly surrounding the RM approach, Piven and Cloward (1979, 1992) have been among the most vocal critics of organization. They criticize RM theory both for overemphasizing the role of formal organizations, to the detriment of a proper consideration of what can be and often is achieved by looser and less (formally) organized collectives, and for failing to recognize the conservative influence which formal organizational structure can have. Their argument is very much the same as that which McAdam makes for external sponsorship, namely, that formality breeds accountability and thus deference towards the political establishment, when real change sometimes requires radical actions which offend the sensibilities of the establishment.

I do not have the space to examine the many debates that have taken shape around the contentions of Piven and Cloward or, indeed, those of Michels (e.g. see Tarrow 1998: 123–38; Barker 2000). It must suffice here to make a couple of common-sense observations. First, formal organiza-tions are by no means necessary to sustain strong political campaigns. The direct action networks referred to earlier in this chapter illustrate that. There are many different ways in which protest activities and even sus-tained campaigns can be organized. Second, it is clear that the dangers that both the pro- and anti-organization camps point to are real. Protest re-quires some degree of organization and coordination otherwise it will not happen. But too much organization, of the formal variety, can lead to oligarchy and bureaucratization, and indeed to political cooptation, such that movements lose their critical edge. Most successful movements, one assumes, pass somewhere between these two extremes, or perhaps counter-balance the tendencies of one against the other, thus avoiding the worse excesses of each.

The network argument

As we have outlined it so far RM is centrally focused upon the role of imported external resources in mobilizing struggle. In some versions of RM theory there is an additional argument concerning the importance of indigenous networks. This argument has been appropriated by many researchers outside the RM tradition and my discussion of it will range into their respective contributions too. I will begin, however, with the formulation of the argument in the classic statement of RM theory posited by Oberschall (1973).

Oberschall's argument on networks involves a deliberate and self-conscious departure from the work of Olson. Olson assumes that the 'communities' out of which collective action emerges are unorganized and loose knit, Oberschall notes. They are at best concentrated populations of distinct and unconnected individuals. This is unrealistic. Human beings live in groups, that is, in communities, networks and other forms of association and mutual interdependency. Some of these forms of network are quite weak, unstructured and disorganized, but this is by no means always the case. They can be strong and organized. This is important because, as with Olson's small groups (see Chapter 4), sanctions and rewards pertaining to participation are much more effectively instituted in closely knit networks than in atomized communities. Free riding can be minimized, if not eliminated, by the 'levers' which human interdependence generates: levers of solidarity, obligation and the threat of ostracism or other easily realized punishments. In addition, Oberschall continues, the networks of everyday life harbour a multitude of resources which can be tapped for the purposes of struggle. With networks and communities come leaders, places of association, communicative channels and means, and often a stock of organizational and administrative materials.

This observation leads one to hypothesize that many movements will grow out of pre-established networks, communities and organizations, and that movement formation will be more common among tightly networked groups than in situations of high social atomization. This hypothesis is borne out in a great deal of empirical work. Much of the work on black insurgency and the civil rights movement in the USA has focused upon the role of black churches, as well as black colleges and the National Association for the Advancement of Coloured People (NAACP), for example (Oberschall 1973; Piven and Cloward 1979; McAdam 1982; Morris 1984). These networks provided the bonds of solidarity out of which a movement could grow. They provided pre-existing lines of communication, not to mention places of assembly and basic organizational and administrative resources, and many of the early leaders of the black movement were key players from the aforementioned groupings (McAdam 1982). Many leading members of the clergy became leading members of the movement, for example. Indeed, as McAdam (1982) has shown, there is evidence to suggest that it was the commitment which such leaders developed for the cause of black resistance, and their capacity to communicate that commitment to others, persuading them to follow, which provided the basis of movement recruitment itself. For many the movement was simply an extension of the forms of communal life and association in which they were already involved. It is perhaps not surprising, in this respect, that the practices of these 'micro-mobilisation contexts', such as the singing of hymns, were evident in the civil rights movement too (Morris 1984).

In a slightly different vein, McAdam's (1988) later work on the 'freedom summer' project, which involved white college students in the USA travelling down to the southern states to lend support to the actions of the civil rights movement, reveals a similar story. Students were far more likely to be successfully recruited and to stay recruited, McAdam found, if others from their friendship networks were recruited too. The bonds of friendship made the dangers and hardships of activism more bearable and thereby lent strength and support to the activists. The recruitment of networks or 'block recruitment', as it is sometimes called, proved far more effective than the recruitment of individuals.

Churches and university campuses are just one type of context wherein networks might develop, and they may not always be the most conducive to the formation of movements. In their study of the uprisings in the former East Germany in 1989, for example, Opp and Gern (1993) found very little evidence to suggest that the churches had served as 'micro-mobilization contexts'. This may be due to the relationships between State and Church in this particular context, they suggest. However, their work did point to the strong effect of personal relationships – which are more insulated from State control – upon mobilization. Personal ties, it would seem, had a direct and strong effect upon the likelihood that an individual would take part in protest events. Opp and Gern muddy the water slightly, however, by suggesting that individual political dispositions may be a factor affecting network formation:

> . . . politically homogeneous personal networks may develop. In everyday communication, subtle signals indicating a partner's political views may be exchanged. Reactions to such signals provide an impression of the partner's political attitudes. If the initial interactions convey similar political views, step-by-step communication may begin that results in the recognition of the partner's critical views and may result in the establishment of a personal relationship.
>
> (Opp and Gern 1993: 662)

This is just a hypothetical description. Political dispositions and the formation of personal networks may interact in many and various ways. The basic point is important, however, and adds a crucial element to the net-work argument. While networks affect mobilization, underlying political dispositions may affect networking. Networks are as much products as producers of social movements.

This notion of community or network plays a central role for Oberschall (1973). Grievances or hardship are often sufficient to stimulate periodic outbursts and perhaps riots, he observes, but for outbursts to become move-ments there must be organization and leadership within an aggrieved popu-lation, and organization and leadership come from whatever pre-existing forms of network, association or community that exist within that popula-tion. To this, moreover, he adds a notion of 'segmentation'. Segmented communities are, for the most part, well integrated internally but are cut off from other groups and, specifically, from social elites. They may be bound to these elites in the respect that they must serve them in some way, either as employees, clients or political subjects, but they do not mix with them socially and are extremely unlikely to experience upward mobility into the elite strata. This is favourable to movement formation on two counts. First, distance between groups means that less intensive forms of social control hold between them. Aggrieved groups have relatively few channels by which to influence elite groups, other than overt protest, and elite groups have little leverage, beyond formal repression, by which to prevent such protest or uprising. They have no access to more subtle means of persuasion, control or appeasement. Second, the lack of mobility between groups means that the more talented and motivated members of the aggrieved group, whom Oberschall believes may become its movement leaders, are not drawn out of the oppressed group and into the elite. Their resources or resourcefulness remain within the aggrieved group, at its disposal.

Again a number of studies support this claim. The aforementioned black churches were able to play the role within the civil rights movement that they did, for example, because of their largely segregated nature and be-cause of the unusually high degree of autonomy enjoyed by the black clergy. As McAdam (1982) notes, studies of a variety of aspects of participation in the civil rights movement indicate that those most involved, at least in the early stages, were those least dependent upon the white community for, for example, a wage, and those thereby least subject to the controlling influ-ence of whites. Similarly the tendency for such groups as students to be-come involved in struggle is often explained on these terms. Campuses tend to be cut off from the controlling influences of, for example, parents or employers, and students are often free of other personal and professional ties, making them 'biographically available' for struggle, as McAdam (1988) puts it.

Snow *et al.* (1980) found a similar pattern, regarding networks, in the re-cruitment channels of a range of movement organizations. The vast majority of movement participants they studied had become involved in the movement or organization by way of networks (e.g. of friendship) they were already involved in. Typically they would be invited by a friend to partake in some sort of activity, without being asked to believe in the cause or doctrine of the movement, and they would then gradually become involved. Notwithstanding this, however, Snow *et al.* also note how 'extra-movement' networks can be an inhibiting factor for a person who might otherwise join or participate in a movement: '. . . the reason for participating or not participating in movement activities once invited is largely contingent on the extent to which extra-movement networks function as countervailing influences' (1980: 793). Other networks, outside the movement network, make demands upon one's time, energy and emotional commitment, for example, such that one has little to give to a movement. Moreover, friends not involved in movement networks may discourage and even punish movement involvement if they do not agree with it or share its broad aims (see also McAdam and Paulsen 1993).

The twin themes of association and segmentation have been developed in a number of ways within the RM and related literature. Tilly (1978), for example, adds to this basic picture by reference to what he calls the 'catnet' factor. Where a group of people live together in forms of close association and networks, he argues, the historical record suggests that they are far more likely to mobilize around an issue of shared grievance than groups who are not networked in this way. The propensity is greater still where this group belong to and identify with a social category: e.g. a community of 'blacks', 'workers' or 'peasants'. We might rephrase this, in more contemporary terms, by suggesting that close-knit networks or communities are more prone to mobilization around a shared grievance where they manifest some form of collective identity.

Most of the empirical work in the field is supportive of the network argument. However, an interesting exception surfaces in Oliver's (1984) work on local community activism. She found that activists tend to be more pessimistic with respect to the possibilities of collective action than nonactivists. It is their pessimism, she argues, which partly motivates them into action – 'If I don't do it, nobody else will.' This pessimism, in turn, derives from having a less integrated position in the community in Oliver's view. Agents with less involvement in the community have less faith in it. Thus, she argues: 'There is a kind of paradox of community life. People with the greatest sense of collective identity and positive regard for their neighbours may not absorb the costs of community activism because they assume that somebody else will take care of the problems' (Oliver 1984: 609). This finding need not call the whole network argument into question but it should remind us that the dynamics of social networks are complex and can pull in different directions. We cannot assume that tight networks have a radicalizing effect upon their members.

Movements, networks and organizations

The implication of the RM approach is not simply that movements 'grow out of' networks or that networks 'foster' movements. Movements are networks and, in the first instance, they are the very networks that they grow out of. Movement formation is less a matter of agents coming together and more a matter of agents who are already together, transforming their network into something different. The emergence of a new movement consists in the mutation of an already existing network. Furthermore, the organizational structures of those networks will tend, in the first instance, to serve as organizational centres of the movements. Thus, as many observers note, the black church, black colleges and NAACP became the key organizations within the civil rights movement in its early days.

This is only at the beginning, however. As a movement develops and gathers momentum the network expands and follows its own course. As Diani (1997) points out, social capital, defined as 'ties which are based on mutual trust and mutual recognition among actors involved in the relationship', can be one of the key outcomes of much movement activity (see also Crossley 1999b). Movements, rooted in networks which resource them, produce networks which will resource them. Furthermore, this will often also entail the emergence of new formal organizations which offer leadership and coordination to the movement. As I found in my own work on anti-psychiatric and mental health survivor movements, the history of any movement is often punctuated by the rise and fall of specific organizations and organizational cells within it, each new group breathing life into the movement and its struggle, directing it in a specific way, before finally dying off or burning out and leaving room for the next contender.

Some of the key work on the network structure of movements has been done by Diani (1990, 1992) and Melucci (1986). Their respective works raise many important issues, too many to explore here. Two issues are particularly important, however. First, as Diani (1992) has noted, the network structure of movements is complex and multifaceted. There are many different types of network or sub-network within an overall movement network. At a very basic level, for example, there are links between movement organizations (e.g. between Greenpeace, Friends of the Earth and Earth First!), and links within these organizations, which constitute their basic organizational structure. There are links between these organizations and outside individuals who variously support them and there are overlapping memberships between different groups. Finally, there are friendships and personal relationships between individuals variously involved in a movement or set of groups. Each of these types of network may affect the movement in various ways. This list should be warning enough that we cannot make broad and general statements about network structures and their effects, at least not until a great deal of empirical work has been done.

A second observation regarding networks, this time from Melucci (1986), concerns their role in the periods of latency that are evident in the careers of most key movements. Much work on movements has focused upon very overt protest activities and is chiefly geared to an understanding of those moments of high tension, Melucci argues. But movements also manifest considerable periods of latency where their overt activities and public profile are minimal. An understanding of networks is crucial to making sense of the way in which they hold together during these periods of latency. It is because movement members are meeting and interacting in their networks during periods of latency, keeping those networks going, that they are then available for mobilization at more active times.

Evaluating the network argument

The argument about networks makes a lot of sense and is supported by much evidence from both within and beyond the RM camp. It does raise a few problems, however. Piven and Cloward (1992) offer three quite pointed criticisms. First, they note the equivocation which some advocates of networks make with respect to their claim. As I noted above, Oberschall concedes that 'outbursts' can occur in the absence of networks and seems only to emphasize the roles of networks and associations in relation to sustained campaigns. This is quite a concession in Piven and Cloward's view and it opens the door to the possibility that a high number of certain sorts of political action occur in the absence of networks. Certainly it implies that networks are not necessary for the translation of political discontent into action. Second, they pick up upon the notion of 'segregation'. Advocates of the network argument generally oppose their position to one which they attribute to Durkheim, Piven and Cloward note. Durkheim and Durkheimians are alleged to argue that protest and movement formation are a consequence of anomie and social disintegration, such that we would expect them to emerge at times when such social strains are in evidence and would predict participants to be malintegrated, alienated and so on. The network argument, which is much better supported by the evidence, seemingly suggests the opposite. It suggests that solidarity and integration are a precondition of movement and protest. Or at least that is what its advocates think. Piven and Cloward, in contrast, argue that the clause about 'segregation' and 'biographical availability' which the network theorists introduce constitutes a major concession to the Durkheimian position. It concedes to Durkheim that integration and tight social networks have a controlling and regulative influence, suggesting that those groups most likely to become involved in movements and struggle are precisely the groups cut off from this controlling influence: e.g. students and, in situations of racial segregation, blacks. There is nothing wrong with being Durkheimian, of course. Piven and Cloward's point is rather that the evidence unearthed by

RM researchers is closer to the Durkheimian view opposed by these researchers than the latter are inclined to admit.

This criticism is further bolstered by a third. The primacy which RM affords to networks, Piven and Cloward argue, is susceptible to many of the same criticisms that RM advocates level against the alleged primacy of strain or grievance in the collective behaviour approach. RM theorists often criticize the notion that strains cause movements because, they argue, strains are a constant factor in social life and one cannot explain a variable, such as protest or movement formation, by reference to a constant. However, Piven and Cloward argue, networks are fairly constant too and the same criticism must therefore apply. Networks and associations are equally ubiquitous and constant as grievances are alleged to be and are therefore no more adequate as explanations of collective action. To give one example:

> Wilson and Orum claim that 'conventional psychological theories', such as relative deprivation, do not explain the ghetto riots of the 1960s and that instead 'social bonds . . . i.e. friendship networks, drew many people to become active participants . . .', but they do not wonder why riots before the 1960s were so rare or why there have been so few since, despite pervasive friendships in both periods.
>
> (Piven and Cloward 1992: 147)

What is less constant, Piven and Cloward add, is the relationship of specific oppressed groups to elites, that is, degrees of segregation. Thus, if we are looking for a variable factor to explain movement emergence and protest we should really be looking for processes which segregate or isolate oppressed groups from the controlling influence of elites. There is more life in Durkheim that networkers assume, they conclude.

Actually there is far more life left in Durkheim than even Piven and Cloward recognize. Before we reflect upon this, however, we must consider some evidence which challenges their assumption about networks. Their charge that networks are a constant, and are therefore no more likely to explain movements and protest than grievances are, is questionable. Migration and a range of forms of social policy, including housing policy, can all have an effect on networks, particularly neighbourhood networks, and in this respect networks can be variable and so could explain mobilization. The optimism about proletarian revolution among certain early Marxists, for example, as Piven and Cloward (1979) elsewhere state themselves, was precisely premised upon the notion that the logic of capitalist development was concentrating ever more workers into ever smaller spaces (e.g. cities and factories) and thus building up the networks which provide the potential for mobilization and revolution. Networks, in other words, were expanding with urbanization. Empirical support regarding the political salience of these processes is found in McAdam's (1982) aforementioned study of the civil rights movement. His diagnosis of the preconditions leading up to the emergence of black insurgency and the civil rights movement focuses precisely upon the trends which led to a concentrated and integrated black population in certain urban areas. Similarly, the aforementioned work of Opp and Gern (1993) on the uprisings in East Germany points to an active process of network building, which again suggests that networks are not as constant as Piven and Cloward suggest. Notwithstanding this, however, the work of Opp and Gern (1993) challenges some of the assumptions of the network argument too. They suggest that networking may be a politically driven process, which implies that networks can be as much an outcome of a movement formation as a precondition. Politically inclined agents may form networks which, in turn, constitute the basis of movements.

By the same token, *contra* Piven and Cloward, segregation can be a fairly constant factor. The segregation of students on campuses far away from their homes has been a fairly constant factor in many countries throughout the last 50 years, for example. And it undoubtedly contributes to the increased tendency towards political activism that can be identified within that group. Nevertheless, there are considerable stretches of time when most students have not been particularly politically active, despite the constancy of both their segregation and their communal concentration and networks (Crossley 2000b).

Networks and individuals?

A further problem with the network argument stems from its relationship to RAT. Like the aforementioned reference to the charitable acts of middle-class liberals, the notion that social agents live within closely knit communities with which they identify, bonded by relations of solidarity, at least insofar as this is taken as a basic assumption of the theory, sits rather unhappily with the atomized and individualistic worldview of the RAT model which RM theory claims to draw upon. Oberschall recognizes this and makes a point of putting clear distance between himself and Olson in this respect. This is a rather big point on which to disagree, however. It presupposes a completely different ontology to RAT and a completely different model of what social agents are. Furthermore, it undermines the logic of the collective action problem, since this is not nearly such a problem when the collective and its bonds of solidarity are already presupposed. A major part of the problem of collective action, for Olson, is as to how self-interested monads could ever be moved into a collective formation. RM theory, by contrast, assumes the existence of a collective as given (see also Cohen 1985). This creates a problem for RM theory but it is not the problem which many critics of the approach point to. Critics such as Feree (1992) and A. Scott (1990) attack RM because of its appropriation of the RAT model. This would be a problem, in my view, if RM had appropriated the model in its pure form, but it has not. It has attempted to mix the model with a more social model. This, in turn, has created two problems. First, RM amounts to an ambiguous and potentially highly contradictory mix of individualist and collectivist ontological assumptions. Second, unlike the RAT model that it borrows from, it has no clear conception of the social agent (which is the virtue of RAT). The RM agent is not the RAT agent, because they 'belong' to a community and are implicated in its 'solidarity' but then what are they? We might add a third point here, which is that RM theory seemingly has no strong theoretical conception of social integration or solidarity, or of what they might entail.

I do not wish to question that the RM theorists are correct in supposing, at least in some cases, the existence of pre-existing solidaristic networks. But the price they have to pay for this is being much closer in orientation to the likes of Durkheim, Mead and Blumer than they might like to think they are. More to the point, RM theory's confused ontology, lack of a coherent model of the agent and inability to shed much light upon issues of solidarity, etc., beyond using them as variables in models of insurgency, suggests that they may actually be in need of some theoretical input from their opponents in the collective behaviour camp. I noted earlier in the book that Durkheim, Mead *et al.* were quite open to the notion that human action is purposively oriented towards goals and even strategic and utilitarian. But, I noted, these writers argue that social agency is produced within society, that human beings always already belong to some form of community, and that their utilitarian inclinations must be balanced against the demands of the group, as they are manifest in the form of conscience and feelings of justice and duty – albeit usually backed up with a fear of punishment. It doesn't take too much probing within the RM perspective, in my view, to see that they are saying the same thing. Or rather, they are vaguely tending in that direction but lack the conceptual apparatus which would allow them to make very much sense of it. The solution to this problem is clear. RM would be much better served if it abandoned its loose and somewhat tenuous grip on RAT and embraced a more appropriate theory of agency.

I want to push this argument one step further by reflecting upon the RM critique of Durkheim. As I noted above, RM theorists have tended to assume that a Durkheimian theory of movements would focus upon anomie, social disintegration and so on; and they have sought to challenge the theory by showing that just the opposite is true. Bonds of solidarity and tight integration are, in fact, crucial preconditions for struggle. If this criticism is intended to do any justice to Durkheim then it fails miserably. It may be that some movement theorists, vaguely informed by Durkheim's work, have sought to explain movement activism and struggle in terms of anomie and disintegration. They are wrong. Durkheim, however, is a much more sophisticated thinker. He is not interested so much in anomie and disintegration as in degrees of integration and normative regulation, that is, in the continuum or variation which is manifest in degrees of integration and normative regulation and their consequences. In this respect alone the finding that movement activity and protest are more common in well-integrated and solidaristic communities is a thoroughly Durkheimian point: just the kind of finding which he would have deemed supportive of his basic position. Building upon this, Durkheim himself pointed to the effects of high integration upon behaviour. The argument of *Suicide*, for example, is not that anomie or individualization cause suicide, though the evidence suggests that they do, but rather that different states of social integration can cause an individual to commit suicide (Durkheim [1897] 1952). And of course this includes states of very high integration, where individuals identify very closely with the group and are prone to what Durkheim calls *altruistic suicide*. This is an important point, not least since political struggles are one of those rare types of situation where we find altruistic suicides: e.g. suicide bombers, hunger strikers and a range of 'high-risk' activists who at least chance death. From a RAT point of view such extreme movement activities are just beyond the pale. Suicide bombers pay the highest price and do not survive to claim any reward. But for Durkheim, who theorizes the relationship of agents to their network, their identification with their category, not to mention the nature of collective beliefs which might persuade agents that they will be rewarded in the next life, these actions can be explained and understood. Finally, when, in his later work, Durkheim explores the process of collective effervescence, a process which he explicitly if only briefly links to both the French Revolution and the rise of socialism (see Chapter 2), he speaks explicitly of the coming together of society (or a group therein), not its falling apart. Collective effervescence entails and requires the coming together of members of a group or network and an increase in the interactions between them.

One final point on Durkheim which is relevant here concerns what we might call movement within networks. We have already noted, primarily with respect to Piven and Cloward's critique, that networks, even if they are a necessary structural precondition for movement formation, are by no means sufficient to explain movement formation. Part of what is lacking in the basic notion of networks, I suggest, is any sense of the transformation that they need to undergo in order to become an effective movement base. Even if the black churches were a basis for mobilization of black insurgency, for example, we need to understand the process by which this happened. This is precisely what Durkheim, with his notion of collective effervescence, and Blumer, with his 'elementary behaviour', seek to do. They examine the creative dynamic which can develop in situations of intense social interaction, which gives rise to new 'definitions of the situation' and to a newly renewed conviction in one's capacity to transform that situation. Without the effervescence which their theories identify and seek to examine, I contend, black churches would simply have remained black churches, that is, places of worship and sites for the production of a conservative form of solidarity.

Resources, networks and the value-added model

Both the resources and the network arguments have been posited, by some advocates, as the key to explaining movement emergence. In this chapter I have sought to explain why both these factors are important but I hope that I have also done enough to put them in their place. Neither resources nor networks, any more than grievances or strains, are sufficient to explain movement emergence, however necessary or important they may be. Sometimes either one of these factors may be the missing ingredient whose emergence sets a movement in process but it is only too obvious that many well-resourced and well-networked communities do not give rise to movements most of the time. Well-resourced and networked groups with no grievances will not mobilize, and the process of mobilization involves a collective effervescence which transforms networks in any case. It is my contention, therefore, that resources and networks must be incorporated into a broader value-added model of movement formation, similar to that argued for by Smelser (1962). In Smelser's terms both networks and resources would fall under the rubric of 'mobilization' factors. I will show how resources and networks fit into my reformulated value-added model in Chapter 9.

To end on a positive point, it is important to note that the RM argument illuminates a different dimension to movements than that identified by most movement theories. Most theories tend to focus upon periods of social unrest and upon the emergence of movements. These factors are important in RM theory too, but it also points to the existence of a more stable and durable field of movement activism (i.e. the movement sector and movement industries) and to the role of established political elites in movement politics. There is less of a sense, in this work, of movements emerging out of nowhere only to sink back there, and more of a sense of a permanent site of movement and fringe political activism which, as it were, sponsors or patronizes new causes. I share the concern of those writers, such as McAdam, who believe that this dimension is overemphasized in RM theory but it is an important aspect of movement politics and one that we should remain alert to.

Summary and conclusion

This chapter has covered a lot of ground. In essence, however, we have considered two arguments. The first focused upon the role of resources in movement formation and suggested that powerless groups require an injection of resources from elite groups if they are to mobilize. The second focused upon the role of networks in mobilization. We also considered a more elaborate conceptual model, which focused upon the role of social movement organizations in meeting the political 'demand' created by a wider population.

Two central criticisms have emerged in the chapter. First, I have noted that neither resources nor networks are sufficient causes for movement mobilization and have suggested that they need to be integrated into a value-added model. Second, I have noted a range of problems with the use of the RAT model of agency within RM theory. In many instances RM is simply not compatible with the assumptions of RAT.

Further reading

Jenkins's (1983) 'Resource mobilisation . . .' paper presents a very good overview of the approach. On networks, Snow *et al.*'s (1980) 'Social networks and social movements' is a classic. For a more critical perspective see Piven and Cloward's (1992) 'Normalising collective protest'.

chapter six

Opportunities, cognition and biography

RM theory is one of two overlapping approaches which emerged in American movement analysis in the wake of the collective behaviour approach. In this chapter I consider the other side of the double act: the political process (PP) approach. Or rather, because the RM and PP approaches share many ideas in common, particularly the network argument, and I do not wish to repeat myself, I discuss a number of concepts and themes, additional to those shared by RM and PP, which the latter has introduced into movement theory. I begin the chapter with a discussion of a paper by Eisinger (1973) which centres upon the idea of 'political opportunity structures'. This is the most central concept in the PP toolbox and Eisinger's paper was one of the earliest to discuss it. In the section which follows this I discuss some of the ways in which the concept of opportunities has been developed, focusing particularly upon the work of Tarrow (1998). Following this, I discuss the work of Doug McAdam (1982, 1986, 1988, 1989). McAdam develops a model which focuses upon the combined effect of networks, opportunities, the action of social control agencies and what he calls 'cognitive liberation'. It is the latter two of these notions that I focus upon in my discussion, and I consider a number of ways in which McAdam has reintroduced a consideration of cultural and psychological dynamics into movement analysis. The chapter ends with a critical assessment of the PP approach.

Protest and opportunity

Eisinger's (1973) research emerged out of the context of civil unrest, particularly among the black population, in the USA in the late 1960s. He was interested in the use of protest among minority and deprived groups. Part of his paper is devoted to an attempt to define protest and distinguish it from forms of collective violence. Protest involves a threat of violence, he argues, but that threat remains largely implicit such that the act of protesting remains legal and has a claim to legitimacy. Indeed, he suggests that protest 'harnesses aggressive impulses' and controls them, where violence gives them free reign. The consequence of this is that protest tends to have a greater political efficacy within the system. Violence is generally illegal and is deemed illegitimate. It therefore both invites criticism and becomes a focal point in its own right, diverting attention away from whatever issue provoked it. Protest, by contrast, insofar as it keeps the threat of violence veiled, is a legitimate act whose form is much less likely to detract from the content of the issues it is focused upon. Continuing this distinction, Eisinger argues that protest is an instrumental form of activity, guided by a cost–benefit analysis, where violence is an 'expressive' form of action in which 'actors . . . have essentially thrown cost considerations to the winds' (Eisinger 1973: 13). This cost–benefit notion, as we will see, is a dominant theme within the 'political process' school.

Eisinger's characterization of protest raises many contentious claims. However, it provides him with a ground upon which to explore the main theme of his study: the relationship of protest to its immediate political environment. Specifically he is concerned with the relationship of forms of protest to the 'political opportunity structures' within their context; that is, '. . . such factors as the nature of the chief executive, the mode of aldermatic election, the distribution of social skills and status, and the degree of social disintegration . . . the climate of government responsiveness and the level of community resources . . .' (Eisinger 1973: 11). These factors, he suggests, variously constrain or facilitate institutionalized political participation for citizens and, as such, have a direct effect upon the likelihood of protest and movement formation. But what sort of political system generates protest? Eisinger considers two competing hypotheses. The first predicts a linear relationship between opportunities and protest. It suggests that protest will be higher in those cities whose political structure is closed and offers few opportunities for participation and change to minority and deprived groups. Exclusion, so this story goes, leads to protest. The second hypothesis, by contrast, predicts a curvilinear relationship between protest and opportunities. It suggests that protest will be highest in cities with a mix of opportunities and constraints, decreasing both in those cities with more repressive and closed systems and in those (to some extent hypothetical) cities with open systems which afford great opportunities for effective political participation. The rationale for this curvilinear hypothesis is multi-levelled. Repression is said to reduce protest because it raises the costs of such action and, insofar as the system is closed, protests prove relatively ineffective in any case. Complete openness, by contrast, removes the need for protest. If demands are acted upon quickly and effectively then protest is unnecessary. These are largely negative reasons for why we might expect a curvilinear relationship between protests and opportunities. They explain why protest levels are likely to be low in closed and open systems respectively. However, Eisinger adds a number of more positive reasons why we might expect higher levels of protest in the middle of the opportunities spectrum. His main argument focuses upon systems which are in transition from a closed to a more open state:

> Protest occurs in a mixed system because the pace of change does not keep up with expectations, *even though change is occurring*. As the political opportunity structure becomes more open, previously power-less groups begin to acquire influence. The acquisition and develop-ment of influence, however, is likely to come slowly. Conventional strategies of political influence may appear too slow and unwieldly to effect significant gratification. In a system which is opening up, the realisation that the system may be vulnerable or responsive to political efforts combined with the persistence of inequalities becomes intol-erable for some groups. Hence these groups may resort to protest to express their impatience, even when the system may be viewed in relative terms as a responsive one.
>
> (Eisinger 1973: 15, his emphasis)

I have quoted this relatively long passage in full because it is quite reveal-ing. First, it ties the curvilinear hypothesis, which is the one Eisinger later endorses, to conditions of change. It predicts protest in an 'opening' rather than 'open' or even 'relatively open' political system. In the situation Eisinger addresses this process of opening involved the efforts of US politicians, stimulated by the civil rights movement and 'ghetto riots', to make the polit-ical system more responsive to the needs and wishes of the black population. This 'process' clause is important both because it strengthens the argument made and because it puts limits on that argument. It strengthens the argu-ment because, in contrast to those approaches which focus narrowly upon either grievances, resources or networks, it does not seek to explain a vari-ant by reference to a constant, that is, it does not seek to explain a change in levels of protest by reference to a factor which is itself stable but rather seeks to explain such variation by reference to a factor (opportunity) which is itself changing. The limit which this imposes, however, is that the model seems better placed to explain protest in those systems undergoing major reform than in systems whose structure of opportunities can be assumed to be relatively stable. This is a difficult point to establish because systems are always 'in process' and thus never stay exactly the same, but it at least alerts us to the responsibility which those who advocate a 'political opportunities' position have to identify the significant changes in the system they are analysing which have brought about increased levels of protest.

There is another important point to draw out of this passage, however, concerning the model of the social actor which is implied in Eisinger's account. Much of his language (e.g. of costs and benefits) suggests a RAT model and his explanations do broadly presuppose purposive action. The notion that repression and political closure inhibit protest, for example, clearly assumes an agent who can weigh up both the costs and benefits of acting politically, and the likelihood of success, such that they are put off by poor odds. There are numerous points in his argument, however, where Eisinger departs from this model. The above passage is one such place. Here Eisinger sounds rather more like a sophisticated advocate of the 'collective behaviour' approach. The agents in this passage are endowed with expectations about the process they are involved in and it is the thwarting of these expectations which prompts them to act. They feel aggrieved by the slowness of the political machine and find the pace of change intolerable. Their protest 'expresses' their 'impatience'. This is not a far cry from what Smelser and Blumer have to say about the raising and thwarting of expectations (see Chapters 2 and 3). Moreover, as in the collective behaviour approach, there is a focus upon the emotional response which specific sorts of factors are inclined to provoke. Repeatedly Eisinger makes indirect reference to what Blumer referred to as 'unrest'. He talks about agents finding the situation 'intolerable', for example, and about their 'impatience'. What is also interesting about Eisinger's paper is that he suggests that protest channels these feelings in a potentially fruitful direction. As noted earlier, he believes that protest has an instrumental rather than an expressive form and that it 'harnesses aggressive impulses'. What this amounts to is a notion very similar to that which I discussed under the rubric of 'rational emotion' in Chapter 3. Emotions feed into the communicative processes which constitute the fabric of the social world and therein their reasonableness is assessed and ways for acting upon them devised. Agents can discuss, for example, whether their feelings of impatience are reasonable, and if they decide that they are then they may elect to act upon them.

To compare and evaluate the linear and curvilinear hypotheses, Eisinger examined protest levels during the summer months of 1968 in 43 similarly sized cities, each of which had been graded in terms of its political opportunity structures. The definition of protest involved was narrowed down, so as to focus only upon local issues. This meant that certain types of protest, such as campus and anti-war/anti-draft protests, were excluded. 120 events, in total, were included. Political opportunity structures, in turn, were gauged through a battery of measures. Cities were assessed on the basis of whether they were run by an elected mayor or a paid professional manager, for example, or upon whether they held ward aldermanic elections, which 'afford residentially concentrated minorities greater opportunity for representation than at-large electoral systems' (Eisinger 1973: 17). Indicators of social stability and organization, such as crime rates, were also included.

The results of this study supported the curvilinear hypothesis over the linear hypothesis. Rates of protest were higher in those areas with a mix of opportunities and constraints than in closed and more repressive systems. Thus Eisinger concludes that repressive and closed systems discourage protest, while mixed systems both provoke and facilitate it. He is careful to stress, however, that at least some of the differences recorded between types of system are not statistically significant, that a considerable amount of the variance in rates of protest is not explained by opportunity structures, and that his research therefore provides only a 'moderately suggestive basis' for the curvilinear hypothesis. In his conclusion he urges caution: 'The conditions which give rise to protest are many and complex, and the structure of political opportunities, insofar as this is measurable by aggregate indicators, plays only one small part' (Eisinger 1973: 28). Among the other conditions which might stimulate protest, Eisinger specifically emphasizes perceived deprivation: a condition which, he emphasizes, can occur in both open and closed systems, as well as mixed states. On this point, again, he echoes certain of the basic insights of the collective behaviour approach.

The opportunities argument raises the question of how agents know that their system is open or opening. One possibility suggested by Eisinger himself is that the openness of the system is communicated back to potential activists by way of the example of ongoing struggles. Successful struggles stimulate further struggles: '. . . the system which responds [positively] to protest is likely by its very responsiveness to encourage protest. Elites who attempt to mobilise people to protest will eventually fail to recruit participants if protests are never successful' (Eisinger 1973: 27). There is a feedback mechanism within the protest environment. The successes and failures of protests communicate opportunity levels back to the political community, offering either encouragement or discouragement to groups within that community who may be considering the possibility of protest themselves. They show that success is 'there for the taking', or perhaps that it is not. This notion of feedback and the idea that the action of one movement affects the opportunities of another has been very important in the uptake of the idea of opportunity structures within movement theory. What is also identified here, moreover, is the equally important notion that what counts is the perception of opportunity. As Tarrow puts it, we must '. . . emphasise elements of opportunity that are *perceived* by insurgents – for structural changes that are not experienced can hardly be expected to affect people's behaviour, except indirectly' (1998: 77, his emphasis).

Opportunity and constraint

The hypothesis that movement activity is affected by changes or perceived changes in opportunity structures has been explored and supported by many writers and a great body of empirical work (e.g. Snyder and Tilly 1972;

Tilly 1978; McAdam 1982; Kitschelt 1986; Kriesi 1989; Tarrow 1989, 1998; Amenta and Zylan 1991; Diani 1996). These studies have also served to elaborate the basic notion of political opportunity structures considerably. One particularly important innovator is Tarrow (1998). He defines political opportunity structures as being composed of both opportunities and constraints, defining opportunity and constraint in the following way:

> By political opportunities, I mean consistent – but not necessarily formal, permanent or national – dimensions of the political struggle that encourage people to engage in contentious politics. By political constraints, I mean factors – like repression, but also like authorities' capacity to present a solid front to insurgents – that discourage contention.
>
> (Tarrow 1998: 20)

Opportunity structures are only one factor affecting the emergence and development of social movements and protest activity in his model. Other crucial factors are networks, resources and 'frames' (see Chapter 7). But opportunities are central. Their effect can be demonstrated in two ways. First, like Eisinger (1973), Tarrow suggests that *protests and movements tend to emerge and flourish in periods when opportunities are being opened up*. This might involve the extension of political rights to new groups, shifts in alignments within the polity or the emergence of cracks within an elite's hegemony. It might involve a decline in the state's repressive power or the emergence of a new external ally whose presence and interests change the shape of the political map. One good example, which illustrates many of these factors coming into play, in interaction, is the collapse of the former Soviet Union. No one could have imagined such a powerful and repressive state giving way under pressure of contentious politics and social movements from within, Tarrow notes. But of course it did and this was triggered by some initially quite minor reforms. These were the small cracks in the system which activists perceived as opportunities and they were just big enough to prompt mobilization. This resulted in a number of minor victories which further opened up opportunities and, perhaps more importantly, made existing opportunities visible to other potential contenders, communicating the possibility of a successful challenge to them. The sort of feedback mechanism identified by Eisinger slipped into place and the movement escalated to the point where the old regime eventually gave way.

The feedback effect of protest is often more complex than this, according to Tarrow. It generally moves in three directions. In the first instance, the action of movements changes the political opportunity structure for both themselves and any potential allies. Second, it potentially provokes counter-movements and/or changes the situation within which already existing counter-movements operate. A successful and support-winning action by pro-choice groups, for example, would usually be detrimental to the opportunities of the anti-abortionists, but a botched campaign might be just what this counter-movement requires to win support. Finally, protest actions open up opportunities for elites. A protest which is highly disruptive and receives a bad press might give politicians the opportunity to introduce more repressive legislation than would ordinarily be deemed legitimate, for example. Each of these factors interacts with the others, of course, and the outcome could go any of a number of ways. The original agents may end up better off, in terms of future opportunities, but they may end up worse off.

These factors concern change in opportunities but Tarrow also makes reference to more stable aspects of opportunity structures, which tend to register in cross-national comparisons of movement activity. This is the second of the aforementioned ways in which the effects of opportunities can be demonstrated. There are *observable differences in the rates, forms and successes of different types of movement*, across different national states, and these differences can be explained, at least to some extent, by the political opportunity structures in those countries. This has been demonstrated empirically in a study by Kitschelt (1986), which compared the opposition to nuclear energy in France, Sweden, East Germany and the USA. Kitschelt compared different aspects of the respective opportunity structures of these societies with the types of protest which emerged, making a case that the latter is shaped by the former.

For Tarrow, the main stable factors in an opportunity structure involve the strength and centralization of the state, as well as the forms of repression it is able and prepared to use. He stresses, however, that this broad brushstroke description glosses over many important details. Different areas of the state may vary with respect to these factors, he argues, and the state may have a different strategy with respect to different sorts of protest and movement. Government and police authorities might be less inclined to use repressive measures in relation to environmental groups, for example, than far right groups, perhaps because they feel a greater force of legitimation behind them in relation to their efforts to control the latter.

One relatively simple hypothesis that emerges in relation to these various ideas is that strong, centralized states, which are disposed to using considerable repression and force to control protests and movements, will tend to discourage the latter, with the effect that visible opposition to them is low in comparison to other states and societies. This hypothesis has common-sense plausibility and is borne out by many examples, such as the low levels of protest in the former Soviet Union during the height of its power. Notwithstanding this, however, Tarrow also refers to the paradoxes of repressive control. Repressive forms of control can have a radicalizing effect upon collective action, he argues, because they sometimes scare away the moderate dissenter, leaving radicals to control the opposition, and/or because they persuade moderates to adopt a more radical stance. Furthermore, *an increase in levels of repression* can generate both increased contention and new movements because it increases the costs of not resisting. Tarrow illustrates this with reference to the growth in Palestinian resistance following the expansion of the Israeli state in the mid- to late-1990s:

> The threat of suffocating in the grip of Israeli 'created facts' was a major incentive to Palestinian protest. Indeed, it might be said that Netanyahu's outrageous move provided an opportunity for popular protest that Yassar Arafat's government could not have mustered on its own.
>
> (Tarrow 1998: 86)

There is a problem in referring to an increase in repression as an 'opportunity', not least that it risks a circular definition of opportunity in which anything would count. I return to this later. For the moment we must consider two further points that Tarrow makes regarding opportunities and repression. First, he argues that the rigidity of repressive states can make them quite fragile and vulnerable to opposition, compared to democratic states, if insurgency begins. Where democratic states can absorb opposition and accommodate new claims, authoritarian and repressive states are often forced to stand their ground and face the consequences. Democratic states can use the power of their opponents against them, as in judo, where repressive states are more geared up to meet force with force. Second, Tarrow adds that centralization and concentration of power can make a state vulnerable to takeover, again if strong opposition is mounted. When power is dispersed it is not as easily seized by an opposition.

There is a great deal of evidence to support the notion that movements are shaped by opportunities. However, we should be mindful of what we infer from this. Two types of study muddy the water. In the first instance, as Tarrow (1998) himself notes, there are studies, such as those of James Scott (1985, 1990), which point to the subterranean resistance cultures that sometimes emerge in the context of highly repressive systems. These cultures may not engage in overt protest action, not least since doing so would lead to incarceration or even execution, but they generate and reproduce resistance identities and beliefs. Within these cultures, Scott argues, gestures and symbols of defiance are woven into the fabric of everyday life. Common place phrases and acronyms can achieve a highly charged significance, for example, and the handshakes and forms of identification of the 'secret society' become a popular vernacular of grassroots resistance. Second, as Taylor's (1989) work on abeyance structures and Melucci's (1986, 1996) work on networks and movement latency each suggest, movements in less repressive societies have ways of perpetuating themselves and biding time during times of low opportunity, in order that they might re-engage when opportunities improve. These studies suggest that we should distinguish between movements and their overt acts of protest, and that we should view opportunities as a factor mediating between movement and protest, perhaps determining the latter in some cases but much less causally efficacious in relation to the former. Movements can form, albeit in a subterranean manner, in a diverse range of opportunity structures, though such structures will shape the ways in which they can be predicted to act and the success they are likely to achieve.

Cognitive liberation and social control

Political opportunity structures are also central elements, alongside networks and indigenous organization forms, in the model of movement analysis developed by Doug McAdam (1982). He adds a number of important elements to this basic model, however. Two are particularly significant. First, he advocates a *longer term and more processual approach*. This has two aspects. On one hand, echoing Blumer (see Chapter 2), he argues for the necessity of tracing a movement from its inception, right through its 'career'. It will not suffice to produce a model which accounts only for the emergence of a movement, he argues. We must be able to account for the various transformations they undergo, the dynamic of their development and ultimately their demise. On the other hand, echoing Smelser (see Chapter 3), he argues that the elements which facilitate movement development may fall into place over an extended period of time and he thus warns against those approaches to movement analysis which focus only upon the immediate events surrounding mobilization. In his analysis of the rise and fall of the black civil rights movement, for example, he charts the gradual and eventually converging processes whereby blacks became concentrated in tightly-knit communities and political opportunities opened up for them. These processes were the key preconditions for movement formation, he argues, but they took a long time coming to fruition.

McAdam's second big contribution to the PP model is *his recognition of the role of 'cognitive liberation' and 'insurgent consciousness'* in the sparking of conflict. These notions are related to his more general understanding of the relationship of theories of social movements to theories of power. He commends the RM approach for rejecting the pluralist view of power implicit within the collective behaviour approach and embracing a more elitist model. Collective behaviour approaches view power and access to political influence as relatively open, he argues, such that protest behaviours which fall outside the mainstream channels appear deviant and are explained as such. RM corrects this. It recognizes the existence of political elites and the necessity which this generates for powerless groups to pursue their political interests outside the mainstream political channels and institutions. What the RM approach fails to realize, however, is the power which seemingly powerless groups could have if they did but recognize it and organized appropriately. Workers, for example, have a great deal of latent power by virtue of the structural contribution they make to the economic life of their society (see also Piven and Cloward 1979). As strikes demonstrate, workers can use their indispensability to generate a structural pressure for change. This all depends upon workers or other apparently powerless groups becoming conscious of their power, however, and perhaps also of their oppressed situation. Part of what is involved here is the subjective or perceptual dimension of political opportunity structures, namely, that they must be perceived to be open or opening in order to affect action. There is more to it than this, however. On the one hand, McAdam incorporates the psychological notion of the 'fundamental attribution error', that is, he argues that agents tend to attribute the misery and misfortunes of their own lives to themselves and/or other specific individuals, rather than to situational or social structural factors. Mobilization will only occur, he argues, when these attribution patterns are transformed (see also Klandermans 1984, 1989; Feree and Miller 1985). Agents must attribute their grievances to changeable aspects of the social world. In addition, borrowing from Piven and Cloward (1979), he argues both that the state or a specific state of affairs must lose legitimacy in the eyes of those subject to it, before they will contest it, and that potential challengers must lose the sense of fatalism, inevitability and personal inefficacy which ordinarily prevails among oppressed groups, so as to develop a sense of their own collective capacity to change society or some aspect of it. Finally, he notes that protest and contention depend upon the way in which agents collectively define their situation: 'Before collective protest can get under way, people must collectively define their situations as unjust and subject to change through group action' (McAdam 1982: 51). When these pieces fall into place communities are 'cognitively liberated'. They manifest an 'insurgent consciousness'.

These cognitive factors, which in more recent work McAdam (1994) has theorized in terms of 'movement cultures', interact with opportunities and networks of solidarity to produce the necessary preconditions of movement formation. They are also shaped by these factors, however, and by the latter in particular. Drawing on a number of empirical studies, McAdam (1982) argues that 'system attributions', delegitimation and feelings of collective efficacy are all likely to be fostered within the context of highly integrated and homogeneous social networks or communities.

It is these same three factors – opportunities, networks/solidarity and insurgent consciousness – which shape and affect the career of a movement beyond its initial emergence, for McAdam. Each interacts with the others in a mutually affecting way. A fourth factor also comes into play at this later stage, however, in the form of the responses of social control agencies. At one level the impact of these agencies may be to quell, facilitate or amplify mobilization processes. A strongly repressive gesture may raise the costs of protest sufficiently to reduce the active support base of a movement beneath an effective level, for example, but it might equally serve to antagonize protestors further and to generate a wider support base for them among sympathetic publics. The effects of social control agencies extend beyond the basic vital statistics of a movement, however, and can reach right to the heart of strategy itself. This is apparent in the history of the black civil rights movement, according to McAdam (1982, 1983). The interaction between the civil rights movement and their opponents progressed in a 'chesslike fashion' (1983: 735). Each move by one called forth a response from the other. More to the point, a pattern emerged in which the movement would devise new and innovative tactics, which caught their opponents off guard and were therefore successful for a period, until their opponents devised ways of dealing with those tactics, which were successful until the movement devised further tactical innovations and so on. A dialogue of actions was generated which demanded constant innovation and improvization from each side. This pattern was particularly fascinating from the point of view of political opportunities, McAdam (1983) notes, because we can see a pattern of booms and slumps in general levels of movement activity, following the periods of innovation and containment. The emergence of successful tactics encouraged greater levels of involvement, while the successes of opponents and agencies of social control decreased it. In this respect responses of social control agencies and their interactions with movements can count as a crucial (perceived) opportunity factor shaping the longer term career of the movement.

Freedom summer

McAdam's account of the emergence of the black civil rights movement and the political process model he builds around it clearly identifies, in the form of 'insurgent consciousness', a number of social–psychological factors which enter into the process of movement and contention. He focuses upon the way in which agents collectively define both their situation and their own agentic capacities and moral status therein. This aspect is further explored in his later study, *Freedom Summer* (1988). The title of this book refers to the summer of 1964, when white American students from leading universities were recruited by black civil rights activists to aid in a variety of political projects in the South. They were to offer basic education to black children, for example, and to both register eligible blacks to vote and encourage them to do so. This was an extremely costly activity in many respects. Three students lost their lives at the hands of racists and many experienced harassment from both white citizens and the police. Furthermore, all had to forego the prospect of earning money over the summer and, in fact, had to support their own activities financially.

Potential participants for this political project were required to fill in a brief application questionnaire and, in some cases, undergo interview, before they were accepted on the project. These files, which covered applicants who were rejected or withdrew, as well as those who participated, were kept, and the freedom summer project was thereby able to serve as a fascinating naturally occurring experiment in movement activism. McAdam was able to follow up applicants, finding out what they had done since freedom summer and comparing those who partook with those who, for whatever reason, did not. Many important insights were gleaned from this study (see McAdam 1986, 1988, 1989). For present purposes it will suffice to outline three.

Shock and the 'freedom high'

In the first instance, his study puts a clear emphasis upon emotion, culture, identity (individual and collective) and the sense of 'shock' which often prompts an individual to join collective actions. In relation to this latter phenomenon, McAdam argues that there is ordinarily a seamless relationship between agents' expectations and the reality they experience. But this was shaken in the case of the freedom summer volunteers when they came face-to-face with the living conditions of the Mississippi blacks and the regime of hatred and injustice to which they were subject, not only by their white neighbours but by the police and other authorities too. And the shock was all the greater when those same representatives of the American system that these young liberals had grown up to respect treated them in the same way. All that they had come to believe about their society, at the deepest level, was thrown into doubt. This, McAdam argues, was a considerable learning experience for the volunteers, which had a profound effect upon them. Such experiences of shock entail a considerable affective intensity. The world of the volunteers was shaken in a way that made them anxious, afraid and angry in equal measure. On the more positive side, however, McAdam discusses the emotional 'ups' of the experience. He refers at a number of times to the 'ecstasy' which the volunteers reported; an ecstasy which, he argues, derived from the process of stepping outside the cultural framework of taken-for-granted assumptions in which they otherwise lived their lives. When events in the world cease to conform to the habitual schemas and expectations of the agent this is experienced as a shock and generates anxiety. But when the agent dares to step blindly out of that habit-world and into the emergent structures of a transgressive project the feeling is 'intoxicating'. This became known as the 'freedom high' among the volunteers and McAdam notes that many of them spent much time in the years after the project attempting to achieve it again.

In stepping out of their taken-for-granted habit world the volunteers did not literally step into a void. They stepped into a resistance culture which had been emerging within the civil rights movement for many years and to whose development they were now contributing. This culture involved new and different ways of perceiving, thinking about and acting within American society. It entailed new schemas of understanding and new forms of know-how. It also entailed rituals, such as collective song singing. McAdam's account focuses particularly upon these rituals. He emphasizes their role in creating and sustaining identities at both the individual and group levels. As with the 'freedom high', this sense of collective identity and togetherness was something which the volunteers often wished to recapture when they returned to 'normal' life. They had come to feel and see themselves as activists and they wanted to be reconfirmed in that identity when they returned to college. Moreover, they wanted to recapture and recreate the sense of collective belonging that the summer activities had created. Many had started to experience the movement as a 'family' to which they belonged and they experienced the break up of that family, at the end of the summer, painfully.

Activist biographies

Because he had data on a group of applicants from both before the project and a long time afterwards (when he caught up with them in the 1980s), and because this involved both individuals who had participated and those who had not, McAdam was able to examine the effect of participation on agents. His conclusion was that participation had a significant effect, both at the level of personal and political lives. The volunteers were much more likely to be active in politics in their later lives, and their personal lives were strongly affected both by this and their aforementioned need to rediscover both the 'freedom high' and the 'movement family'. We must be careful how we interpret these findings. Although, in a paper specifically focused upon biographical impacts, McAdam argues that there were no significant differences between participants and withdrawals, prior to the project, his later work does suggest certain differences, including a longer previous history of political involvement and a greater ideological commitment to the project. Nevertheless, all applicants for the project were very politically involved and committed, and the differences between their respective biographical trajectories do seem to be attributable, in some measure, to the effects of involvement in the project. The shock caused by involvement and the emotional intensity of the project, combined with immersion in the resistance culture, seemingly functioned to resocialize the participants, breaking down many of the conventional habits of the American citizen and generating new and radical habits: a disposition towards and a competence in the alternative politics of social movements.

It is also evident, in this connection, that involvement in the project bestowed a particular form of status or political capital on the participants, which allowed many of them to emerge as leaders and stars of the subsequent student movement and the various 'new social movements' which emerged out of that movement. This is an important theme which McAdam and Debra Friedman explore elsewhere, in a more general paper on movements and identity (Friedman and McAdam 1992). Engaging with the broad theme of the incentives, selective or otherwise, which draw agents into activism, they argue that specific political identities often involve a degree of status, such that agents are motivated to compete for them. In some cases this is of little consequence. Agents can acquire the identity simply by labelling themselves as such. In some cases, however, SMOs manage to limit the 'supply' of a specific identity by stipulating conditions which its incumbents must meet to achieve it and this can be a valuable lever for motivating agents into action.

The path to activism

McAdam also explores the role of biographical and socialization factors in relation to the process whereby participants were recruited for freedom summer. Much work on the process of recruitment emphasizes the importance of 'structural' over psychological factors, he notes. In particular, as we noted in the last chapter, social networks are identified as central. However, this work has tended to focus upon relatively low-risk and, indeed, low-cost forms of activism. In this context, McAdam argues, it is not surprising that structural factors are the main determinant. An agent whose friends are all partaking in a political project, even if they are not so bothered about the politics of the event themselves, will tend to go along because the cost of doing so is much less than that risked, in the form of social chastisement, if they do not. This would not apply to the same extent, however, if the risks and costs of participation were much higher. Involvement in high-risk activities tends to depend upon greater levels of ideological commitment. But this high level of commitment may itself be explained through involvement in lower risk forms of activity and an activist 'history'. Any social agent will have a certain disposition towards politics on account of her family socialization, McAdam notes, but this disposition can be modified by way of (even reluctant) participation in political activities:

> First, through his friends, he will almost surely meet activists whom he did not know previously, thus broadening his range of movement contacts and increasing his vulnerability to future recruiting appeals. Second, in talking with others at the rally and listening to the scheduled speakers, our budding activist may well develop a better and more sympathetic understanding of the . . . movement. Finally, the behavioural norms of the rally may encourage the recruit to 'play at' being an activist for the duration of the event. However, as self-perception

theory . . . and the research on identity transformation suggest, it is precisely these tentative forays into new roles that pave the way for more thoroughgoing identity changes. Playing at being an 'activist' is a prerequisite to becoming one.

(McAdam 1986: 70)

Involvement in the activity disposes the agent both towards further involvement and towards the forms of belief and identity which correspond with and reinforce it. Moreover, McAdam postulates a process of circular reinforcement and amplification in this process, whereby each successive act of involvement commits the agent towards more costly and risky forms of activism: '. . . each succeeding foray into safe forms of activism increases the recruit's network integration, ideological affinity with the movement, and commitment to an activist identity, as well as his receptivity to more costly forms of participation' (McAdam 1986: 70).

McAdam's work on recruitment to the freedom summer project is by no means an adequate test of this theory, nor does it claim to be. By contrasting the participants with the withdrawals, however, he was at least able to see if their characteristics were consistent with what this theory would predict. They were. Taken as a group, all of the applicants for the freedom summer project had a greater ideological commitment to the civil rights cause than the average student, as well as connections with other applicants and a higher than average degree of prior involvement in political activities. The key factors which distinguished the applicants who went South from those who did not was the extent of their prior activism and their levels of manifest commitment. Those who went had generally been more involved in struggle in the past and, perhaps as a consequence, had a greater commitment to the project. This 'proof' is far from watertight. A critic might argue that some as yet unnamed disposition must explain the greater prior history of activism among those who went; that this explains why they carried through their application to the project, when others did not; and that this also explains their greater subsequent involvement in politics after the project. There is a genuine 'chicken and egg' problem here. Nevertheless, McAdam posits a very strong case for breaking this particular causal circle in the way that he does and, in the absence of anything more substantive to support the hypothetical alternative, his is the most plausible case.

Evaluating the political process model

The political process model is persuasive, insightful and well supported by evidence and research. However, there are a number of problems with it. I will focus upon two broad areas of difficulty. The first concerns the idea of political opportunities. The second focuses upon issues of agency and structure.

Political opportunities?

The concept of political opportunities has been used in two different ways. The first concerns the emergence of movements and, specifically, the timing of their emergence. It is argued that movements emerge at moments when political regimes are opening up and new opportunities for change are consequently appearing. The second concerns the way in which different types of movement or protest emerge in different types of society. Different polities afford different opportunity structures, it is argued, and therefore different types of protest and movement emerge. Studies which address this second type of question say nothing about the emergence of movements or its timing. Indeed they cannot as they generally assume a fairly constant opportunity structure in the societies they are comparing.

My first set of comments addresses the first of these two uses only, that is, those which seek to explain the emergence of movements. The key examples of this mechanism of movement formation tend to involve fairly considerable shifts in political systems which are, at least in respect of the movement population involved, relatively repressive in the first instance: e.g. the authoritarian state in the former USSR and the Jim Crow system of racial segregation in the American South. These are important periods of social transition and serve as very dramatic and lucid examples of the opportunities argument. One can readily imagine that the average rational actor in the USSR would have decided against protest when that might lead to incarceration in the gulag, and similarly one can imagine how a relaxation in that system, once proven trustworthy, would lead to an escalation of protest. Such big changes are relatively few and far between, however, and it is not as obvious that protest and movement formation will be sensitive to smaller changes in opportunity, particularly in societies which boast a reasonable degree of democracy in the first place and near universal suffrage among their adult populations.

More to the point, protests and movements are emerging most of the time in these societies, sometimes at a greater pace than others, without any obvious changes in the basic opportunity structure, or, indeed, when opportunities might be perceived to be contracting. I have no systematic evidence on this and am prepared to be proved wrong but a relatively safe anecdotal example can be gleaned from the Thatcher years (1979–90) in the UK. If the Thatcher government had any effect upon political opportunities in the UK it was to contract them. It is commonly argued that power was centralized during this time and a series of laws were introduced to limit and regulate opportunities for public assembly and protest. I do not have the data to indicate whether overall levels of protest and activism increased or decreased during this time and would concede that levels of industrial action were reduced by new trade union legislation. Nevertheless, a number of significant and high-profile protest activities emerged during this more repressive period. Among these were the formation of the longstanding women's peace camp at Greenham Common; a year-long, highly volatile and sometimes violent miners' strike; two bouts of inner city rioting in a number of major cities; and an 'anti-poll tax' movement, with associated widespread riots and skirmishes with police, which arguably contributed to Mrs Thatcher's own personal political demise, if not that of her party (Bagguley 1995b). Furthermore, the attempts of the subsequent Major government to limit rights of public assembly was a key factor in the emergence of the Reclaim the Streets group, which has played such a central role in more recent anti-capitalist protest (Klein 2000), as well as a number of further key currents of resistance within UK society (McKay 1996). My basic point here is that the importance of political opportunity structures, and particularly the opening of these structures, is by no means as obvious in relation to relatively democratic political systems as it is to those which are 'on the way' to democracy. Political openness may be a precondition of protest and movement formation in these former cases, and thus a crucial element in the value-added process which generates struggle, but it does not explain emergence or its timing to anything like the same extent.

It may be argued, following Tarrow (1998), that my Thatcher example actually illustrates the way in which repression or closure, in moderate doses, itself creates an opportunity for struggle. This brings me to my second worry with the opportunity model. The notion that repression creates opportunities for protest and movement formation is peculiar. Extreme acts by elites or oppressors may create opportunities for movement leaders to recruit and mobilize new members but this surely has more to do with an increase in 'grievances' or a transgression of moral and political expectations than with the political opportunities of the society in question. Movement leaders have a greater opportunity to mobilize the masses only because the masses are more aggrieved or outraged than previously. Though Tarrow may refer to this in terms of an increase in the 'costs' of not resisting, his own use of the term 'outrageous' in relation to the expansion of the Israeli state (see above) clearly indicates that we are not dealing with a process of cold, economic calculation. 'Increasing costs of not resisting' is just a cumbersome way of saying 'increased grievances' or perhaps of pointing to what Smelser referred to as 'precipitating events'. There is nothing wrong with this at all but we should be clear that this is what we are saying. Twisting the language around to maintain a focus upon opportunities only does the theory of opportunities a disservice in the long run because it renders the language of opportunity so loose as to make it meaningless. I would prefer to argue that grievances and opportunities are both variable and that changes in either can be consequential in relation to movement formation and development.

This brings me to my third point. The PP approach is extremely close in form to the value-added model discussed in Chapter 2, but remains vague on issues which the value-added model could clarify. Recall Smelser's six preconditions of movement emergence:

1 structural conduciveness;
2 strain;
3 formation of generalized beliefs;
4 precipitating factors;
5 mobilization of participants;
6 operation of social control.

The notion of 'political opportunities' is clearly very similar to 'structural conduciveness'. Both notions seek to identify the manner in which social structures variously repress, constrain and facilitate protest. Similarly, the notion of 'cognitive liberation' and 'insurgent consciousness', though their value accent is different, are very close to what Smelser means by the 'formation of generalized beliefs'. Both identify the importance of processes of situational definition and blame attribution. Finally, McAdam follows Smelser in identifying the central role of agencies of social control in shaping and containing or amplifying struggle. If we add to this that the network and resources arguments discussed in the previous chapter mirror Smelser's concern with 'mobilization', and, as shown above in relation to Tarrow, that the PP approach tends to smuggle grievances back in, under the guise of 'increased costs of not resisting', then it is evident just how much overlap there is between the PP approach and Smelser's value-added model.

I do not mean to deny, in arguing this, that both the PP and RM approaches put a great deal more meat upon the bones of the model, nor that the empirical work they have generated has contributed a great deal to our understanding of movements and their preconditions. PP and RM approaches have advanced our understanding of movements considerably. But in doing so they have sailed ever closer to the model (i.e. Smelser's) they purport to reject. More to the point, there is still more to learn from Smelser's value-added model. It remains important, on one hand, because it draws all of the preconditions distributed across a variety of PP and RM models together, combining their scattered insights into a centralized and coherent synthesis. On the other hand, it remains important because of the emphasis that Smelser puts upon both the analytic status of the elements of the model and the possibility that they may combine, in practice, in a variety of different orders. Proponents of RM and PP seemingly assume that movements are triggered by a single factor or by a cluster of factors but in a determinate order. It is networks that are the real cause of struggle, they argue, or opportunities. And their analyses are often insufficiently abstract, failing to recognize that the same event or process may serve a number of interrelated functions in relation to movement formation. Smelser is more flexible, more abstract and therefore more persuasive. He identifies the functional precon- ditions which must be met if movements/protests are to emerge, without conflating those functions with concrete events/processes, and he thereby remains open to the possibility that a single event may fulfil more than one function. In addition, he recognizes that, empirically, the events which fulfil these various functions may emerge in any order. Thus, in certain cases of movement formation, where all elements of the value-added model are in place except for a strain or grievance, the emergence of a strain or grievance may be sufficient to generate insurgency. In other cases, by contrast, a grievance may be harboured for decades before the further conditions that allow it to be transformed into conflict fall into place. So it is with all elements in the value-added model.

My final concern about 'political opportunity structures', which applies to both of the uses of the model referred to above, involves its relatively narrow focus upon political structures. As I noted in Chapter 2, modern societies are highly differentiated and thus involve multiple levels or sites of opportunity and restraint. Tarrow recognizes this, in part, when he argues that the different branches of the state may entail differing forms and levels of opportunity. My point is that we need to extend our view beyond the state to incorporate other structures. To anticipate a point from the next chapter, consider the media. In a modern society the media is a crucial site of social activity, not least for social movements. The media offers the key to publicity, good and bad, and everything that goes with it. In this respect the media generates opportunities for movements. But the media is a relat- ively autonomous 'game' or social structure whose opportunities are by no means stable or evenly distributed. It works in particular ways, with its own 'currency' and is subject to various cycles and trends. For example, the probability that a movement will achieve high levels of good publicity within the media is greatly dependent upon the media currency of 'news value'. Movements which are legally or politically very viable may be 'no hopers' in relation to the media because they lack 'news value', and if so they will simply not get coverage. Conversely, a struggle with very little legal or political claim may push the right buttons in relation to the media and achieve masses of publicity. Furthermore, this, in itself, is not a stable matter. If the journalistic 'market' is flooded with high-value stories a movement will need more novelty or whatever to succeed than in periods where the competition is low. And what counts as news value will change. In other words it makes sense to talk of variable 'media opportunity structures'. And we need not halt there. Social movements and protests have emerged in a diverse range of social spaces, from the psychiatric system, through the school, to the workplace, each of which afford their own structures of opportunity, and these struggles have spread to a range of further sites, such as the media, courts, parliament or the academic field, wherein they have again encountered a distinct game and opportunity structure. Some movements have found the law an opportune site of struggle, others the academy or media. While I agree that opportunities are a very important factor in determining movement activity, I see no reason to limit our focus to specifically *political* opportunities. Having said this, if we are to recognize the existence of multiple forms of opportunity then we need a more differentiated conception of society and a better understanding of its sites of action than the PP approach affords.

It is important to add here that in each of these cases 'opportunity' is a relational property, a function of the fit between the resources of agents and the state of the social space in question. Openings in the media will be more of an opportunity for those with the know-how and resources to make something of them. This means that certain SMOs will have more opportunities in relation to certain fields than others.

Structure and agency

The failure of advocates of the political opportunity approach to consider this wider range of possible opportunities/constraints stems from their broader failure to engage with the differentiated nature of modern societies and is, as such, a problem with their conception (or lack of a conception) of social structure. Like RM advocates, PP advocates are proudly 'structural', and yet like RM advocates their concept of structure is quite narrow and ignores much of what usually belongs to 'structure' in sociological work. As in RM this also extends to the issue of structural strain. PP advocates distance themselves from concerns with 'strains' or 'grievances' to such a point that their model fails to locate struggles or movements within the structures and structural tensions of the societies from which they emerge. It is interesting in this respect that many PP advocates tend to draw strongly from Marx and to identify their position as one inspired by him. If anything characterizes the Marxist position it is the tendency to locate the possibility for a proletarian movement and uprising in terms of the system (capitalism) and systemic contradictions and crisis tendencies which produce the parties to struggle, set them in opposition to one another and aggravate this condition through the generation of specific grievances (e.g. wage depression and unemployment). Marx recognizes the importance of networks, etc., as his emphasis on the class-forming effects of urbanization testify, but the structural conditions of struggle, in the broader sense of 'capitalism and its contradictions', is what most distinguishes his approach. The Marx-inspired PP approaches do not address these issues at all. At best they tend to take it for granted that there are fundamental conflicts of interest in modern societies, between classes, genders and races, for example. This is problematic on three counts. First, it means that we forego an important opportunity to link social movement analysis to broader reflections upon the nature of society, social order and social conflict. Second, it amounts to a tendency to ignore the grievances which give rise to struggle and lend them their intelligibility. Finally, it fails to address important questions about the changing nature of the underlying structural conflicts within society. As we will see in Chapter 8, many theorists of 'new social movements' believe that the contradictions and structural strains identified by Marx no longer hold in the contemporary era, at least not in the manner identified by Marx, and that new structural determinates of conflict have emerged. Whether they are right or not, these are clearly important issues which social movement analysis ought to be able to address, but the PP approach does not prepare us to do so.

Agency too is a problem in relation to the PP approach. At one level the approach remains wedded to the extremely problematic RAT model. This is evident in the language of 'costs and benefits' that most advocates use and in the basic assumption that the chief determinant of movement activism is the opportunity/constraint structure within the polity. Mindful of the problems of RAT, however, and perhaps more open-minded than the average RAT, many PP advocates have begun to explore the role of identity, emotion, culture and biography in relation to movement involvement. This has been most evident, in this chapter, in relation to the work of McAdam (1988, 1989, 1994) but he is by no means alone (see A. Scott 1990; Morris and McClurg Mueller 1992; Johnson and Klandermans 1995; Jasper 1997). There is much to commend this move. It opens up neglected movement dynamics to analysis and constitutes a first, if largely unacknowledged, step to recover some of the important but buried insights of the collective behaviour approach. It is amazing how close McAdam sails to Blumer, and such notions as a movement's *esprit de corps*, without acknowledging or discussing the fact. However, the problem with this is that it leaves us without a clear concept of agency. The agent is no longer a rational actor, at least not in the minimal sense proposed by RAT, but no other clear conception, over and above ad hoc additions of 'emotion', 'identity' and 'culture', has yet emerged. The PP agent is thus stranded in a vague and unclear position somewhere between RAT and a better alternative. This is a problem if we believe, as I do, that social movement analysis should be able to transcend eclectic and empiricist compilations of the 'facts' of movement formation to offer a coherent theoretical framework which incorporates and explains those facts.

Summary and conclusion

This chapter has considered the key elements of the 'political process' model of movement analysis. The early part of the chapter focused upon the notion of 'political opportunity structures', as developed by Eisinger and Tarrow. This was then followed by a discussion of McAdam's work: specifically his reflections upon 'cognitive liberation', social control and the biographical impact of struggle. The chapter concluded with a sympathetic critique of the political process approach. It clearly has a great deal to offer to the analysis of social movements but it also manifests significant weaknesses which must be addressed.

Further reading

The best overall text for the political process approach is Tarrow's (1998) *Power in Movement*. Eisinger's (1973) paper 'The conditions of protest in American cities' remains important as a discussion of the notion of political opportunities. On biography and movements see 'Recruitment to high risk activism' and 'The biographical consequences of activism', both by McAdam (1986, 1989). For a more critical reflection on the political process approach see Jasper's (1997) *The Art of Moral Protest*.

chapter seven

Repertoires, frames and cycles

In the previous chapter I considered the basic position of the political process approach. In this chapter I follow that up by outlining and discussing three key concepts which have emerged out of that tradition and have shaped its research agenda to a considerable degree: 'repertoires of contention', 'frames' and 'cycles of contention'. These are important concepts because they allow us to dissect movement activity in new and interesting ways. In the case of the first two, however, they are also problematic concepts which we need to be wary of appropriating too readily. Their value, I suggest, lies more in the questions they raise than in the answers or solutions they present. It is also noteworthy, and will be emphasized, that they sit very unhappily with the RAT model of agency which has tended to dominate the PP literature, thus raising further questions about both the internal cogency of that position and the value of the RAT model. I begin my discussion by examining repertoires, followed by frames, before finally focusing upon cycles. In each case I will present a brief exposition and then an evaluation. As in the previous chapters I conclude the chapter with a brief summary and overview.

Repertoires of contention

The concept of repertoires of contention, which was developed by Charles Tilly, was first posited in a paper which surveyed and compared forms of contentious political action in the Burgundy province of France over a 300-year period (Tilly 1977). Since then Tilly has revisited and revised the concept many times (Tilly 1978, 1986, 1995), as have many others (see Traugott 1995a). The concept seeks to capture the historical peculiarity of the methods of protest that agents use. The way in which agents protest,

Tilly observes, reflects both their historical and national–geographical location:

> The word *repertoire* identifies a limited set of routines that are learned, shared and acted out through a relatively deliberate process of choice. Repertoires are learned cultural creations, but they do not descend from abstract philosophy or take shape as a result of political propaganda; they emerge from struggle. People learn to break windows in protest, attack pilloried prisoners, tear down dishonoured houses, stage public marches, petition, hold formal meetings, organise special-interest associations. At any particular point in history, however, they learn only a rather small number of alternative ways to act collectively.
>
> (Tilly 1995: 26)

Five points are noteworthy from this definition. First, there is a suggestion that repertoires constrain behaviour and choice. Although Tilly elsewhere makes reference to improvization in relation to repertoires it is evident that he believes protest to be bounded by the repertoires that protestors have learned. Indeed, one of his hypotheses with respect to repertoires is that 'the prior history of contention [in a given geographical/social arena] constrains the choices of action currently available, in partial independence of the identities and interests that participants bring to the action' (Tilly 1995: 29). Second, on the other side of this same point, there is a tacit recognition of the know-how or acquired competence involved in specific forms of protest. Protesting requires a certain degree of skill in specific techniques of protest. Third, there is an emphasis upon the practical constitution of repertoires. They do not emerge out of abstract thinking but rather out of struggle and the activities of everyday life. Traugott's (1995b) study of barricades illustrates this well. The use of the barricade in popular protest, most famously associated with the French Revolution, developed, he shows, out of a routine and everyday method of 'neighbourhood protection' in sixteenth-century Paris. Fourth, a notion of deliberate but constrained choice is introduced. Protestors choose their repertoire from the available stock. Finally, to reiterate the main point, repertoires are identified with specific historical periods.

Repertoires are not so much forms of action as of interaction, however. They connect and belong to sets of actors:

> The action takes its meaning and effectiveness from shared understandings, memories, and agreements, however grudging, among the parties. In that sense, then, a repertoire of actions resembles not individual consciousness but a language; although individuals and groups know and deploy the actions in a repertoire, the actions connect sets of individuals and groups.
>
> (Tilly 1995: 30)

What Tilly evokes here, I suggest, is similar in some respects to the notion of the 'moral economy of the crowd' discussed in Chapter 3. His reference to shared understandings, memories and agreements suggests that contention is, in certain respects, the expected punishment to which elites are subject when they overstep a culturally determined mark. And this entails a sense that the aggrieved have a 'right', however grudgingly accorded them, to defend their interests in this way. In addition to this, however, there is a sense both that the protest follows an expected path and that it works, in part, by way of a communicative power which is afforded it by the aforementioned shared expectations. Repertoires are language games (Wittgenstein 1953) in which specific moves or actions have particular meanings and effects. There are, in effect, legitimate and illegitimate moves in protest, which all parties, perhaps unwittingly, adhere to. This entails that repertoires are, to a degree, institutionalized, and Tilly extends this notion by noting the 'fit' between repertoires and other institutionalized aspects of the social world: e.g. 'police practices, laws of assembly, rules of association, routines for informal gatherings, ways of displaying symbols of affiliation, opposition . . . means of reporting news and so on' (Tilly 1995: 26–7). Repertoires are shaped by these other institutions, he argues. But they also play a part in shaping those institutions. Or rather, the institutionalized space for legitimate protest is carved out by way of protest itself. As an example of this Tilly makes reference to the struggles in Britain during the nineteenth century over what counted as acceptable and legal forms of strike activity. Contemporary strike activities take place in the 'space' forged by these earlier struggles.

Given the emphasis that Tilly puts upon historical differences and comparison it is obvious that he will need some account of how new forms emerge within a repertoire and how old ones either die away or are modified. He actually says relatively little with respect to this issue, but insofar as he does his focus is upon innovation. Contenders are constantly innovating, he argues, but this is usually at the 'perimeter' of existing repertoires. Moreover, even when they do generate new forms of protest these forms will often fail. If, however, they are successful and other actors perceive them to be so and appropriate them, then they will enter and modify the repertoire.

Much of Tilly's work on the concept of repertoires has been concentrated on the emergence of what he takes to be the general features of the broad repertoire of the modern era in France and Britain. Contentious politics in these two national contexts, prior to the mid-eighteenth century, was parochial, he argues. Local people addressed local issues and insofar as national issues were breached this was generally by way of the mediation of a local elite – who was pressured to act for the local people. This was reflected in the fact that repertoires were quite particular, both to specific types of struggle and, to a lesser extent, to specific geographic regions. By the mid-nineteenth century, however, contentious politics had become national in focus, with ordinary citizens acting on their own behalf in the national arena. Again this was reflected at the level of repertoires, which had become more modular: i.e. the same type of protest served many different agents, in different localities, pursuing different interests and concerns. Thus, in modern societies, Tilly argues, there is a general repertoire: a repertoire belonging to those societies *qua* modern societies. Perhaps more importantly, however, what emerges out of this discussion is a sense in which social movements themselves are modern and are aspects of a specifically modern repertoire of contention. Although agents have pursued their interests by contentious means for as long as we care to look back, it is only more recently that they have tended to do so by banding into the relatively durable networks of agents that we recognize today as social movements (see also Tarrow 1998: 29–70).

The concept of repertoires clearly involves linguistic or discursive forms of behaviour. The act of petitioning is a form of discourse, for example, as is the chanting which often occurs on marches. Steinberg (1995, 1999) has extended this further by focusing on the various forms of rhetoric and argumentative strategy which seem to become institutionalized in various types of struggle. One can identify acquired rhetorical forms of argument within and across struggle as surely as one can identify acquired behavioural forms of protest, he argues. Similarly one can trace the history of contention that has shaped these 'fighting words'. Thus the concept of repertoires must be expanded to incorporate these forms of talk. We must be alert to the phenomena of 'discursive repertoires'.

Repertoires assessed

The concept of repertoires is both interesting and important. It enables us to take a step back from the protest activities we study as social movement analysts and to reflect upon their social form. Tilly looks behind the apparent spontaneity and transgression of protest to reveal a stable social structure within it. Moreover, he poses questions and raises problems which have prompted movement analysts into a range of fruitful lines of empirical enquiry. Notwithstanding this, however, there are problems with the concept which we need to be mindful of. I will briefly outline two of them.

The first is not so much a problem with the repertoires concept as an observation on its relationship to the broader concepts and concerns of Tilly's work. There have been few movement analysts more critical of Durkheim than Tilly, and few who have so aggressively pursued a rational choice alternative. Indeed, in the book which offers the first extended discussion of the repertoires concept, *From Mobilisation to Revolution*, Tilly (1978) both rejects Durkheim out of hand, suggesting that there is little of value in his work, and engages enthusiastically with both the early

Utilitarian forerunners of rational choice theory and its most recent apologists and advocates in game theory. This is odd since the concept of repertoires confirms much that Durkheim sought to argue and to juxtapose to the naiveties of the Utilitarian position (see Durkheim [1893] 1964, [1924] 1974). The Utilitarian and rational choice theorist alike are methodological individualists. Like Margaret Thatcher, and for the same reasons, they believe that there is no such thing as society, only individuals – she added families to this inventory but they do not. Durkheim sought to challenge this idea by identifying a realm of 'social facts', irreducible to individuals *qua* individuals, among which he numbered such emergent social forms as rituals and collective representations, that is, ways of acting which pre-exist individual actors, will outlive them, and whose meaning and logic are collectively constituted (Durkheim [1895] 1965). Repertoires of contention fall into this category. They are socially inherited ways of acting in specific sorts of situations. Furthermore, in referring to repertoires as 'constraining', Tilly uses the exact same language as Durkheim uses in relation to social facts ([1895] 1965). In addition, it is clear that protest action, when described in terms of repertoires, is not 'utilitarian' in any normal sense. Agents do not choose the most efficient means for pursuing their ends. At best they choose the most efficient means from a learned cultural repertoire, but more particularly they participate in a 'game' in a sense quite removed from that of game theory. They orient to shared meanings, expectations, understandings and, what amounts to the same thing, norms. In this respect, again, Tilly inadvertently sides with Durkheim, whom he professes to be critical of, against the Utilitarians, whom he professes to admire. One of the key themes of Durkheim's sociology was the insufficiency of utilitarian conceptions of the social world to account for its order, because they lacked any notion of shared social norms (Durkheim [1893] 1964). These interpretative/theoretical matters are important because they contribute to both the critique of RAT that I have attempted to develop in this book and to my attempt to rescue a Durkheimian element in movement theory. Tilly's efforts to make sense of protest force him, in spite of himself and without acknowledgement, to put a lot of distance between himself and RAT and tacitly to take up a Durkheimian position. Or rather, I contend that Tilly's position and the concept of repertoires more specifically is torn between the two mutually incompatible alternatives of Utilitarianism and a Durkheimian position. This leads to ambiguities in the concept itself. For example, Tilly describes repertoires as 'learned' ('people learn to break windows in protest'), suggesting that they are internalized and become second nature to us, and yet that they are 'chosen', which would imply that they remain 'external' objects of choice for us, akin to tools we may select from.

My second criticism concerns the issue of repertoire selection. What Tilly identifies with the concept of repertoires is a very broad range of methods of protest which, he seems to imply, all agents within a national–geographical area during a broad historical era choose from in the course of struggle. This is important but we need also to be sensitive to the social dynamics of the processes by which agents and groups select from that repertoire. Certain groups or agents, even from within the same struggle, consistently select particular methods of protest and reject or do not even consider others. They develop their own habitual and more specific 'repertoire of contention'. This often corresponds to other broad aspects of what we might call a movement or protest style. Some groups or agents manifest a radical style, which involves radical beliefs and a radical identity, as well as more extreme protest methods; others are more reformist. Some are 'outsiders', others insiders, etc. Within the animal rights movement, for example, there are those who pursue their objectives within the confines of the law, by petition and lobby, and those who adopt more extreme tactics, such as the 'liberation' of animals from laboratories and attacks upon known vivisectionists.

It is not just individuals and groups who manifest stable differences in repertoire choice. Differences can be identified across different types of struggle, across differently resourced groups and across generations of activists and movements. With respect to the former, different contexts clearly facilitate different types of struggle. One can only strike if one has labour or some form of cooperation to withdraw, for example, and one can only liberate caged animals if they are there to be liberated. Piven and Cloward put this point succinctly:

> ... institutional roles determine the strategic opportunities for defiance, for it is typically by rebelling against the rules and authorities associated with their everyday activities that people protest. Thus workers protest by striking. They are able to do so because they are drawn together in a factory setting, and their protests consist mainly in defying the rules and authorities associated with the workplace. The unemployed do not and cannot strike . . .
>
> (Piven and Cloward 1979: 21)

This point about the unemployed also leads to the second point, which is that the actions open to agents depend upon their resources. One cannot withdraw labour if one has no labour to withdraw. Activists' statuses, skills and social connections all shape their possibilities for protest and this is reflected in their different ways of doing so. Finally, styles of protest can change as an effect of what Mannheim (1952) refers to as political generations. Different generations practise politics differently, Mannheim argues, because the conditions of their political socialization endow them with different dispositions. Whittier (1997) observes some examples of this in her work on the feminist movement in the USA and I have a noted a similar phenomenon in relation to the UK mental health survivors' movement

(Crossley 1999c). The first wave of the movement, whose context was largely shaped by conditions of industrial conflict and the dominance of traditional left groups in opposition politics, tended to appropriate the forms of protest appropriate to that context. Thus the first key SMO of the movement was the Mental Patients' Union and this grew out of a strike, by both staff and patients (who withdrew their cooperation with hospital administrators) at a London day hospital (Crossley 1999a). By the time of the second wave of the movement, however, though industrial conflicts were still in evidence, the context of high-profile protest was increasingly dominated by gay activists and feminist critiques of domestic violence and child abuse. This manifested itself in the mental health movements in the respect that the language (and practice) of 'unions' and 'strikes' had been abandoned in favour of a language of 'survivors' and a tendency towards such symbolic protests as candlelight vigils and the laying of wreaths (Crossley 1999c). It should be added here that many of the mental health activists I spoke to noted the peculiar restraint that they were under, regarding their choice of tactics, on account of their (mental health) status. They argued that the public were disposed to see them as violent and threatening, or else perhaps not to take them seriously as 'schizos' or 'nutters', and that this precluded them from using more disruptive or excited forms of protest, because such forms would invite the familiar stereotype (Crossley 1999c). This illustrates my earlier point about resources. These mental health activists are constrained in repertoire choice by their (perceived) status deficit or stigma. They cannot 'get away' with what other protestors get away with. These internal differentiations in repertoire appropriation cast some doubt upon Tilly's contention that we can speak of a repertoire, in the singular, belonging to a specific society.

So should we abandon the notion of 'repertoires of contention'? I am in no hurry to adopt it. On the other hand, however, it is quite clear that Tilly has marked out an interesting set of observations and questions with this concept, which we would be well advised to pursue further. In a very qualified way, therefore, the concept does remain useful and should be maintained.

Framing contention

The next concept I will consider, framing, is drawn from Goffman's (1974) *Frame Analysis*. As with many of his key concepts, Goffman is extremely vague in his definition of framing. In essence, however, what he seeks to identify is a meta level of categorization of the objects of experience, which affects the meaning which they have for agents and, consequently, the way in which they act towards them. Bateson's (1972) discussion of play-fighting among otters, which influenced Goffman, provides an instructive path in to this idea. Otters fight with one another, Bateson notes, but they also play at fighting. Play fighting involves all of the same posturing and snarling but the punches, so to speak, are pulled. The animals will nip each other without fully biting, even if they look as if they are going to bite. For this to be possible, Bateson rightly points out, each otter must not only read and respond to the actions of the other but must also frame that reading more broadly in terms of a definition of their situation as play. A lunge forward must be perceived as an attack, so that defensive manoeuvres can be mobilized, but only as a pretend attack, so that the defensive retaliation is not too severe. The meaning of each gesture depends upon the broad definition of the situation as a play fight, and the combatants must maintain some form of metacommunication between themselves which maintains that definition of the situation. The same thing happens in a multitude of forms and contexts in the human world, including the theatre. What happens in the theatre may, to the naked eye, be indistinguishable from 'real' acts of, for example, murder or trickery. And audiences must be sufficiently convinced if they are to be taken along by a play and emotionally moved by it. Notwithstanding this, however, they must simultaneously perceive events on the stage as imaginary if they are to refrain from heroic interventions. We joke about the individual who stands up and shouts 'he's behind you' to Julius Caesar during a performance of Shakespeare's play. Theatrical events are framed, both for us and by us, so that we do not take them for reality. Framing, in this sense, moreover, is a communicative process. Just as Bateson's otters must have a way of communicating to each other that 'this is just play', we tend to demarcate such things as theatrical performances (e.g. by way of a stage and curtains) so that their frame is apparent.

Frames are not merely a matter of 'reality' or 'fantasy', however. Within the bounds of what we take for reality our perceptions of events can be framed in different ways, which causes us to read that event in different ways, attributing blame and responsibility in different ways. The sight of a young person begging on the street may convey, at a very basic perceptual level, injustice and structural social failure to one individual, while it 'shouts out' individual moral failing to another. The same event is framed by a different agent in a different way. It is this latter level and form of framing which has been of particular interest to social movement scholars. Acknowledging the basic truth of the interactionist claim that agents act in situations in accordance with the way in which they perceive that situation, it has been argued that framing is crucial to mobilization and the sustaining of activism. The individual who reads the beggar as proof of the evils of capitalism is more likely to be mobilized into anti-capitalist actions, for example, than the individual who sees only individual fecklessness. It is not simply others that we see in this way, moreover. The notion of framing connects directly with the notion of 'cognitive liberation' which we discussed in relation to McAdam's (1982) work in the previous chapter, and thus to processes of self-interpretation and attribution. If we perceive our own misfortunes as evidence of personal failing we are much less likely to challenge it politically than if we frame it in terms of broader system failings. In this respect 'framing' rekindles the issue of 'grievances' and rejoins the concerns of those scholars who have argued, against pure RM or RAT approaches, for a focus upon processes of grievance interpretation (Klandermans 1984, 1989). Moreover, it reintroduces into movement analysis issues of situational definition and generalized belief, such as were explored by the collective behaviour theorists. The notion of framing is freed of the irrationalism of Smelser's account of generalized beliefs but the general point, that movements depend upon particular ways of defining situations, attributing blame, etc., is identical, as, indeed, it is with the concern with situational definition in Blumer's interactionist account.

The earliest appropriations of 'framing' within the social movements literature tended to come from within the RM camp, in the context of an exploration of the way in which SMOs mobilize support. SMOs, it was argued, must attempt to link their frames with those of their potential constituents ('frame alignment') if they are to secure the support (and other resources) of those constituents (Snow *et al.* 1986). They must tap into 'sentiment pools' by way of a mobilization of resonant symbols. Snow *et al.* (1986) outline four basic possibilities for alignment. First, in cases where constituents hold consistent but unconnected frames to SMOs, SMOs can align themselves with those constituents simply by contacting them, informing them of whatever issue is at stake and drawing out the connections for people (*'frame bridging'*). Groups or populations with a strong concern for civil rights might be prompted to partake in a new civil rights campaign, for example, simply by having the issues presented to them as civil rights issues. However, sometimes this is not enough. It might be necessary to draw a population's latent sentiments and schemas into sharper relief (*'frame amplification'*). This might involve persuading individuals that their already existing values logically require them to subscribe to a particular cause, or perhaps rekindling those values through subtle provocation. Alternatively, it may involve an attempt to 'amplify' beliefs about, for example, the causes of specific problems and the possibilities of solving those problems. From the other side of the coin it may be necessary for SMOs to extend their own basic frame, to incorporate the interests of their constituents (*'frame extension'*). They may, for example, align themselves with popular and fashionable causes, in the hope that this will win over those committed to these causes to their own. Or it may involve an SMO aligning itself with the culture or practices of a particular group, as when SMOs align themselves with fashionable music, through benefit gigs, in an effort to draw young people into their frame. Gramsci's (1971) important analysis of the rise of Italian fascism illustrates this. The fascists came to power at a time when Marxist theories might have a predicted a growth in the left, he argues. This was because the fascists were prepared to involve themselves in the traditions and the religion of the people, defining themselves as defenders of those traditions, while the Marxists denounced tradition and religion on philosophical grounds. The 'people' rejected Marxism because Marxism, by rejecting Catholicism and Italian cultural traditions, rejected them. Finally, and more drastically, in some cases '... *new frames may have to be planted and nurtured, old meanings or understandings jettisoned, and erroneous beliefs or "misframings" reframed*' (Snow *et al.* 1986: 473). This may involve total conversion experiences, such as we usually associate with religious cults, or it may involve more detached and detachable 'chunks' of the agent's lifeworld. Appropriating a concern for civil rights may affect many sectors of one's life and experience, for example, but many will be relatively unaffected. One would not ordinarily abandon one's family and the 'outside world' as one would if joining a cult, for example.

Some frames are movement- or even group-specific. In a later paper, however, Snow and Benford (1992) make reference to what they call 'master frames'. These are less specific frames which might be appropriated or used by any of a number of different groups and perhaps even movements. The most obvious example of this is the civil rights frame. This frame is ordinarily linked to the emergence of the black civil rights movement in the USA in the 1960s. As Snow and Benford (1992) point out, however, it was quickly appropriated by a number of other movements and groups, including women's groups and native North American groups, as it achieved a high and popular profile.

Tarrow (1998) has extended this notion of frames. Movement organizations need to maximize their support, he notes, and to do this they must engage strategically with the symbols and more broadly the culture which mediates agents' perceptions and understandings of the world. They must, to use the language of Snow *et al.* (1986), create a 'bridge' between themselves and their potential constituents: 'Out of the cultural reservoir of possible symbols, movement entrepreneurs choose those that they hope will mediate amongst the cultural understandings of the groups they wish to appeal to, their own beliefs and aspirations, and their situations of struggle' (Tarrow 1998: 109).

What Tarrow adds to this is an account of the central role of emotion in both collective action and framing. He makes three basic claims regarding this issue. First, reflecting upon the process of grievance interpretation, he notes that grievances, particularly but not exclusively when suddenly imposed and dramatic, can generate emotions which the agent needs to channel and manage. Frames, he argues, are precisely about this. They make sense of emotions and direct an agent's course of action in such a way as to channel that emotion. Related to this point is a second point that emotions are very often a crucial source of the energy which fuels movement activism and engagement. It is because agents feel injustices and feel wronged – or that others are wronged – that they are moved to action. Or rather, it is because their feelings are framed as feelings of injustice that this occurs. Finally, he notes that processes of frame alignment must attempt to tap into those symbols which are emotionally invested if they are to be effective. This, for Tarrow, explains the force of both religious and nationalist symbols in movement struggles:

> Because it is so reliable a source of emotion, religion is a recurring source of social movement framing. Religion provides ready-made symbols, rituals and solidarities that can be accessed and appropriated by movement leaders. The same is true of nationalism: lacking the fine mechanical metaphors of class dialectics, nationalism possesses a much greater emotional potential [than socialism].
>
> (Tarrow 1998: 112)

This emphasis upon emotion is important because, again, it (re)connects with key themes from the collective behaviour approach. Smelser's account of generalized beliefs, for example, was very much focused upon the way in which such beliefs give meaning and direction to the feelings stirred up by stresses and strains. Furthermore, in identifying the link between affect, solidarity and religious/nationalist symbolism, Tarrow invokes a strong theme of the work of the later Durkheim ([1912] 1915). Though he does not make the link to political mobilization, Durkheim is centrally concerned with the manner in which religious symbolism mediates and mobilizes feelings of group solidarity.

Framing takes place, Tarrow continues, within a context of struggle. Movement entrepreneurs must compete with those parties whose vested interests lie in the status quo, and with the dominant symbolic systems which prop it up. Meaning making and sentiment tapping are competitive and contentious forms of activity. The battleground on which much of this takes place, he suggests, is the mass media. If movements are to win hearts and minds on the scale which they require then they must work through the media. However, Tarrow is sceptical with respect to the operation of the media. Even if it is not true, as some have claimed, that the media necessarily represents the interests of the ruling class, he argues, nevertheless it does not represent the interests of social movements:

> . . . the media are far from neutral bystanders in the framing of movement events. While the media may not work directly for the ruling class, they certainly do not work for social movements. In a capitalist society, at least, the media are in business to report on the news and

they stay in business only if they report on what will interest readers or viewers, or on what editors think will interest them.

(Tarrow 1998: 116)

In particular, the concern for newsworthiness and news values ensures that the media seeks out the more sensational aspects of movement activity, such as violence and the more eccentric extremes, and this necessarily distorts the portrayal of movements.

I do not entirely agree with Tarrow on this latter point. It is only some movements, some of the time, which are disadvantaged in this way. In my own work on mental health movements, for example, I found that the news value of what some journalists dubbed 'mad lib' constituted an important source of publicity for the early (and explicitly anti-capitalist) mental health groups, on which they were able to 'cash in' for increased membership and legitimacy (Crossley 1999a). Coverage of their cause generated a process of 'media amplification' in which many more people became involved. And it helped to frame their cause as a serious political agenda which could not be dismissed lightly. A similar point is also drawn out in McCarthy's (1994) analysis of US anti-drink driving groups, but he adds an important note on timing. The emergence of these groups was sparked by the tragic death of the child of one lead campaigner in particular, McCarthy notes, but there had been equally tragic and very similar deaths prior to this which had not lead to movement formation. The question therefore emerges of why some incidents lead to movement formation and others do not. The crucial factor in this case, McCarthy argues, was the prevalence, within media discourse, of a 'drunk driving' frame which construed driving accidents in such a way as to invite moral condemnation and action for legal change. The dominant discourse prior to this time had portrayed road deaths as tragic but unavoidable accidents, thus inciting grief but not political action. In other words, the media facilitated movement formation by virtue of the frame which prevailed within it at the time. In this respect the notion of framing contributes to my argument regarding media opportunity structures outlined in the previous chapter. Media campaigns and/or the particular frames which predominate in the media at a particular point in time can variously help or hinder the attempts of SMOs and activists to achieve publicity for their cause.

The other side of this, as Diani (1996) notes, is that the effectiveness of particular frames can itself be the product of particular structures of political opportunity. He cites a number of possibilities but one important example is that anti-system and anti-establishment frames have more resonance and more effectiveness at times when cleavages in the social system are high, while opportunities for working within it are low. In other words, agents are more persuaded by anti-establishment frames when the establishment is both more antagonizing and more resistant to change. Populations are more amenable to different frames at different times as a function of their changing experience of the structural constraints and opportunities in their immediate environment.

Framing assessed

Like the notion of repertoires, the notions of framing and frame alignment are important. They put questions of meaning, culture and interpretation firmly on the analytic agenda. Like 'repertoires', however, they are also problematic in certain respects. I will outline five key problems here, beginning with the tendency for framing theorists to view the role of frames in struggle in purely instrumental terms.

Frames are portrayed, in many accounts, simply as means by which populations are mobilized in order to address specific issues. This overlooks the extent to which frames may themselves constitute a stake in struggle. An integral element of the struggle of mental health movements, for example, has been the attempt to change the way in which people with mental health problems are perceived, that is, the frames applied to them. In some cases and to some extent this is motivated by a concern with the knock-on effects of public perceptions but it also involves a more basic politics of recognition. The aim of the movement is to have their members perceived as human beings rather than 'nutters' or 'madmen'. This is not just a matter for mental health movements. As Melucci (1986, 1996) has argued, many contemporary movements are intrinsically concerned, either in part or wholly, with questions of recognition, representation and the dominance of certain cultural codes in institutionalized contexts of framing (see also Honneth 1995). Thus, if we look at the struggles of feminists, black activists, the disability lobby and many others, we find a central concern with the way in which groups are represented, by whom, in what contexts, etc.

A further implication of this point is that the media and other cultural fields assume a far greater importance for these movements than the RM and PP approaches are generally inclined to admit. Cultural opportunities and outcomes are far more important than political opportunities and outcomes, at least in any narrowly defined sense of those terms. More to the point, the aim of movements is often to bring about changes within these particular social fields, rather than, or as well as, in the formal political and legal fields. The aim of the movement is to change public perceptions or media and cultural representations, and legal and big 'P' political changes may have a marginal or instrumental role in this struggle, if they have a role at all.

A second key criticism, which has been argued for by Steinberg (1999) in particular, is that accounts of framing often pay insufficient attention to the historical emergence of the discourses, rhetorics and meanings that mobil-ize movements and, more particularly, to the dialogical and conflictual nature of their context of emergence. Frames are often written about as if they were self-contained and pre-given packages of meaning or discrete and unchanging tools of interpretation, Steinberg argues, when the reality of symbolic and semiotic politics is much more processual and perhaps also innnovative. Through his notion of 'discursive repertoires', which was dis-cussed earlier, Steinberg makes a very similar point to the framing theorists: that struggles are mobilized through shared meaning. He adds, however, that movement discourses are not just aimed at potential supporters but also adversaries, who are challenged to disagree with the claims that a movement raises. The construction of a discursive repertoire entails proleptic anticipation of objections and a targeted focus upon the vulnerable areas of one's opponent's beliefs. And, as his analysis of the 'fighting words' of a group of nineteenth-century weavers reveals, these repertoires emerge gradu-ally in the course of a conflict, constantly evolving to keep up with dialogical exchanges between activists, their constituents and their opponents.

I would also add to this that accounts of framing can appear to separate questions of meaning and symbolism from questions of power, ignoring the central role of forms of symbolic power in the process of struggle. Acts of communication presuppose certain rights of expression on behalf of agents and take place within a context where speakers enjoy unequal degrees of legitimacy and privilege (Bourdieu 1992b). Who gets to say what and to what effect is crucially affected by social structures and imbalances of power. This is particularly pertinent in relation to those contemporary struggles, including ecology and pro-/anti-abortion struggles, where activists find them-selves in conflict with designated authorities on particular issues, whose voice is generally privileged. These struggles often hinge upon scientific arguments and must contend with the power of dominant paradigms or 'regimes of truth' (Foucault 1980) and their expert systems. However, it can be of equal relevance in relation to cases where the accent or 'linguistic code' (Labov 1969; Bernstein 1975) of an oppressed group connotes inferi-ority to those whom they must attempt to persuade of their case. They do not get a fair hearing because what they say cannot be separated from the way that they say it and the way that they say it sounds inarticulate and thus ill thought out to their audience.

This point leads us to the relatively murky issue of 'persuasive com-munication'. Writers such as Snow *et al.* raise a crucial point when they observe that SMOs must attempt to 'bridge' their own perspective with that of potential constituents but they really only scratch at the surface of the issues raised by that task. They offer a broad typology of strategies of persuasion, from bridging to total conversion, but their account, and most others in the field, fail to explore the deeper dynamics of persuasion. More problematically still, as Gamson (1992) has observed, Snow *et al.*, in particular, tend to slip between different epistemological positions in their account, thereby making their position inconsistent and untenable. The notion of framing, Gamson rightly argues, rests upon a constructionist epistemology, that is, it suggests that our perceptions and knowledge of the world are, at least in part, a function of active processes of construction on our own behalf and the various cultural schemas and categories which we habitually and pre-reflectively or unconsciously deploy in that process. The consequence of adopting this epistemological position is that our arguments must avoid reference to a real objective world which agents have access to. The world that agents have access to and which affects them is the world as they perceive it, a world affected by their own interpretative activities – be they individual or collective (Klandermans 1992) – and the aforementioned social schemas which shape these activities. When discussing the efficacy of particular frames, however, Snow *et al.* sometimes make reference to the 'empirical credibility' of frames, an argument which seemingly supposes that agents have access to the world independently of any interpretative frame, such that they can compare and assess the validity of frames against it. This argument is self-contradictory (Gamson 1992). Although frames may strike agents as more or less plausible and can be argued over, the process by which agents are persuaded of new frames, or aspects of them, must necessarily consist in an attempt by movement activists to connect with the interpretative schemas of their potential constituents. As Klandermans (1992) has argued, this can have the effect that movements very often only persuade those who already share many of their sentiments and schemas, or, putting that more forcefully, 'consensus mobilisation often consists of preaching to the converted' (1992: 91). Notwithstanding this, however, drawing on McAdams's (1988, 1989) *Freedom Summer* work, among other sources, Klandermans adds that protest activities can have a significant effect in changing certain of the basic dispositions and schemas of a social agent, making them more available for future persuasion.

A further problem with the framing approach concerns its relation to the issue of agency. As Steinberg (1999) argues, considerations of framing are often 'added on', in the movements literature, to a Utilitarian (RAT) theory of agency. The framing theorists tend to treat frames and questions of meaning as if they were resources akin to material resources which could be manipulated in the same way. There are crucial differences between the utilitarian conception of resources and the notion of framing, however, such that this combination results in self-contradiction. Frames are not objects or utensils in the objective world, which agents can pick up and use like tools. They are constitutive aspects of the subjectivity of social agents which those agents cannot get behind or detach themselves from. Among other things, the presumption otherwise leads to an 'excessive voluntarism' in the theory of agency:

> . . . the underlying epistemologies of [frame theoretical] and rational
> actor accounts of collective discourse are not easily reconciled. It is prob-
> lematic to characterise social movement framing as both an exercise in
> reality construction of genuinely held senses of injustice and identity,
> while simultaneously holding that activists and SMOs strategically
> manipulate and align frames to mobilise consensus. This can create an
> excessive voluntarism, vitiating the understanding of discourse as a
> stock of contested codes and meanings that impose boundaries on the
> way in which people understand and represent their life.
>
> (Steinberg 1999: 742)

Steinberg's basic point is that agents cannot choose the way in which they
perceive self and world or think about them, since choice itself presupposes
a vision and conception of the world, and consists in thought. Agents'
constructions of reality cannot strike them as constructions, or else they
would lack the accent of reality and some further definition of the 'real'
reality would be presupposed. To put that more concretely, a feminist does
not 'frame' male domination as unjust in an effort to win support, nor does
she put on and take off her feminist identity as a coat. She sees and feels the
world to be one which is unjustly dominated by males, and she really
believes both in feminism as a cause and in her own identity as a feminist.
This notion need not preclude the possibility that the feminist will con-
sciously manipulate symbols and meaning in an effort to advance her cause
and recruit more agents to it, nor does it preclude the possibility that her
deeply held beliefs, frames, etc. are forged through strategic interactions. It
does, however, suggest that the schemas and dispositions which structure
struggle operate at a deeper level than that suggested by the framing theorists: a pre-conscious or pre-reflective level. Or perhaps, rather, that their
focus upon PR, spin and advertising in movement mobilization really only
scratches at the surface in relation to the role of meanings and symbols in
movement struggles.

The general conclusion to be drawn from this argument is that we must
abandon the commitment to the RAT model and embrace rather a perspective which puts interpretative schemas and dispositions at its very heart.
This is not to deny that social agents act purposively in pursuit of goals but
it suggests that we cannot take for granted the ways in which they make
sense of their environments, what their goals are, how they reflect upon
their situations, etc. We thus return to the arguments that I made, against
RAT, in Chapter 5.

As a final point of criticism I would like to emphasize the vagueness and
sometimes quite lightweight feel of the notion of frames, particularly as
Snow *et al.* develop it. They are absolutely right to say that SMOs, not to
mention other agitators, must 'connect' with potential constituents. But the
notion of frames seems inadequate to express the depth and richness of that

which must be connected too. It is not simply a matter of cognitive frames, but of deeply held and embodied dispositions: an ethos: in Weber's ([1956] 1978) sense, and ultimately a way of life.

The work on framing in movement analysis is of undoubted importance for reopening questions of meaning and culture in movement analysis, and 'framing' now belongs to our everyday ways of talking about these issues so will undoubtedly remain. The criticisms that I have considered cast considerable doubt on the utility of 'frame analysis' as such, however. They suggest a need to go much further into the world of meanings and symbols than has hitherto been achieved. They also suggest, however, that doing so is not compatible with remaining in the RAT 'frame'. Once again then we find evidence to suggest that PP and RM approaches risk theoretical inconsistency and that their model of the agent, insofar as it is a RAT model, is more of a hindrance than a help.

Cycles of contention

The final concept I will outline in this chapter is 'cycles of contention'. This concept, which was first developed by Tarrow (1989, 1995, 1998; Della Porta and Tarrow 1987), engages with a number of important observations about movements and protests. First, they are not evenly distributed across time. At certain points in history we can see a great deal of movement activity, involving a great many movements, while at other times movements and protests are much fewer in number. The periods of heightened conflict often begin with core struggles or movements, which McAdam (1995) refers to as 'initiator' movements and Tarrow (1998) calls 'early risers', but this quickly spreads out across both geographical and social boundaries, as 'spin-off movements' or 'latecomers' enter the fray. This connects with our sense of the more dramatic 'moments of madness' (Zolberg 1972) in political history, such as the Paris Commune or the events of Mai '68, where regimes look close to toppling and, as Zolberg (1972) puts it, 'anything seems possible'. At these times, Tarrow argues, political activity appears to 'speed up': '... during periods of increased contention, information flows more rapidly, political attention heightens, and interactions amongst groups of challengers and between them and authorities increase in frequency and intensity' (Tarrow 1998: 146).

Furthermore, it has been argued that the dynamics of political interaction change during these periods. Where a moderate level of repression might serve to quell a movement or protest campaign outside a cycle, for example, it often has the opposite effect during cycles, such that only the harshest forms of repression serve to quell activism (Brockett 1995). This is not just a matter of the 'usual suspects' lining up to partake in actions. These periods typically entail a politicization and mobilization of previously inactive and (perhaps) disinterested agents, as well as an emergence of new groups, organizations and causes (Barker 1999). Some writers have identified a temporary transformation in the collective psychology of a population during cycles. Tarrow (1998), for example, writes of the festive and even ecstatic atmosphere which can develop in cycles, while Barker (1999), drawing upon Luxemburg's (1986) account of the 'mass strike' in the USSR, refers to an increase in popular (political) confidence and combativity – what Lenin referred to as a 'festival of the oppressed'. Finally, related again to this, movements themselves seem to be identified with specific 'families' which, in turn, can be identified with these specific points of intensified political activity (McAdam 1995). The 'movements of the sixties' are the most obvious example of this. *It is this clustering of processes and events which movement analysts seek to capture by the concept 'cycles of contention'* and much of the work in the field has been devoted to an analysis of their emergence and spread.

The concept of cycles has emerged within the PP literature and most advocates of it have therefore tended to explain the emergence of cyclical upturns in the same terms that they would use to explain the emergence of a single movement: by reference to networks, organization, political opportunity structures and 'cognitive liberation' or frames. This combination of factors is said to give rise to an initiator movement or a cluster of early risers who begin the usual movement business of protest and contention. What effect these early risers have depends, to a large extent, upon what follows. Tarrow suggests three ways in which 'early risers' draw 'latecomers' in, generating a cycle:

> First, they demonstrate the vulnerability of authorities to contention, signalling to others that the time is ripe for their own claims to be translated into action. Second they 'challenge the interests of other contenders, either because the distribution of benefits to one group will diminish the rewards available for another, or because the demands directly attack the interests of an established group' . . . Thirdly, they suggest convergences amongst challengers through the enunciation of master frames.
>
> (Tarrow 1998: 144)

The first two points raised here resonate with the political opportunities paradigm: early risers both signal the existence of opportunities and, at the same time, increase the costs of not acting. They indicate to others that there are rewards to be got from action and that they will get all those rewards, to the detriment of others, unless those others act. These points are rejoined by Koopmans's (1993) comparative work on cycles in West Germany, Italy, the Netherlands and the USA. In all cases, Koopmans argues, basic elements of the opportunity structure (repression, facilitation, etc.) played a central role in shaping the dynamic of the cycle. However, we must be wary of extending the role of opportunity structures too far. McAdam, for example, argues that the dominance which initiators can achieve within the political and media fields, and the attention they can command, are often highly detrimental to the opportunities of other, later groups, such that opportunities actually have very little influence on those late arrivals to the struggle – though, of course, what really counts is perceived opportunities, which is a different matter. Furthermore, he notes that the geographical spreading of contention during cycles often crosses national borders into areas where the opportunities which sparked the initiator movement are not in evidence. Against the notion of opportunity, and connecting with Tarrow's third point, therefore, he emphasizes processes of cultural and cognitive diffusion. Frames, repertoires and the general culture of contention all spread during cycles, from the initiators to the spin-offs and potential spin-offs. Very often this happens, he argues, because emergent movements give birth to further movements, from which further movements 'spin off' and so on. The American student movement of the 1960s, for example, was born in large measure out of the involvement of some students in the black civil rights movement, and particularly freedom summer. And the student movement itself spawned a number of movements, including the anti-Vietnam movement and the second-wave feminist movement (McAdam 1988). Furthermore, tactics, frames, etc. are diffused through existing movement networks. As his own point about the international diffusion of contention illustrates, however, these are not the only channels by which these cultural forms are transmitted. They must be transmitted through the mass media too. In these latter cases diffusion may depend upon what McAdam calls attributions of similarity, that is, 'spin-offs' will be inspired by initiators and inclined to follow their lead to the extent to which they identify with them and see them as similar.

Snow and Benford (1992) rejoin this basic position in their aforementioned paper on 'master frames'. Initiator movements will tend to spark spin-offs and a consequent protest wave, they argue, when and if they generate a frame which both appeals and can be transferred to a wide range of struggles. The central role which the civil rights frame was able to play in a range of struggles during the sixties is their key example of this. It is commonality of frame, moreover, which lends movements belonging to a particular cycle their 'family' feel. They seem to belong together because they share a common master frame.

Why cycles come to an end is less discussed in the literature. Tarrow (1998) suggests four reasons. First, basic exhaustion, weariness and disillusionment. The excitement of the struggle dies away and it becomes less easy to sustain. Second, institutionalization: struggle alters the institutional context and many of the more successful and more moderate movements and activists can find a place for themselves within the newly revived political system. Third, factionalism: it is evident in many cycles that self-defeating factions emerge between, for example, moderate and radical wings, and that this divides them against themselves, reducing their level of effective organization, detracting them from their 'external' battles and ultimately draining their energy. Finally, the role of agencies of control and, particularly, the state plays a large role. In particular, Tarrow argues, states can feed into the divisions which form within movements, rewarding the moderate sections with concessions and adopting a more repressive stance towards the more radical groups. Snow and Benford (1992) add to this, continuing their notion of the centrality of master frames, arguing that cycles may come to an end when a particular master frame loses its appeal. They do not particularly explore the reasons why this would happen, but we can at least speculate that part of the value of frames is their capacity to make us perceive issues in new ways and to seem new and exciting, all of which will fade a little each time the frame is applied to a new issue or area. The more often a civil rights frame is invoked and the further it is stretched, for example, the weaker is its capacity to shock and outrage.

However, cycles do not disappear without trace. Many movement scholars argue that they make important and lasting contributions to both political life and society more generally. In his work on the Italian cycle of the late 1960s, for example, Tarrow suggests that it reinvigorated, indeed modernized, democratic politics in Italy. Outcomes may not always be quite so profound as this. Most researchers agree, however, that cycles are periods of great innovation which spawn new repertoires and frames, as well as new agents and organizational forms. Many of these innovations will not survive the end of the cycle. Some, however, will and they will assume a 'tried and tested' status as a consequence. In this respect cycles achieve permanent change in the movements field.

Cycles assessed

McAdam (1995) has argued that the concept of cycles calls for a fundamental realignment of movement analysis. Movement analysis has tended to focus upon single movements, he argues, assuming that the same basic theories could be applied to them all. The notion of cycles changes this. It implies that we must learn to think about how movements develop together. We need to account for the differences in the way in which movements emerge at different points in a cycle. Theories which apply to initiator movements, as we have seen, may not apply to spin-offs, and so on. I am not convinced about this particular implication, not least because my basic acceptance of a value-added approach to movement analysis leads me to reject the notion that the causes or preconditions of movement formation, whether at the same point in a cycle or not, necessarily fall into place in the same order. Some initiator movements may be triggered by an opening of political opportunities, but in situations where opportunities are already relatively open another factor, such as a new grievance, may be the last piece to fall into place; and the same is true of spin-off movements. Nevertheless, it is evident that the notion of cycles does have profound implications for our understanding of social movements and should be given strong consideration in our research agendas and designs. We need to be sensitive to cycles in interpreting our data and to recognize that they raise important research questions in their own right. It is important to add here, however, that it is not simply the cyclical highs that are of importance. We need also to know how movements survive and fare through the quieter moments in political history and what Melucci (1986, 1996) has referred to as their periods of latency.

I have no specific criticisms of the cycles idea, as such, except to make the somewhat obvious point that many of the ideas discussed here overlap both with Durkheim's ([1912] 1915, [1924] 1974) notion of collective effervescence and with Blumer's (1969) notion of social unrest. In some respects the cycle theorists suggest a different timing to the collective behaviour theorists. Where Blumer views social unrest as a precipitant of movement formation, the PP theorists seemingly argue that unrest is an effect of 'early rising movements', which in turn stimulates further movement developments. This is a more persuasive account, in the respect that, as Blumer's notion of agitators suggests, unrest does need to be stirred up. Nevertheless, the collective behaviour theorists do have something to offer back in this exchange. They identify the different dynamics of interaction which come into play during unrest. In particular they alert us to the manner in which many of the usual self-imposed constraints upon interaction are suspended, giving rise to more intense and also more creative and socially generative interactions. New things come out of cycles because the mechanisms which otherwise impose order and continuity are temporarily put out of play. Habits and the self-imposed social controls of self-consciousness are lifted.

Summary and conclusion

In this chapter I have outlined and discussed three central concepts which have emerged, in recent years, within the movements literature: repertoires of contention, frames and cycles of contention. Each of these concepts raises new and interesting insights and questions for movement analysis and, as such, each is extremely valuable. With the exception of cycles, however, they prove inadequate to answer the questions that they raise and, as such, have a rather limited value. We should use them to open issues up but not allow them to close those issues down. We have also seen that these concepts generate problems for both RM and PP approaches, insofar as they sit unhappily with the RAT model of the agent otherwise embraced by the advocates of these positions. The time has come, I suggest, to go beyond RAT and with that, we must necessarily go beyond both PP and RM too.

Further reading

Traugott's (1995a) edited collection, *Repertoires and Cycles of Collective Action*, is an excellent starting point for discussions of both repertoires and cycles. It includes papers by the respective architects of these two concepts, Tilly and Tarrow, as well as a range of clear and well-written papers which variously apply the concepts, connect them and explore their implications. Chapter 5 of Tilly's (1978) *From Mobilisation to Revolution* offers an early formulation of the notion of repertoires, which is still important and allows the reader to grasp some of the background to the notion. Tarrow's (1989) *Democracy and Disorder* is the most extensive study of a cycle of contention and puts a great deal of flesh onto the basic conceptual bones of the idea. Snow and his colleagues are perhaps still the key reference point with respect to framing: see especially Snow *et al.*'s (1986) 'Frame alignment process, micromobilisation and movement participation', and also Snow and Benford (1992) 'Master frames and cycles of protest'.

chapter eight

New social movements

Most of the debates and issues covered so far in the book have stemmed from the American context, albeit an American context increasingly engaged with and influenced by European theorists and ideas. In this penultimate chapter I consider what has probably been the major issue in European debates on social movements: the question of 'new social movements' (NSMs). The term 'new social movements' is rapidly approaching its sell-by date. It refers to a cluster of movements that began to emerge out of the student movement of the 1960s, that is, the peace movement, the environmental movement, second-wave feminism, animal rights, anti-psychiatry and so on. Many of these movements are now in a period of latency, if they have not disappeared altogether, and others have achieved a foothold in the political system and/or the more local sites of struggle in which they emerged. None are particularly 'new' any more. Furthermore, other 'even newer' social movements have emerged in more recent years, some of which are quite different in form to the NSMs (Tarrow 1998). However, the debate about the NSMs remains important because of the very different slant which it puts upon movement analysis and the types of question it involves. It raises issues not discussed elsewhere in the literature and opens up a further dimension of movement analysis. Furthermore, in doing so it allows us to question further the adequacy of the RM and PP approaches.

I begin my discussion of NSMs with the inevitable question of what is deemed to be new about them. I approach this question at a general level, reflecting broadly on a number of NSM theorists. Having done this I then focus upon one NSM theorist in particular, Jurgen Habermas, and offer a more detailed exposition and critique of his argument. Habermas is perhaps an unusual choice, given that he has less to say about movements than certain other key NSM theorists, such as Touraine and Melucci, and, unlike them, has not explored the NSMs empirically. It is necessary for me to select out one theorist to discuss, however, in order that we can move beyond a superficial gloss of the theory towards a more detailed account, and I have selected Habermas because, in my view, his work focuses most squarely upon what is important about the NSMs debate. I also find his arguments clearer, more cogent and thus better to engage with than those of the other key theorists of new social movements.

What's new?

The central question raised in the NSMs debate is whether the above-mentioned movements, which emerged in the 1970s, herald a new era in movement politics in any substantive sense and, if so, what sense exactly this is. The key figures associated with the notion of NSMs, Alain Touraine (1981), Jurgen Habermas (1987) and Alberto Melucci (1986, 1996), all argue that the NSMs do represent a new era. The issue has been whether they are right and, if so, in what respect? In what sense are NSMs new?

It is important at the outset of our discussion to dispense with one line of argument that the NSM concept has attracted: the historical critique which points out that most of the repertoires, issues and organizational forms NSMs have adopted can be identified way back in the history of what, by implication, we are forced to call 'old social movements' (Tucker 1991; Calhoun 1995). It is argued, for example, that what is supposed to be new about social movements is their reluctance to engage in big 'P' politics, their emphasis upon internal democracy and their focus upon everyday ways of acting and relating, but that it can be shown that many radical movements of the nineteenth century shared these exact same concerns (Tucker 1991; Calhoun 1995). This is an important critique because it brings interesting data to light and questions any simple-minded conception of NSMs which we might wish to advocate. It is flawed, however, because it misconstrues the NSM thesis as an empiricist thesis about the observable properties of a specific movement cluster. The critics overlook the extent to which the NSMs argument represents a paradigm shift among a particular strand of European intellectuals, namely, the Marxists. Marxists maintain that capitalist societies are based around a fundamental conflict between their two major classes, the bourgeoisie and the proletariat, and that the 'historical mission' of the proletariat, their predefined role in history, is revolutionary overthrow of that order. Whatever surface conflicts between whatever groups we may identify, Marxists argue, the major fault line of conflict in capitalist societies is between workers and capitalists. The workers' movement is *the* social movement of capitalist societies. The NSMs argument is a rejection of this very specific historical thesis. It is an attempt by what we might loosely call 'post-Marxist' writers both to move beyond the tendency to afford a theoretical privilege to the working class in social movement analysis and to identify other schisms, conflicts and movements *at the heart of the modern social order*. Societies have changed, NSM theorists argue. They no longer conform to the model outlined by Marx. The proletariat, as defined by Marx, has been pacified and the labour movement, to which Marxists attributed a revolutionary role, has been integrated into society as a part of it: e.g. in the form of labour parties. The break with Marxism is by no means total, however. Though NSM theorists reject the notion that the working class is destined to be a key agent of change and that labour relations are the major fault line of social order, they nevertheless maintain that there is a major fault line of the social order, a new fault line for a new order. And in some cases they still seek to find *the* movement or agent change which emerges out of that fault line. Alain Touraine's studies, for example, are focused upon an attempt to find *the* movement of the contemporary era and *the* struggle. Each type of society or 'mode of historicity' entails a central movement struggle, for Touraine. In industrial society that struggle was between the bourgeoisie, who exercised effective control over the means of material production, and the proletarian movement, which sought to seize control over it. Society has moved beyond that stage now, however, and is moving into a post-industrial or 'programmed' type of society. This raises the question of the movement which will be central to this type of society:

> . . . the practical aim of our research: to discover the social movement which in programmed society will occupy the central position held by the workers' movement in industrial society, and the civil liberties movement in the market society by which it was preceded.
>
> (Touraine 1981: 24)

This discussion of *the* social movement, in the singular, is not intended as an empirical claim that only one movement exists, any more than Marxists claimed that all empirically identifiable struggles and conflicts were between workers and capitalists. Touraine concedes both that there are a plurality of movements and political interest groups in the present, and that there were throughout the industrial era. His point, right or wrong, is that every society centres upon a particular mode of organization, which he terms its 'historicity', and that this gives rise, in every case, to one central conflict and struggle. The thesis of NSMs, in this respect, is a thesis about the shift in the mode of historicity in western societies and the corresponding shift in the central struggle of those societies. It is this mode of historicity and its faultlines which lends NSMs their 'newness', rather than any particular empirical feature of those movements.

NSM theory parts company from Marxism in yet one more respect, however. The Marxist discourse on social movements was traditionally focused upon issues of state and revolution. Very crudely put, it was believed that the proletariat would liberate themselves by forcefully seizing control of the centralized state apparatus, which would in turn allow them to bring the means of economic production under collective control. NSM theory, by contrast, generally focuses upon the ways in which social movements seek to achieve change in cultural, symbolic and sub-political domains, sometimes collectively but also sometimes by way of self-change. It takes seriously the feminist slogan that 'the personal is political'. This is not to say that NSMs are any more concerned with local and sub-political issues than certain branches of the labour movement were. Nor does it necessarily mean that some branches of the labour movement were any less sceptical with respect to the likely outcomes of revolution or rigid party structures. As I noted above, historical critiques of NSM theory have identified significant examples of 'identity politics' far back in the history of the labour movement. The point is that NSM theory, as a paradigm of movement analysis, has been instrumental in drawing that aspect of movement activity into clear relief. It has abandoned the model of politics developed within Marxism, wherein it necessarily centred upon parties, revolutions and states, and has sought to explore the broader territories of movements and politics.

This debate between Marxism and NSM theory – and it remains a debate rather than a foregone conclusion – is important because it brings to light aspects and dynamics of movement theory that remain submerged or ignored in the US perspectives. Two points are important. First, many RM and PP writers profess to a Marxist influence and this is evident in their tendency to operate with a very narrowly political definition of movement activism and protest. In recent years, as we have seen, this approach has been 'softened' to include more consideration of culture and identity, but still culture tends to be regarded in instrumental terms, as a means through which agents are mobilized into political struggle. There is little recognition that some movement struggles begin and end in specific cultural fields, that they are focused upon issues of representation, recognition and other cultural or symbolic stakes, and focus, as Melucci (1985: 810) notes, upon 'pushes toward the renewal of cultures, languages, habits'. Culture may be a means to political ends, for RM and PP advocates, but it is not yet fully recognized as an end in itself. The NSM paradigm is as much of a challenge to RM and PP approaches as to Marxism in this respect, whatever concessions to culture and identity the former now makes.

Second, despite borrowing from Marxism, RM and PP approaches, perhaps because of their aversion to 'grievances', have not tended to focus explicitly upon the broad societal bifurcations and fault lines which foster specific clusters of movements at any one time (see also Cohen 1983, 1985). They would not, for example, typically ask whether post-industrial societies give rise to different forms of movement to industrial societies. Melucci (1985) has expressed this difference by suggesting that the RM and PP approaches focus upon the 'how?' of movement emergence, while the NSM approaches focus upon the 'why?'; that is, the NSM approach considers the problems and issues around which movements tend to mobilize, while the

RM and PP approaches tend to reflect upon the conditions which enable and facilitate mobilization. This is a useful way of putting it, providing that we bear in mind that the NSM theorists also seek to identify their 'problems and issues' with the current state and developmental trends of society taken as a whole. This wider vision of society as a whole and the tensions and struggles it gives rise to is important because it reconnects movement analysis with the broader focus upon order, change and structure within sociological analysis. It widens the scope of movement analysis by introducing the 'big picture'. It is also important to note, however, that it reintroduces the question of 'grievances' or 'strains' quite centrally into the picture and gives us good reason for supposing that they are important elements in analysis. The standard argument of the RM and PP theorists was that grievances are relatively unimportant because, in effect, they are relatively constant. The analyses of the NSM theorists contest that claim. They seek to show that different types of society give rise to different types of grievance and strain.

Habermas

There are many overlaps between the competing theories of NSMs, but also many differences. It would be impossible to do justice to all of these accounts in one chapter. For this reason I have decided to narrow my focus to one thinker: Habermas. Habermas has had less to say about NSMs than other key theorists, notably Touraine and Melucci, and unlike them he has not engaged in any systematic empirical analysis of these movements, with the exception of an early study of the student movement (1989b). It is my view, however, that Habermas's account of the structural transformation which has given rise to the NSMs is the clearest and most robust to be found in the literature. I have many disagreements with his argument but believe that it is a relatively clear and parsimonious thesis with which we can engage. Furthermore, although of all the approaches its roots in Marxism are the clearest, it avoids the highly problematic assumption, which we find in Touraine, that there is or will be a single social movement in the new type of society that we are moving towards. Habermas remains under Marxist influence in the respect that he seeks to identify the central structural problems of modern society, which give rise to NSMs, but he does not follow Touraine down the problematic path of attempting to distinguish a key movement or 'universal class' among the plurality of movements that his analysis identifies.

My exposition of Habermas will unfold in four stages. I will begin by reflecting upon the basic theoretical background to his approach. I will then outline the structural conflicts which, in his view, give rise to movements. Third, I will consider the movements themselves and their relationship to these structural conditions. Finally I will consider some problems with Habermas's approach.

Theoretical background

Habermas theorizes the rise of NSMs as a response to both 'the colonization of the lifeworld' and 'cultural impoverishment'. To understand these
conditions fully we must first discuss his theory of society and, in particular, his contention that it can be understood, for analytic purposes, to
consist of two distinct 'levels': system and lifeworld. Confusingly, Habermas
draws this distinction between system and lifeworld in two different ways.
System and lifeworld are two different 'parts' of society but there is also
a distinction between systemic and lifeworld modes of analysis and – here's
the potentially confusing bit – the lifeworld can be regarded as a part of the
system from the point of view of a systemic analysis. In this brief exposition
I will focus mainly upon the distinction between system and lifeworld as
'parts' of society, but it is important to be mindful of the other distinction
too.

   All of society, system and lifeworld, consists in interaction for Habermas.
However, interaction can assume different forms and contexts, thus giving
rise to different levels of social organization. The lifeworld consists in direct
'symbolic' interactions which are coordinated by way of the mutual understanding achieved between agents and their common orientation towards
shared norms and values. It is held together by traditions and the various
obligations and duties which they impose and, *qua* the communicative space
of society, is also the area of society wherein those traditions, along with
other aspects of culture, knowledge and identity, are reproduced. As a site
of symbolic interaction the lifeworld invites hermeneutic analysis. This is
what Habermas means by a 'lifeworld analysis'. Lifeworld analyses seek to
uncover the meanings which social actions have for the agents who engage
in them. As noted above, however, Habermas believes that the lifeworld
is amenable to a systems analysis. This broadly amounts to a functional
analysis and Habermas's own schema of functional analysis comes very
close to that of Parsons. The lifeworld, in effect, assumes the 'integration'
and 'latency' functions of Parsons's (1966) AGIL schema. It is a normative
order and thereby coordinates action at the ground level ('integration') and
it is a communicative order which reproduces the cultural patterns, dispositions and resources, such as language, which make social life possible and
which other 'parts' of society require ('latency'). For example, the economy,
which we will discuss shortly, presupposes agents who are motivated by a
'work ethic', but this in turn presupposes symbolic and socialization processes which instil such an ethic in successive generations. The lifeworld
'provides' or rather consists in these processes, at least when viewed from a
systems point of view. Where Habermas differs from Parsons is that he
draws attention to the possibility of crisis tendencies within the lifeworld,
when considered as a social–cultural system (Habermas 1988). Specifically
he refers to the possibility of 'legitimation crises', wherein norms are brought

into question and contested, losing their integrative power to a degree which the political system is incapable of dealing with, and also to 'motivation crises', in which the lifeworld ceases to reproduce the basic dispositions, such as the work ethic, required by the societal system as a whole.

The lifeworld is constituted through 'communicative action'. This, to reiterate, is a form of linguistic interaction oriented towards the achievement of mutual understanding and agreement. Habermas divides this action type into two sub-categories: norm-conformative action and discourse. As its name suggests, norm-conformative action involves a more or less habitual and unnoticed adherence to shared social norms. Agents conform to the shared social expectations which apply to whatever types of interaction they are involved in. Discourse, by contrast, designates those moments at which agents reflexively turn back upon their habits and assumptions to subject them to a communicatively rational interrogation and evaluation. Habermas's conception of communicatively rational discourse is, in effect, a more elaborate version of the same notion that we identified in the work in Blumer and Mead. It entails a contest between agents in which both attempt to persuade the other of their view by recourse to logic and the exchange of reasons alone.

When groups of agents come together to bring normative arrangements into question they form a 'public sphere'. This is a key concept in Habermas's theory. In an early study he identified the famous salons and coffee shops of eighteenth-century Europe as an important, if ultimately bourgeois and male-dominated, prototype of an effective public sphere. It was effective, he argued, because it seemed to generate a genuine pressure for social change (Habermas 1989a). Much of his work and his critique of contemporary society, however, focuses upon the demise or non-realization of an effective public sphere. Norms are only legitimate for Habermas, as for Mead (see Chapter 2), insofar as they are thrashed out in open arguments between all who are or will be affected by them (Habermas 1987, 1992). But this simply does not happen in modern societies.

Habermas (1987) situates his account of communicative rationality within a broader account of historical rationalization. Communicative rationality is, he argues, a historical achievement. As the history of science most clearly demonstrates, our ways of reasoning, arguing and making sense belong to the realm of culture and the learning processes evident within the history of culture. The advent of modern patterns of reasoning, he continues, has made a discursive democracy possible. It has opened up the possibility of a society whose norms, including most centrally its laws, are the outcome of a genuinely communicatively rational debate. Furthermore, areas of social life once deemed 'beyond argument', particularly those pertaining to power and authority, are now open to argument and contestation. Prior to rationalization and enlightenment political structures and laws were rooted in and legitimated by reference to religion, which was itself not open to question or argument. The feudal king did not claim legitimacy for his laws by reference to their reasonableness, which would have left them open to question by reasonable subjects, but by reference to God, whom nobody was entitled to question. Through the process of rationalization this changed. Political elites increasingly claimed legitimacy for their authority and decisions by reference to their reasonableness. The laws of the land are not the laws of God but rather what any reasonable individual would accept as fair and appropriate. Notwithstanding this, however, to return to the point about public spheres, Habermas does not claim that the reasonableness of authority and political decisions are, in practice, contested and argued over. Indeed, he believes the opportunity for genuine public participation in politics is shrinking. This could lead to problems, he argues. Specifically it could generate a 'legitimation crisis'. But this tendency is offset by the 'civil privatism' of most citizens. That is to say, most citizens, most of the time, are more concerned with their own private domestic interests and projects than with politics and public issues. It follows that legitimation would only be endangered if this disposition towards civil privatism were to be undermined or disrupted in some way. Legitimation crises must be precipitated by motivation crises.

The process of rationalization is also central to what Habermas refers to as the 'system' part of society. In traditional societies, he observes, all aspects of society were subsumed within the lifeworld. This meant that both political and economic activities were strongly regulated by religion and tradition, which lent them a framework of meaning and morality. One did not trade freely with the highest bidder in one's economic transactions, for example; goods tended to be passed around in accordance with tradition and obligation. Integral to the process of rationalization, however, has been an uncoupling of these two forms of activities from the normative core of society, such that each has become an arena for relatively free utilitarian action, rooted in instrumentally rational calculation. As political and economic agents, in modern societies, we make a choice about what is best for us and then pursue that choice in a strategic fashion. We are not or at least need not be bound by normative considerations or traditions. Furthermore, each of these domains of life, economy and polity has been further rationalized through the emergence of new communicative media peculiar to them: i.e. money in the case of the economy and rationalized political power in the case of the polity. These new media have transformed economic and political relations in both quantitative and qualitative ways, Habermas notes. The emergence of a standardized national currency, for example, links all the members of the nation in question much more tightly than previously in a mutually affective network and thereby gives rise to a whole range of new social dynamics. The numbers of people linked through a common currency are much greater, as is the strength of the link, and the ways in which people (indirectly) affect and impact upon one another are transformed.

The net effect of all of this, for Habermas, is that a new form of societal integration, which he terms 'system integration', has emerged. The lifeworld, to reiterate, is integrated by virtue of the mutual understanding achieved between interlocuters in local interactions. This is 'social integration'. System integration, by contrast, is a more impersonal matter of balance being achieved between inputs and outputs, supply and demand, at the macrocosmic level. In the political system, for example, all citizens have a degree of power which they 'spend' at elections and other participation contexts, in whatever way they wish. This constitutes a transfer of power to the state, which in turn is then mandated to impose policies and laws upon those same citizens. Integration is achieved to the extent that the state accumulates a sufficient mandate to execute whatever policies it is required to make. Similarly in the economy, all economic actors are freed to pursue wealth and then spend it in whatever way they wish. They act, or at least can act, selfishly and without a thought for anybody else. The system is integrated to the extent that people are sufficiently motivated by the desire for wealth to supply the goods that others demand in sufficient amounts such that these two sides of the picture, supply and demand, balance.

Crisis and old social movements

The situation described here is akin to that famously described by Adam Smith. Agents selfishly pursue their own ends, without a care for 'the system' as a whole, and yet the 'invisible hands' of the market ensure some degree of integration ('system integration'). Supply more or less meets demand. However, like Marx, Habermas recognizes that the economic system is founded upon a fundamental conflict of interest, between capitalists and workers, and is subject to periodic crises, such as 'overproduction' crises. Within modern capitalist societies, he argues, the agents of the state have sought to offset these tendencies by assuming a role of economic management. However, this only shifts the crisis tendency from the economy to the state. The state becomes subject to potential crises of economic management or what Habermas calls 'rationality crises'. Both economic and rationality crises are what Habermas calls 'system crises', and he contrasts them, as such, with the two types of lifeworld (or social) crises discussed earlier: legitimation crises and motivation crises.

System crises may be understood, narrowly, as a failure to 'balance the books', but systems are lived through by living human agents, such that a failure to balance the books often means unemployment, depressed wages and misery for a section of society. Because of this, system crises can be converted into 'social crises', such as legitimation crises. The most pertinent example of this is the emergence of the labour movement during the mid-nineteenth century. As workers were increasingly concentrated in large factories and urban areas, such that they could develop a common identity and a collective sense of their shared grievances, a labour movement began to take shape which contested the legitimacy of the status quo. Workers formed unions which allowed them to challenge unacceptable working conditions and the broader movement generated a pressure for change at the governmental level. For Marx and many who have followed him, the eventual outcome of the agitation of the labour movement should have been revolution. Habermas, however, notes that the labour movement was increasingly incorporated into the political structure of society. The labour movement fought for representation within the political system and gave rise to labour parties who were committed to defending the interests of labourers through the conventional political channels. Moreover, having started with a broad range of moral and political concerns about the organization of society and social life, labour parties and unions became increasingly narrowly focused upon securing material rewards for their members, that is, increased wages and better working conditions. A major turning point, in this respect, was the formation of the welfare state, which guaranteed workers a minimal standard of living and basic rights to welfare. This development, motivated in large part by the revolutionary threat of the workers' movement, served to stabilize class conflict, pacifying workers and giving them an investment in 'the system' (Gough 1979).

Colonization of the lifeworld

The formation of the welfare state has clearly had many benefits for workers. However, it also generates many problems, according to Habermas. It contributes an essential element to what he terms 'the colonization of the lifeworld'. What he means by this is that the state now permeates ever more areas of our life, exercising a surveillance and regulatory role. Integral to this is a process of 'juridification', whereby ever more areas of life are becoming subject to legal regulation and legal regulation itself is ever more internally complex and differentiated. Following Weber's remarks on the 'iron cage' of the modern bureaucratic society, Habermas argues that this results in a loss of both freedom and meaning. The cultural narratives and symbolic forms which give existential meaning and ethical direction to our lives are increasingly trampled into the ground by bureaucratic procedures which offer no comparable vision or comfort and which simultaneously reduce our room to choose and manoeuvre. This is compounded by the 'cultural impoverishment' caused by an increased specialization and differentiation of the knowledge and cultural base of society. The basic social processes in which we are involved and which impinge upon our lives have become so complex and specialized that it is no longer possible for us to comprehend them fully or weave them into a coherent narrative. Our conscious grasp upon the social world is thus both incomplete and fragmented.

These arguments regarding colonization and impoverishment very much overlap with the arguments of both Melucci and Touraine, even if the language which each theorist uses to express the point is different. All share a sense in which the world of everyday life is increasingly subject to bureaucratic and technological (in a broad sense which includes social technologies) regulation. Normative and existential questions are being reduced to technical problems and the traditions and culture which previously 'answered' them for people are being eliminated or eroded. The advantage of Habermas's version of this thesis, in my view, is that he links this process, at least in part, to the formation of the welfare state, which was in turn a response to the threat of both economic crisis and the labour movement. This gives us more of a sense of the dynamic lying behind the process. Moreover, it marks out both the continuities and the discontinuities between the old and the new most clearly. Habermas argues that the imperative towards bureaucratic expansion is fuelled by the need to achieve control over the anarchy of capitalist markets and to pacify the potential for social conflict which this generates, 'buying' the legitimacy which the system needs to survive with the currency of paternalistic support.

The extension of the legal apparatus and welfare state is only one branch of the 'colonization of the lifeworld' for Habermas, however. It is matched by an extension and intensification of the economic system. Just as the state extends further into the lifeworld, so too does the market. Juridification is paralleled by commodification. The worlds of leisure, sport and even personal relationships, for example, are increasingly commercialized. New agencies have emerged who seek to package and sell them to a consuming populace (Klein 2000).

The colonization of the lifeworld amounts to a penetration of those (economic and political) systems which had become uncoupled from the lifeworld back into it in a way which corrodes it. Economic colonization, for example, does not entail a new normative regulation of economic life. Rather it entails the uncoupled market mechanism extending further into the lifeworld, ploughing down cultures and replacing traditional forms of social interaction and relationships with (self-interested) financial transactions. This is problematic, sociologically, because economic transactions cannot fulfil the important symbolic functions performed by tradition and communicative engagement, such as the reproduction of a sense of identity and purpose, and their substitution for these latter social forms therefore has devastating effects.

Related to these processes of colonization and impoverishment is a decline of the public sphere. This decline takes two forms. First, echoing the view of many neo-liberal thinkers, Habermas believes that politics, in the context of the welfare state, has ceased to address issues of truly public concern and has become a vehicle through which sectional groups pursue their own private demands and interests. 'Truly' political issues have become merged with economic and domestic interests. The state is akin to a 'nanny', doling out rewards and punishments to children who have become dependent upon it, and serious political debate, which could only be conducted by autonomous citizens, freed of these domestic concerns, is thereby stultified. At a further level, however, he is concerned with the general degeneration of the level of political debate and the increased incorporation of the techniques and technologies of the advertising industry within it. Public communication by politicians, he argues, has become a glorified public relations exercise, and genuine public opinion is drowned in the sea of manufactured opinion generated by the pollsters and image consultants.

New social movements

Though the picture is grim, Habermas identifies a glimmer of hope in the form of new social movements which have emerged within this colonized and culturally impoverished context:

> In the past decade or two, conflicts have developed in advanced Western societies that deviate in various ways from the Welfare State pattern of institutionalised conflict over distribution. They no longer flare up in domains of material reproduction; they are no longer channelled through parties and associations; and they can no longer be allayed through compensations. Rather, these new conflicts arise in domains of cultural reproduction, social integration, and socialisation; they are carried out in sub-institutional – or at least extraparliamentary – forms of protest; and the underlying deficits reflect a reification of communicatively structured domains of action that will not respond to the media of money and power. The issue is not primarily one of compensations that the welfare state can provide, but of defending and restoring endangered ways of life. In short, the new conflicts are not ignited by distribution problems but by questions having to do with the grammar of forms of life.
>
> (Habermas 1987: 392)

This may make the new movements sound reactionary or defensive and Habermas believes that some of them are. However, he is clear to distinguish between reactionary responses by largely conservative traditionalists and nimbys ('Not In My BackYard'), on the one hand, and more progressive resistance by groups who seek a rational reconstruction of the lifeworld. These latter groups do not defend traditions. They question them and, in doing so, both remoralize and repoliticize politics, simultaneously revitalizing the flagging public sphere. They generate a public debate about matters of public morality and social organization, contesting the norms by which we live our lives. And they are genuinely 'public' in the respect that they stand outside the stage show and bureaucracy of the political system. It is this latter group that Habermas is particularly focusing upon when he refers to NSMs. They are the product of the aforementioned (communicative) rationalization of the lifeworld. They demonstrate the truly emancipatory potential of critical rationality.

Though Habermas is not perfectly clear on the matter, I suggest that the links between the colonization of the lifeworld and the rise of NSMs are threefold in his account. The first link centres on the somewhat obvious fact that *colonization is the cause of the various grievances and strains that the NSMs mobilize around*. In addition to the general problems of 'loss of meaning' and 'loss of freedom' he identifies three broad areas of contention generated by colonization:

1 ' "Green" problems', among which he includes 'the impairment of health through the ravages of civilisation, pharmaceutical side effects and the like' (1987: 394);
2 'problems of excessive complexity';
3 an 'overburdening of the communicative infrastructure' (1987: 395).

It may be objected that this account presupposes, somewhat naively, a direct link between grievance and mobilization, such as has been repeatedly criticized in the social movements literature. I will return to this issue later. For the moment, however, it must suffice to note that the argument need not be read in a strictly causal sense. Habermas is identifying new grievances to which new movements have responded but he is not necessarily suggesting that grievances are sufficient to explain the emergence of the movements. He is not claiming to specify the mechanisms or dynamics of mobilization. His intent, rather, is to locate the NSMs in relation to structural changes and the problems they engender; to allow us to understand these positions rather than strictly explaining them; and to draw out the normative significance of their challenge.

The second key link between colonization and NSMs concerns the way in which the *administrative advances associated with colonization destroy once unquestioned traditions*, inadvertently politicizing the domain of life to which those traditions belonged by opening them up to planning and, in doing so, drawing citizens out of their 'civil privatism' into the public–political domain:

At every level administrative planning produces unintended, unsettling and publicising effects. These effects weaken the justification potential of traditions that have been flushed out of their nature-like course of development. Once their unquestionable character has been destroyed, the stabilisation of validity claims can occur only through discourse. The stirring up of cultural affairs that are taken for granted thus furthers the politicisation of areas of life previously assigned to the private sphere. But this development signifies danger for the civil privatism that is secured informally through the structures of the public realm.

(Habermas 1988: 72)

This is a very interesting point which does touch upon the issue of mobilization. Groups become mobilized, Habermas is suggesting, when their expectations and assumptions are breached and/or raised to a thematic level. And this is precisely what happens when the administrative structures of society extend into new areas, disturbing and uprooting the traditions and culture which ordinarily regulate and legitimate action in those areas. Moreover, he is emphasizing that traditions, having been uprooted in this way, will not settle down again, at least not immediately. Having been raised into discourse they can only be resolved in discourse, that is, through rational argument and debate. It is not simply the case that the administration breaks down traditions and traditional legitimations, however. As a political structure of society it equally politicizes those issues, drawing them into the domain of political discourse. The expansion of the political system into 'everyday life' politicizes everyday life. A political focus upon the family, for example, problematizes and politicizes the family. And this is why, or at least part of the reason why, we have seen the emergence of movements, NSMs, focused upon the politics of everyday life.

The third link between NSMs and colonization concerns the fact that, having ploughed down traditions and stirred up a hornet's nest of political issues, the *administrative system proves largely unreceptive to public opinion and pressure*. The public sphere, as we have said, has been largely eroded through the process of colonization, and the bureaucratic structures of the system are indifferent to communicative action and debate. Thus, the system frustrates the very same projects that it sets in motion, amplifying the intensity of these projects and their tendency to follow 'alternative' and 'contentious' routes.

The response of those involved in these new conflicts and movements, according to Habermas, is largely to reject the institutionalized structures which seem incapable of handling their claims, and to pursue their objectives in the extra-parliamentary domain. They protest or construct sites and spaces for the development of alternative ways of living and dealing with the problems of modern living. However, the issue of protest, at least as conceived in narrow and instrumental terms, is secondary to the role of the NSMs in generating, outside the domain of the institutionalized political channels and official mass media, an active debate on matters of public concern which then translates into an effective pressure for change. The NSMs constitute a new public sphere or spheres and thereby serve to regenerate the vitality of the normative structure of society. They resist colonization precisely by raising and contesting the legitimacy of the actions of the administration. And they thereby revivify the promise of the enlightenment: that reason might prevail and indeed organize society.

A critique of Habermas

There is much of value in Habermas's work. He posits an important account of the structural context in which the NSMs have grown up and points to important links between context and movement. However, his account is partial and incomplete, and quite seriously so in some places. It is important to draw out at least some of the problems. For the sake of clarity and convenience I have arranged my main criticisms under four headings.

Mobilization

The approach which Habermas takes to the problem of social movements is very different to that of the writers discussed hitherto in this book. He is interested in the place of the NSMs in the bigger picture: their relationship to the type of society we live in and the period of history we are living through. He is trying to think of them as Marx thought of the proletariat, not simply another empirical phenomenon to be explained but rather a reflection of the structure of the world in which we live. Moreover, he is attempting to build a normative social theory which can engage with the moral issues raised by the trends and organization of modern society. Given this it is perhaps unfair to wheel out all that we have learned from the American traditions of movement analysis as a way of pointing to the empirical inadequacies of his position, that is, its weaknesses both as an empirical account of the rise of movements and as a framework which might be used to explain or analyse specific movements. Nevertheless, we need to be clear not to confuse Habermas's account with an attempt at empirical explanation or to suppose that it could serve as such an explanation. Habermas does not engage with the myriad debates regarding grievances, networks, resources, etc. that we have been examining in this book, nor does he reflect upon either the history of the specific movements he refers to or the cycle of contention (that is, the sixties' cycle) out of which they emerged. He does an important job in identifying the structural changes contemporary societies are undergoing and charting the various forms of strain, grievance and conflict of interest they give rise to but there is another story of the NSMs that he does not and arguably cannot tell: an empirical–processual story about specific movement mobilizations and protests.

We may summarize this point, using Melucci's (1985) aforementioned distinction, by arguing that Habermas focuses on the why of movement formation but not the how. It is not only the 'how?' question that he ignores, however, but also the 'who?' Repeated studies since the sixties, covering a range of countries, movements and SMOs, have consistently identified an overrepresentation of the new middle class of service workers within the ranks of the NSMs (for overviews of this literature see Bagguley 1992, 1995a; Rootes 1995; Byrne 1997). Habermas appears to recognize this bias but fails to reflect upon either its causes or its significance. This is a serious omission, not least because it suggests that the 'old politics' of class remains alive within the 'new politics' and because it raises important questions regarding the interests involved in NSM struggles. Do the NSMs represent the interests of everybody or just the class fraction out of which they emerge? Are their successes indications of genuine democracy or just another indication of the domination of the middle classes within the political field? Habermas does not tell us.

It is worth adding here that many of the distinctions which Habermas introduces into his account, such as that between system and lifeworld, are analytic distinctions which serve the requirements of his moral philosophy admirably but do not map neatly onto the somewhat more messy and mixed reality of the empirical social world, thereby generating considerable problems for those who wish to operationalize them in empirical work. It is far from obvious how we might operationalize Habermas's ideas empirically in any tight or rigorous manner.

The dynamics of reincorporation and disentanglement

At a more substantive level we need to be wary of assuming that NSMs necessarily and always stand outside 'the system', not least because of the dynamic which tends to pull them back in. I have observed this with respect to my own work on psychiatric survivor movements. Many of the more radical survivor groups desired to stay outside 'the system' but were drawn back into it. Often this was because they needed money to survive and had little option but to register either as charities or as small businesses, which, in turn, required them to take on board many of the procedures and attributes of the rational economic organization. At other times it was because their struggles entailed using parts of the system to attack other parts. Some brought legal cases against the psychiatric establishment, for example, but in doing so were forced to conform to the 'rules' of the legal game. In this respect they contributed to the process of 'juridification', albeit in the context of a challenge to psychiatry, since their successes effectively amounted to a further extension of the law into the realm of psychiatry. The psychiatric groups are not alone in this respect. The effect of much ecological campaigning has been to extend the legal regulation of behaviours affecting the environment, while feminist debates over pornography and its regulation indicate a similar tendency and 'problem' there (Chester and Dickey 1988). Indeed, most NSMs contain SMOs, such as civil rights groups, who never intend to work outside 'the system' in the first place.

We should also note, however, that processes of reincorporation can be met with renewed efforts to escape from the system. The emergence of new and more radical environmental movements over the last 20 years, such as Earth First! and Reclaim the Streets, for example, point to a resurgence of the more anarchist strand of that movement, which was lost as the earlier wave of the movement gave way to green parties and organized (often quite hierarchical) pressure groups, such as Greenpeace. Indeed, at my current moment of writing it would be difficult to deny that more loosely organized cells and networks of activists are the chief form adopted by those movements engaged in the most high-profile forms of direct action. In this respect Habermas's notion of resistance to colonization remains important but must be extended. The dialectic of colonization and resistance is evident within movements as they variously emerge, grow, institutionalize and then bifurcate.

The old and the new

My point about incorporation blurs the distinction that Habermas wishes to draw between old and new movements. If new movements too are drawn back into the system then their potential and significance is arguably little different from the old movements. Furthermore, Habermas's account of the incorporation of socialist movements fails to recognize how the channels of communication and networks provided by fringe leftist organizations often served as the seedbed for the growing of the new movements and concerns, and, indeed, how the emergence of the NSMs was anticipated by a mutation within the culture of the left. In the UK, for example, we already find the development of a new left, concerned with broader 'non-economic' issues, by the late fifties: a new left who sponsored many of the early key thinkers of the counter-culture and the NSMs. Within the pages of the *New Left Review* during the 1960s, for example, we find important articles on feminism and the politics of the family and psychiatry. Moreover, in Britain at least there was always a close association between the left and the Campaign for Nuclear Disarmament. I do not mean to deny, in saying this, that there is a genuine difference between old and new movements, or indeed that they are not periodically prone to come into conflict with one another. It is important to appreciate the extent to which they overlap, however, and to which the new movements grew out of the old – albeit sometimes also out of disgruntlement with the old movements and their own particular brand of conservatism.

State and market

Although Habermas views the process of colonization as involving an extension of both state and market into the lifeworld, his emphasis is often upon the state. And, unusually for a left-wing academic, his critique is often levelled at the welfare state. The rise of the NSMs, for Habermas, is primarily an attempt to protect our lives from the encroachment of the state and also to free politics of the burden of its newly acquired domestic responsibilities. This thesis raises a multitude of important issues. The destructive consequences of the welfare state must be balanced against its positive role in maintaining decent standards of living for the majority, and we must be wary of the liberal inclination of separating public–political and private issues. I do not have the space to discuss these issues. What is important from my point of view is that the balance of state and market within western societies, and indeed globally, has swung considerably over to the side of the market in the period since Habermas first formulated his views on both colonization and NSMs. New right governments, particularly in the UK and USA, have 'rolled back the frontiers of the state', at least economically, within their own national boundaries. And at the global level, massive multinational corporations have gained an increasingly prominent role. As Naomi Klein (2000) has argued, these corporations have begun to behave in new ways, focusing their 'brand image' ever more deeply within the domain of lifestyle and identity. If we are to use Habermas's thesis today, I suggest, we must be mindful of this shift. The colonization that he refers to continues, but its leading edge is much more at the level of the global market than he himself suggested.

Having said this, if we interpret this changing pattern of economic life as a new phase in the history of the colonization, there is good reason to suppose that Habermas's argument about the relationship between colonization and new movements holds strong. As Klein (2000) has shown, the new 'brand' economy has seemingly generated a range of struggles, from a resurgence of campus politics in the USA, through such famous trials as the McLibel trial in the UK, to the large-scale protest parties of Reclaim the Streets. The most recent and perhaps most significant manifestation of this has been the series of international protests centred upon global economic institutions, the most publicized of which, to date, have taken place at Seattle, Washington and Prague. Quite how these new movements relate to the NSMs of the 1970s remains an open question. However, their emergence and dynamics fits the theory outlined by Habermas. These movements quite explicitly challenge the colonization of both their own and others' lifeworlds (especially the lives of workers in the third world).

Summary and conclusion

My main concern in this chapter has been to stress that the NSM theorists ask a different question to the other movement theorists we have discussed and that this is an important question which we must not lose sight of.

Habermas, Touraine and Melucci each take a step back from the usual battery of questions regarding the dynamics of movement mobilization and seek to identify both the key movement clusters belonging to any given era and the main structural tensions which those movements form around. This is an important step because it relocates our understanding of movements within an understanding of society more generally and because it raises additional questions about the significance or meaning of the movements we study and the normative claims which they raise. In addition, it reaffirms the importance of 'grievances' and 'strains'. PP and RM theorists argued that strains are not important to movement analysis because they are constants. NSM theorists, by contrast, argue that societies change and, with them, so too do sources of strain. Thus strains are important because they are variable.

In the latter part of the chapter I sought to offer some constructive criticisms of Habermas's specific theory of NSMs. A number of criticisms were raised. More positively, however, I argued that his claim that NSMs are a response to the colonization of the lifeworld has an important contemporary resonance, providing that one shifts the emphasis in his work from political to economic colonization.

Further reading

The nub of Habermas's argument about NSMs is contained in a few pages at the end of the second volume of his (1987) *Theory of Communicative Action*. To get the whole story of colonization, etc. it is necessary to read the whole volume and, for a fuller picture still, both volumes, but the few pages on NSMs were published separately in the *Telos* journal (1981, vol. 49: 33–7), under the title 'New social movements'. That article can be read as an introductory 'stand alone'. I offer a more sustained account of colonization and its consequences in Chapter 5 of my (1996) *Intersubjectivity*. Touraine's account of NSMs is most fully expounded in his (1981) *The Voice and the Eye*. Though not his most recent exposition, Melucci's best account remains his (1986) *Nomads of the Present*. For a good collection of by now classic articles see the special issue of *Social Research* (1985: 52(4)). Naomi Klein's (2000) *No Logo* is an excellent journalistic account of some of the 'even newer' social movements emerging on the political stage and the 'ever newer' strains to which they are responding.

chapter nine

Social movements and the theory of practice: a new synthesis

In this final chapter I reflect back upon the issues and models discussed throughout the book and seek to develop a synthetic framework for movement analysis. I argue that a major fault line in all the theories we have discussed hitherto is the problem of agency and structure and I suggest that the most fruitful resolution of this problem lies in Pierre Bourdieu's (1977, 1992a, 1998a, 2000a) theory of practice. My argument with respect to Bourdieu is threefold. On one hand I believe that his theory of practice is strong on agency, structure and the connection between them, such that it provides a more persuasive general theory from which to engage in movement analysis than any we have considered hitherto. On the other, I believe that his theory provides a tidy and parsimonious framework, which is able to accommodate and locate many of the various scattered insights of movement analysis that we have discussed in this book in a cogent and economical fashion. However, the advantages of Bourdieu's position are at the level of general theory. He has relatively little to say about movements and protests, and what he does say is sometimes problematic. I therefore also argue for an incorporation of some of the central insights of movement theory into the theory of practice. Specifically I develop a reconstructed 'value-added' approach to movement analysis.

The chapter therefore seeks to demonstrate the potential of the work of Bourdieu to answer some of the more pressing problems of movement theory, while also considering how the insights of movement theory might be incorporated into his theory of practice, so as to extend and deepen it. Lest this sound dangerously eclectic I should emphasize that I take Bourdieu's basic problematic as my ground, reading the insights of other approaches and drawing them in through the lens of his theory. Insofar as I incorporate alien concepts into the theory of practice it should be understood that these concepts are to be read in light of that theory.

Problems of agency and structure

Each of the theories I have examined in this book manifests problems in relation to the issue of structure, agency or both. These problems have been examined in detail earlier in the book but it would be useful to begin these concluding reflections with a brief recap. This recap is not comprehensive but rather selects those problems most pertinent to my proposals for the development of movement theory.

I noted two problems with Smelser's theory. First, though he recognizes that 'strains' may be a more or less permanent feature of some social systems, he nevertheless fails to recognize that struggle and conflict may be integral and constitutive elements of such 'systems'. Strains or conflicts arise when things 'go wrong' for Smelser. They are not integral aspects of the social world. This is a problem with his concept of structure and it derives primarily from his functionalist orientation. Second, agency all but disappears from his account, being subsumed under system elements or reduced to mechanistic psychodynamic processes. Both structure and agency are problems in Smesler's account therefore.

Blumer's account of movement formation is very much agency-based but he has no account of structure. He does not seek to explain the 'strains' which trigger movement activity in terms of the organization of social systems or structures, for example. Indeed he does not elucidate upon them at all. This is to the detriment of his account of agency too, however, as he fails to embed either agents, movements or struggles within the structures and systems of the social world. He fails to locate his agents in terms of class or status group, for example, and he offers no reflection on the array of constraints and opportunities that they experience as they wage their conflicts in such arenas as the media, parliament and the courts. Again then, both agency and structure pose problems in Blumer's work.

Similar problems occur, in a more extreme form, in rational actor theory (RAT). Many of the philosophical assumptions of RAT, such as its methodological individualism, are extremely problematic, and the minimalism of the model of agency it proposes render it incapable of asking some of the more interesting sociological questions that social movements raise. In particular the tendency of RAT to bracket out a consideration of agents' schemas of interpretation and preference, and their origins, precludes consideration of important questions about the origins of movements themselves. This is most clear in McCarthy and Zald's (1977) definition of social movements. They understand movements as a demand for certain sorts of change, akin to economic demand, but never inquire into the origin of that demand.

In effect they thereby overlook some of the most interesting questions in movement theory, and begin their story halfway through. This is compounded by the fact that the demands sometimes raised by movements are not obviously self-interested in the manner RAT must predict.

RAT attempts to offer an account of structure and certainly opens up the question of structure, when it recommends that we seek out the explanation for changes in social behaviour in the changing balance of opportunities and constraints in the social environment. This account is extremely vague and underdeveloped, however, such that we are forced to conclude that RAT is as weak in relation to questions of structure as it is to agency. Furthermore, in contrast to Smelser, it makes no attempt to identify the structural roots of the strains or grievances which give rise to movements. Structure too is a weak point of RAT therefore.

The resource mobilization (RM) and political process (PP) approaches both start from the RAT model. Some versions therefore manifest just the same problems. Not all versions of RM and PP are guilty on this count. Some, particularly more recently, have added various features and considerations to the model, which allows it to circumvent the more obvious problems of RAT. This creates its own problems, however, as many of the additions, including such central notions as 'repertoires' and 'frames', violate the basic assumptions of the RAT model and thus push the model of agency into an unclear and eclectic no man's land. Furthermore, the additions are made in an ad hoc fashion, without consideration of the basic underlying theoretical model they presuppose. It is therefore unclear what exactly the advocates of these more advanced RM and PP positions think agency is. Agency is a problem.

There is also a structure problem in these approaches. The vehemence with which RM and PP advocates have attacked the strain-reaction or 'grievance' model of movement formation has led them to more or less neglect the question of grievances altogether and, with this, the question of the structural 'contradictions' or tensions which generate those grievances. This becomes most obvious if we contrast RM and PP approaches with the work of the new social movement theorists discussed in Chapter 8. The attempt of these latter theorists to ascertain whether changing social structures have given rise to new forms of movements reveals a level of structural analysis which completely bypasses the RM and PP models. Though they have a concept of structure it does not extend to reflections upon these matters. Finally, RM and PP approaches have tended to assume that the activities of social movements, their struggles, take shape in a single and unified space, 'the polity', failing to address properly the differentiated nature of contemporary societies and the plurality of distinct spaces in which struggles are waged. Movements may wage their wars in the media, the courts, parliament, the laboratory and many other such social spaces, each of which affords a different array of possibilities, opportunities and constraints. Social movement analysis must be sensitive to this fact if it is adequately to address its subject matter. This, again, is a problem of structure.

The theories of new social movements take a very different approach to all the American paradigms and ask a fundamentally different question. As such, many of the criticisms I have raised in relation to the American paradigm do not apply. Notwithstanding this, the NSM paradigms do not help to resolve the problems raised in my critique and the specific theory of NSMs that we examined, that of Habermas, raises many of its own problems. There is much to commend Habermas's work, including many points I have not had the space to discuss. In particular he provides a strong basis for the normative theorization of movements and their place in a democratic society. Nevertheless, as I noted in the previous chapter, Habermas's model is not well suited to an empirical investigation of movements and, as such, falls short of much that we require of a paradigm of movement analysis.

Bourdieu's theory of practice

It is my contention that Pierre Bourdieu's (1977, 1992a, 1998a, 2000a) theory of practice provides a framework through which we might seek to address these problems. Bourdieu is important because he provides the elements of a basic theory of social practice which can be turned to the service of movement analysis and which allows us to ground that analysis in a more satisfactory way. I have begun to develop this argument with reference to empirical materials elsewhere (Crossley 1998a, b, 1999a, b, c, 2000a; Crossley and Crossley 2001). Here I offer a more general theoretical argument.

In *Distinction* Bourdieu offers a highly schematic 'equation' to explain his theory of practice: *[(habitus) (capital)] + field = practice* (1984: 101). There are many problems with this formulation, not least its bogus implication that the elements of practice enjoy a precise mathematical relationship to each other, but it is helpful in some respects. In effect, what Bourdieu is arguing is that social practices are generated through the interaction of agents, who are both differently disposed and unequally resourced, within the bounds of specific networks which have a game-like structure and which impose definite restraints upon them. This needs to be unpacked.

The concept of the habitus is multi-levelled, complex and has evolved through the course of Bourdieu's work. At one level it refers to the fact, recognized by Durkheim ([1912] 1915) among others, that the experience of social life transforms the basic nature of human beings, giving rise to a second nature (i.e. habitus). Human beings have sentiments, morals, preferences and competences which reflect their involvement in a social group. More specifically, this connects with the notions of habit and habitus developed in the phenomenological and pragmatist traditions of philosophy, which suggest that the history of an agent sediments within their 'body', understood as an active and sensuous structure, in the form of perceptual and linguistic schemas, preferences and desires, know-how, forms of competence and other such dispositions (see Crossley 2001a, b). The way we see, think and act, these traditions suggest, is shaped by our personal history. This is intended as a theory of active agency, but it is an approach to agency which seeks to avoid the overly voluntaristic overtones of such writers as the early Sartre (1969). Human action does not emerge out of 'nothingness', for Bourdieu, but rather out of a habitus formed by way of the history of the agent. On the 'agentic' side this conception emphasizes that we make ourselves through our various ways of acting; our habits are a residue of our previous patterns of action. Nevertheless, we make ourselves in particular ways, in response to the conditions we find ourselves in, and this means that we are always 'something' rather than the pure 'nothingness' of the Sartrean schema, that is, we are always characterized by concrete preferences, schemas, dispositions, interests, know-how, etc.

Any agent's habitus will manifest certain idiosyncratic features as no two life histories are the same. Individual history is but a strand in broader collective histories for Bourdieu, however, such that we may speak of group-specific habitus and may analyse the habitus of individuals in terms of their belonging to such collective formations. Different groups will tend to manifest different habitus because they have had to make a life for themselves in different circumstances. Bourdieu has tended to focus upon the class specificity of habitus in particular, emphasizing the role that the possession of different forms of 'capital' or resource (including economic, symbolic, cultural and social resources) has upon agents' circumstances, but this might equally apply to nations, eras and status groups. Each of these collectives may manifest a distinct habitus. *Distinction*, which maps out clear differences in aesthetic, lifestyle and political dispositions between classes and class fractions, remains Bourdieu's key study in this respect (Bourdieu 1984). Here he charts differences in class habitus, explains their origin in the different material conditions in which classes must make their lives, and traces the consequences of these different habitus, with specific reference to the forms of symbolic power which allow some groups to define the products of their own habitus as superior to those of other groups.

As outlined so far the concept of the habitus has at least three dimensions. On one hand it has a phenomenological dimension. It consists in the schemas, typifications, know-how and practical interests which structure agents' understandings of the world. Like the various interactionist and phenomenological schools of sociology, Bourdieu is alerting us to the necessity of identifying and engaging with this phenomenological level if we hope to explain why agents act as they do. Agents act in situations in accordance with the way in which they define those situations and they define their situations in accordance with the schemas, interests, know-how, etc. that comprise their habitus. 'Habitus' is our conceptual tool for mapping the structures and processes of subjective sense-making and, in this respect, has certain affinities to the phenomenological notion of the lived world or 'lifeworld'. Where much (but by no means all) phenomenological sociology is content to explicate and explore the sense-making procedures that social agents use, however, Bourdieu pushes his project further by calling for an 'objectification of subjectivity' and an analysis of the generative processes which give rise to specific habitus. This, in itself, constitutes the second dimension of the habitus concept. The habitus is something we may map and such maps will help us to explain the activities of social agents. But specific habitus are phenomena which, in turn, we must attempt to explain. This might involve a biographical and social–psychological explanation. However, Bourdieu's concern with the generative processes which give rise to habitus is intimately interwoven with a recognition that different aspects of the habitus manifest a social distribution and are thus 'social facts'. We can approach the question of the formation of habitus from a sociological point of view because particular dispositions, schemas, styles, know-how, etc. are more common among some groups than others, prompting the question of why members of 'this' group share 'that' disposition and so on. Habitus are differentiated along social structural, historical and geographical lines because individual biographies are woven into a social fabric. This adds a third dimension to Bourdieu's concept, which is that it can be used to refer to individual sets of dispositions and schemas and/or to the collective interpretative resources and lifeworld of specific social groups and communities. Just as the behaviour of individual agents is governed by their subjective interests, definitions, etc., so too with groups and communities.

Habitus and social movements

At this early stage in our exposition we can identify four broad areas of movement theory which connect with Bourdieu's account. First, the notion of the habitus points to *the importance of individual and group lifeworlds in shaping action* and thus coincides with what Smelser, Blumer and Edward Thompson have to say about these matters. To understand how human beings behave, Bourdieu is arguing, one must understand how they perceive and evaluate their world (individually and collectively) and one must ascertain the (inter)subjective interests which animate them. This means, as Smelser, Blumer and Thompson all suggest, that the 'strains' or grievances that groups mobilize around will only function as such insofar as they disrupt the structure of the lifeworld and/or otherwise come to be defined as strains within the terms of the lifeworld. Events which are of great and obvious significance for the academic may have little or no significance for the populations analysed by the academic and may not even be noticed at all.

Second, for this same reason, the notion of the habitus engages with what has been said, in the more recent literature, regarding *grievance interpretation and framing*. Indeed, Bourdieu himself has emphasized the importance of political agents sharing or engaging with the habitus of their potential constituents ('frame alignment'), and he anticipated Klandermans's (1992) claim that SMOs effectively preach to the converted:

> . . . the successful prophet is one who formulates for the groups or classes he addresses a message which the objective conditions determining the material and symbolic interests of those groups have predisposed them to attend to and take in. In other words, the apparent relationship between prophecy and its audience must be reversed: the religious or political prophet always preaches to the converted and follows his disciples at least as much as they follow him, since his lessons are listened to and heard only by agents who, by everything they are, have objectively mandated him to give them lessons.
>
> (Bourdieu and Passeron 1996: 25–6)

Having noted the similarity of this observation to that of the framing theorists, however, we should note that Bourdieu's account surpasses theirs in at least three respects. First, Bourdieu explicitly links habitus and the frames they entail to specific social groups and classes, thus extending the social psychological insights of movement theory in a more sociological direction. Second, as this passage at least hints, he raises the question of the material and social circumstances which lead different social groups to have different habitus and frames in the first place. Again this raises important sociological questions which are overlooked in the framing literature. Third, a point not evident in the passage above, Bourdieu advances a strong theory of symbolic power which examines the manner in which certain 'frames' (not his term) are elevated and politically backed, at the expense of others. The efficacy of frames is not merely a matter of their 'resonance', therefore, but equally of the power and interests which invest them.

These observations bring us to the next point of overlap between Bourdieu and movements theory, which concerns *the embeddedness of social agents*. I have argued above that many theories of agency, within the movements literature, particularly Blumer and the RAT model, do not and cannot account for embeddedness. And yet, the empirical findings of movement research consistently point to it. Consider, for example, the observation, encountered numerous times in this book, that the educated middle classes are more prone to become involved in new social movements and to serve as conscience constituents for a range of further movements. Both RAT and Blumer are ill-placed to make sense of this observation, given that it is not a straightforward question of resources, as their respective agents are generic agents. There is no difference at the level of agency between the middle classes and the working classes, for them. And yet there are differences, sometimes big differences, and this social fact of differential degrees of involvement in movements is one of them. Bourdieu, I suggest, provides an opening by which we can begin to explore this issue. I do not mean to suggest by this that the habitus is the final answer to this question. To say, for example, that the middle classes are more prone to movement involvement on account of their habitus is really to say little more than that they are prone because they are prone. My point is, however, that a conception of agency rooted in the concept of the habitus would lead us to predict such differences and enable us to frame a project exploring the genealogy of these particular dispositions.

We should add here that Bourdieu himself, in *Distinction*, identifies the 'over-involvement' of the educated middle classes in the political (as well as artistic and literary) public sphere (see also Eder 1985, 1993), and stresses the middle-class nature of that political space in contemporary societies. Just as the children of the educated middle classes are brought up in an environment rich in art and aesthetic sensibility, such that they inherit aesthetic dispositions, he argues, so too are they brought up in political environments, where they acquire the taste, disposition and know-how, not to mention the inherited 'ticket' of cultural capital, such as a university degree, required for involvement in the political public sphere.

Finally, the notion of the habitus is extremely suggestive in relation to the various studies of *the biographical root and impact of movement involvement*. In particular it provides a framework within which to make sense of McAdam's fascinating but largely untheorized observations on the manner in which involvement in protest further disposes an agent towards involvement. This is precisely what one would predict on the basis of the concept of the habitus. Involvement in political and movement activities generates habits which further dispose and enable one to engage in politics.

The value of the habitus concept is not simply that it allows us to probe further into these various issues of framing, biography, class bias, etc., though this is important. More important still is the fact that it provides a coherent and parsimonious means of drawing these scattered insights together in the context of a unified theory of agency. The concept of the habitus captures the basic interpretative aspects of agency flagged up by Blumer and drastically missing in RAT, and it surpasses both by embedding agents within the structures of the social world. Agents act, think, reflect, desire, perceive, make sense, etc. but they always do so by way of habits inherited from the social locations in which they have socialized, which are in turn shaped by wider dynamics of the social world. It is for this reason that specific frames can be resonant or not, and that some hardships will count as grievances or strains for some groups, where others may not. It is also for this reason, as just noted, that social movements can have a biographical impact: because they are one context within which certain structures of the habitus may be remade. The contrast with RAT is particularly instructive here. The RAT agent cannot be influenced by participation in a social movement because it approaches each and every situation in the same instrumentally rational fashion. The concept of the habitus, by contrast, reminds us that we are historical beings who are affected and transformed by significant life events.

Habitus and strategy

It is important to emphasize that the concept of the habitus does not involve a 'culturally dopey' model of agency. The structures of the habitus are intelligent and multi-track dispositions (Crossley 2001a, b). They entail forms of embodied competence or know-how and constitute a basis for improvized and innovative action. The agent is not akin to a blind follower of traditions but rather to a skilled game player, with a 'feel for the game' which allows her to pursue strategic ends in skilful ways. The implication of this point, at a very basic level, is that Bourdieu's conception of the habitus encourages us to view social movements and political activities as the collective work of skilled and active agents. Boudieu's agents, in contrast to those of Smesler, act strategically and skilfully. They 'build' movements and 'do' protests, with all that this implies in terms of purposive action and a requisite skill-base. In this respect they have something in common with the agents posited in RAT. However, Bourdieu provides a welcome alternative to this perspective too. His agents are not minimal 'calculating machines'. They are social beings endowed with forms of know-how and competence, schemas of perception, discourse and action, derived from their involvement in the social world. They are beings with personal histories, which affect them and which are woven into broader collective histories which affect them too. More to the point, their actions are not rooted in abstract logical calculations of utility but in a 'feel for the game' which they have acquired through involvement in the social world. Their experiences have given rise to a 'second nature' and new, social instincts which they draw upon to act. The concept of the habitus thus allows us to preserve what is useful about the RAT model but also to eject those aspects of it which constitute an obstacle to a useful model of agency and to embrace other useful insights which it precludes.

The metaphor of social agents as game players is crucial to Bourdieu. It captures well the subtle blend of active, strategic agency and arbitrary social form which, he believes, we find in the social world. Like a footballer, social agents 'play the game', which entails both that they act strategically and innovatively, with improvisation, but also that they tend to stick within the parameters of the game. This metaphor has an additional interest in our case, however, in the respect that it maps onto Tilly's conception of 'repertoires of contention' (see Chapter 7). Tilly's definition of repertoires, particularly insofar as it emphasizes shared expectations and likens repertoires to a shared language, comes very close to a 'game' model of protest, in the sense of 'games' used by Bourdieu. When events in the normal games of everyday life either permit or necessitate, the protest game kicks in, as all parties to it expect that it will – at least this is so in fields, such as those of labour relations, where there is a degree of institutionalization of protest. And all parties 'know', in the pre-reflective and habitual sense of know-how, how to play that game strategically, and to win. Through the concept of the habitus, however, we are able to ask and raise research questions that Tilly's conception does not extend to. In particular, through the notion of a habitus built up through a combination of biographical trajectory and class belongingness, we are able to begin to make sense of the patterns of repertoire appropriation discussed in Chapter 7. Repertoire choice, we may hypothesize, is a function of a player's feel for the protest game, which is, in turn, a product of their specific biographical trajectory.

Agency and structure

Structuration

Thus explained the habitus is a conception of agency. However, it is more than this. It is a hinge between agency and structure. The habitus, Bourdieu argues, is both a structured and a structuring structure. By structured structure he means that habitus are formed in structured social contexts whose elements they incorporate and embody. An agent who is taken around art galleries as a child, for example, by parents who value art and have the know-how to interpret and discuss it, and to enjoy doing so, is herself much more likely, statistically, to acquire this same 'love of art', with all that it entails (Bourdieu *et al.* 1991). She will incorporate the structures of the art world within her own manner of being-in-the-world: her habitus. Similarly, having been exposed to the language of her native society, as a child, she will incorporate that too, and it will become a structure of her habitus. She will think 'in' that language and it will reside on the hither side of her being, a means of thought rather than an object of it. Having incorporated such structures, however, she is disposed to reproduce them, thereby 'giving back' to the social world the structures she 'borrowed' from them. Her perceptions, thoughts and actions will embody and enact the structures of the social world. She will reproduce the language and linguistic structures of her society by way of her speech, for example, and indeed also by passing that language on to others (e.g. her children) and demanding it of them in interaction situations. And she will contribute to the reproduction of the art world through her interest and continued participation in it. This is the sense in which the habitus is a generative or 'structuring' structure, and it provides the crucial link between agency and structure. To put it bluntly, and omitting for sake of space issues of historical evolution and change, structures form agents who reproduce structures through their actions and so on.

It is important to add here that structures are products of interactions rather than actions. Our hypothetical agent does not reproduce either language or the art world on her own. She occupies a position relative to others and, perhaps in competition or conflict, they reproduce that structure of practice together. One consequence of this is that the dispositions of our agent's habitus can exist in relative degrees of harmony with the environment (formed by other agents) in which she interacts. She might have tacit expectations about the duty of an artist or gallery, for example, and feel shocked or offended if those expectations are not met. Similarly, she may find that her 'perfectly tuned' linguistic habitus runs into difficulty if she travels to a different country or perhaps even too far from her usual social circle.

Fields

However, the habitus is only one part of the picture for Bourdieu, albeit an integral part, and the individual agent is an abstraction. Human individuals have always lived in collective groupings or societies and these societies manifest irreducible or *sui generis* properties and dynamics. On this point Bourdieu follows Durkheim, and he also agrees with the latter that the growth and development of societies has effected a process of internal differentiation. This has entailed, on one hand, hierarchical differentiation, which Bourdieu traces in terms of what he calls different 'species' of capital: i.e.

- economic capital: e.g. money, property and precious commodities with a monetary value;
- cultural capital: e.g. cultural goods and dispositions, including educational qualifications, which have a value in specific social fields (see below) and which allow their holder to procure further goods;
- symbolic capital: e.g. statuses and reputation, which again have value or generate power in specific fields;
- social capital: e.g. connections and ties which can be used to the agent's advantage in specific fields.

Different agents and groups of agents (classes) possess these various forms of capital in differing amounts and ratios and, as a consequence, enjoy different life chances and opportunities. On the other hand, differentiation has assumed a horizontal form, dividing society into discrete social spaces or 'fields' which Bourdieu variously likens to 'markets' or 'games': e.g. the religious field, the political field, the artistic field, the educational field, etc. Each of these fields entails exchanges of the various forms of capital, sometimes highly specific, which circulate within them, Bourdieu notes, and they are structured through the various distributions of these forms of capital. At the same time, however, each field is like a distinct game, which involves its own objects of value, rules and objectives. The way one plays the legal game, for example, is quite specific and far removed from the way in which one plays the scientific or political game, and in each case, though broad and generic forms of capital and class are highly significant, highly specific forms of capital are also generally in play. A law degree is invaluable to players in the legal field, for example, but much less so for players in the scientific and sporting fields. The concept of the habitus is of relevance in this respect since the habitus is the 'feel for the game' which agents acquire through playing it and then subsequently rely upon in their actions. Field presupposes habitus, since there is no game without players who are both motivated and know how to play, and yet this habitus is acquired through play and individual 'moves' have meaning only by virtue of the game: kicking a ball into a net only counts as a goal, after all, in the game of football.

The notion of fields mirrors Smelser's notion of systems in many important respects. However, it also overcomes the central weaknesses of that conception. Four differences between the two conceptions are crucial. First, as the metaphor of the game suggests, fields are sites of strategic and innovative action rather than dumb rule following. Second, they are hierarchically differentiated. Their players enjoy unequal opportunities and positions within them, both because of their specific organization and because of the broader context of class inequality in which they take shape. Third, partly as a consequence of this, certain fields are constitutively conflictual and competitive. Conflicts are not deviant but normal. Finally, insofar as stability is maintained, Bourdieu understands this not in terms of 'functionality' but in terms of power and domination. The relationships between agents and groups in different social fields are power relations and stability is not a result of system equilibrium but rather of effective domination.

The differences between Bourdieu's 'fields' and Smelser's 'systems' make the former a much better starting point for movement theory than the latter. The obstacles which haunt Smelser's account are removed. More specifically, however, I would suggest that the notion of fields has a fivefold significance in relation to social movement analysis. First, like Smelser's conception of social systems, Bourdieu's account of fields affords us the leverage to *identify, map and explore the structural conditions* which give rise to specific strains and grievances in a very detailed and focused way. For present purposes we may identify two ways in which such an explanation may work. On one hand, the concept of fields admits a consideration of the 'internal' tensions which generate strains and grievances in specific arenas of social life. It may be, for example, that the relations of domination in the psychiatric field constitute the strains in that field which are necessary, if not sufficient, to explain the emergence of the anti-psychiatry and psychiatric survivor movements. Certainly any analysis of these movements would want to know what was going on in this field at the time the movements emerged. Were things getting worse? Better? Unchanged? Similarly, our understanding of labour movements must necessarily attend to the 'contradictions' and periodic 'crises' of the economic field. On the other hand, it may be, as Habermas's (1987) notion of the 'colonization of the lifeworld' (Chapter 8) suggests, that strains and stresses are generated by the infringement of one field, perhaps the economic field, upon other fields. Strains and grievances may be generated through an interaction of fields, in other words, and we can thus grasp the broader structural trends affecting movement formation, such as those described by the theorists of new social movements. It is interesting in this respect that much of Bourdieu's recent work has focused upon the infringement of the economic field upon such fields as the artistic and media fields (Bourdieu 1998b; Bourdieu and Haacke 1995). In particular, sounding very similar to Habermas, he has argued that the autonomy of these fields is undermined by economic encroachment and that so too, therefore, is the potential for free and critical discussion which might otherwise be facilitated.

Bourdieu's own view of movement formation and development, as I note below, tends towards a simple and problematic strain model. To jump the gun of my argument in this chapter slightly, however, I want to argue that the notion of fields also opens the door to a more differentiated account of the other value-added elements that variously facilitate and constrain movement formation and development. Specific fields will often have their own forms of social control, their own structures of opportunity and their specific types of resource, and thus the possibility of movement formation, development and success within them may be quite specific to them. While psychiatric patients were locked up in a punitive asylum system and subject to harsh and intense forms of social control, for example, the possibility of them coming together to form effective movements for change was extremely limited, whatever the wider state of the political field. What counted, for them, were the opportunities, controls, resources, etc., within their own specific fields. This is the second contribution of the field concept. It offers a framework for thinking about *conditions of struggle and the value-added elements of movement formation in a differentiated society*.

We can push this argument one step further, to make a third point. Struggles often spread to different fields, wherein *different constraints and logics* come into play. As I noted earlier in the book, for example, a campaign which is eminently newsworthy in the media field may be quite hopeless from a political or legal point of view, and vice versa. The media game is quite different from the legal game, which is different again from the parliamentary game, and we need to be attentive to this if we are analyse struggles which traverse these domains. Movements may experience a different balance of opportunity and constraints in the various fields in which they engage and they will most certainly find that they are required to play a different game in each of these fields. It is perhaps for this reason that many SMOs specialize in particular types of intervention or, in the case of the bigger ones, have specialized 'departments' dealing with specific fields. Within the mental health movements I studied, for example, some SMOs, such as the Schizophrenia Media Agency and Mental Health Media, were devoted entirely to media campaigning, while bigger SMOs, such as MIND, have media, legal and parliamentary departments.

The concepts of capital and habitus are important here also, because one's opportunities in a particular field and one's ability to play well within it will be dependent upon one's feel for that game and the resources available to one. To give an extreme example, one campaigner I studied in my work on mental health movements was an award-winning journalist. It would be difficult to overstate the advantage this secured for her in media campaigning, relative to other campaigners. She had greater know-how and a range of social, symbolic and cultural resources to draw upon. This boosted her campaigning power outside the media field as well as in it. But her contacts, status and 'feel for the game' were, nevertheless, largely specific to the media field and, at the very least, served her best there. She was not well equipped, for example, to engage in legal battles – unlike the civil rights lawyers who had become involved in other groups in the field.

Fourth, the concept of fields suggests *a model of movements in its own right*, allowing us to connect with some of the important themes that McCarthy and Zald (1977) raise in relation to social movement industries and sectors. That is, we can appreciate that and how movements, insofar as they achieve any size and duration, can become sites of internal competition and 'games'. McCarthy and Zald conceive of this in very narrowly materialistic terms and, as I noted in Chapter 5, this is problematic because the material rewards for many forms of protest are slight and some activists quite clearly eschew the economic field that McCarthy and Zald try to link them to. They do not pursue donations and market share. The notion of fields is more flexible, however, and invites us to reflect with an open mind upon the type of game members of a specific movement (or sub-movement) are pursuing, with the stakes and goods this involves. We could begin to shed light upon the action of tunnel protestors, for example, by exploring the games their actions belong to and the various 'goals' and taken-for-granteds that it involves.

Finally, again rejoining McCarthy and Zald to an extent, Bourdieu (1992b) has an explicit, if underdeveloped, concept of the political field, which allows us to put specific movement fields into broader relief. His account of this field is, interestingly, quite similar to that suggested by RM. It entails a notion of *political entrepreneurs in pursuit of 'profit'*, though Bourdieu is prepared to accept that these profits are quite specific to it. Political agents seek political rewards. Not everybody will pursue the rewards which politics offers, nor indeed perceive them as rewards. There is much that I could say with respect to this notion of the political field. For now I want to emphasize that it is useful, if we interpret it broadly, such that it incorporates movement politics, since it indicates the existence of a wider and perhaps more durable (than specific movements) social space of movement politics. Many of the theories that we have examined in this book offer a two-dimensional picture of social movements. They emphasize change, eruption, emergence, etc., as they must, but they also tend to point to a more durable field of movement politics which pre-exists and aids such eruptions, which may be modified by them, but which will also outlive them. Thus, in the midst of his account of social unrest Blumer makes reference to 'agitators', that is, a class of agents politicized prior to the emergence of unrest who variously provoke and enable struggle among the less initiated. Similarly, in RM theory, accounts of how insurgency and protest outbreaks are stimulated by the injection of external resources make explicit reference to a liberal political establishment which pre-exists the struggle and which is responsible for injecting those resources and patronizing parties to the struggle. Or again, more particularly in the work of McCarthy and Zald (1977), new movement developments are framed in terms of a broader understanding of movement 'industries' and 'sectors', that is, more permanent fixtures of the field of movement politics. The precise details of these 'permanent fixtures' raise too many controversial issues for me to discuss here. Nevertheless, I would suggest that this basic two-sided picture, in which movements involve both spontaneous, new and fast moving forces, on the one hand, and more durable structures of radical and movement politics on the other, is an important one. To see the movements picture properly I believe that we must 'hold it properly', 'from both sides'. More to the point, I would suggest that Bourdieu's account of the political field is a useful framework for grasping the 'structure' side of this particular equation. The 'political field' entails all that we may wish to discuss under the rubric of 'movement industries', 'sectors', etc., but it theorizes these aspects of movement activism in a more sensitive and instructive way than the overly economistic models of RM provide for.

[(Habitus) (capital)] + field = movements?

To summarize the position so far: Bourdieu suggests a model of the social world in which it is differentiated into specific 'fields', each of which is a game in which suitably disposed agents engage, in accordance with their forms of 'capital' and their 'feel for the game'. Agents, *qua* players, incorporate these games in the form of habitus, which predispose them to play the games, thereby reproducing them. Thus the social world is reproduced. I am suggesting that we might use this model in a threefold manner in social movement analysis. First, I am suggesting that this account provides us with the tools to make sense of the basic preconditions of movement emergence and development. An analysis of fields and their various interactions allows us to make sense of the strains, opportunities, resource flows, etc., which can give rise to movements. Second, I am suggesting that this model is also peculiarly well placed to allow us to conceptualize the diverse and differentiated range of arenas in which movements wage their struggles. Many movements will struggle in the media, in parliament, in the courts, in the fields from which they originally emerge, and in each case they will encounter a different 'game' which demands different dispositions and resources from them. Media struggles demand a whole different set of resources and skills to legal struggles and both are different again from struggles in the academic field. Finally, I am suggesting both that the internal environment of a movement may assume a field structure, and that there is, within our society, a more permanent field of movement and political activism, a political field, wherein various movements stake their claim. Thus, for example, the environmental movement involves its own basic internal struggles and games, and it is located in a wider movement and political game, along with pacifism, feminism, animal rights, etc.

A crisis theory of movements?

The first part of my argument in this chapter has now been made. Traditional movement theories, of whatever persuasion, have failed to develop or identify a general theoretical framework for dealing adequately with issues of agency and structure. Bourdieu offers us a much more credible perspective in this respect and, in my view, the most credible in contemporary social theory. In addition, his relatively simple theory proves capable of integrating into a coherent conceptual framework a whole range of scattered insights that have been thrown out by various movement theorists, concerning such issues as frames, grievance interpretation, biography and repertoires. As I noted in the introduction to this chapter, however, Bourdieu fails to develop an adequate account of movements within the context of his theory of practice, such that we are required to effect a two-way dialogue between his ideas and those of movement theory. Movement theory must adopt Bourdieu's theory of practice as a conceptual basis for research and theorization, but we must be sure to reincorporate back into this new synthesis the many insights of movement theory that Bourdieu, himself, has not arrived at. This point requires unpacking.

Bourdieu actually says relatively little, explicitly, about movements in his work. Or rather, he has perhaps said more in his capacity as a political activist than as a sociologist (Bourdieu 1998b, 2000b). More to the point, what he does say is problematic insofar as it seems to imply a relatively straightforward 'crisis' theory of movements, such as has been strongly criticized in the movement literature. This crisis theory stems from his perspective on domination, legitimation and the public sphere. The public sphere is an important political space for Bourdieu, as is illustrated by a number of his more recent studies, which identify and criticize its erosion in

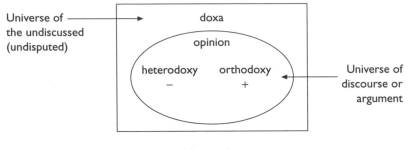

Figure 9.1 Doxa, orthodoxy and heterodoxy
Source: Adapted from Bourdieu (1977: 168)

contemporary societies (Bourdieu and Haacke 1995; Bourdieu 1998b). Political power is at least nominally legitimated on the basis of rational agreement in modern societies, he argues, and this means that it can and should be called to account before a potentially critical public. However, this level of discursive engagement is underpinned by habitus in at least two ways. In the first instance, referring back to a point raised earlier, he notes that certain social groups are more disposed towards and better resourced for engagement in the public sphere than others. The field of political debate is not a level one. Second, and more generally, the thematic issues raised in public discourse are but the tip of an iceberg with respect to legitimation, for Bourdieu. Beneath this level, supporting it, is a much deeper and broader level of unspoken and pre-reflective or unconscious 'doxic' assumptions which allow political society to function without calling it into question. This is represented diagrammatically in Figure 9.1.

Discursive persuasion is not necessary for effective legitimation most of the time because much of the consent which agents grant to the state and the *status quo* is granted at the level of habitual assumption. Agents do not decide anew, each day, to support the status quo. Insofar as the social world conforms to their expectations of it they do not question it at all. Or rather, their questions and criticisms do not suffice to raise serious legitimation issues. Like a game player they reproduce the game with skill and competence, but without ever having to think about the game. The concept of 'public opinion' suggests that democratic states are actively and reflectively supported by their citizens, Bourdieu notes, and this is seemingly supported by the many opinion polls which catalogue and collate 'views'. However, this is misleading. Opinion polls, for the most part, generate an appearance of public opinion by asking citizens to tick boxes on questionnaires but this does not necessarily reflect any deeply held beliefs of citizens. The support and legitimation which citizens offer to the state is much less active and much less reflective than liberal political thinkers suppose.

However, what is taken for granted and habituated now may not always have been. Today's 'common sense' might have been fought over furiously yesterday, and may only have become common sense or doxa to the extent that these fights have been repressed from historical memory:

> What appears to us today as self-evident, as beneath consciousness and choice, has quite often been the stake of struggles and instituted only as the result of dogged confrontations between dominant and dominated groups. The major effect of historical evolution is to abolish history by relegating to the past, that is, to the unconscious, the lateral possibles that it eliminated.
>
> (Bourdieu 1998a: 56–7)

Legitimation and stability are not inevitable therefore, but are rather the contingent and observable effect of a dying down of struggle and a forgetting of it from historical memory. More to the point, they are not buried for ever. Bourdieu often makes reference to the possibility of crises, such as 'Mai '68', in which a dissonance emerges between subjective expectations and objective outcomes which, in turn, stimulates the possibility of critique. In such situations, he argues, doxic and embodied assumptions are brought into the sphere of discourse:

> The critique which brings the undiscussed into discussion, the unformulated into formulation, has as the condition of its possibility objective crisis, which, in breaking the immediate fit between the subjective structures and the objective structures, destroys self-evidence practically . . . the would-be most radical critique always has the limits that are assigned to it by the objective conditions.
>
> (Bourdieu 1977: 169)

Two points are important to note here. First, Bourdieu recognizes that the expectations of a particular group's habitus may slip out of alignment with the objective goods they can secure in particular fields, thereby shocking them out of their habitual acceptance of that field and into a more critical attitude. Second, he perceives the effect of this as a general calling into question of doxic assumptions and beliefs. When the 'fit' between objective structures and subjective expectations is broken the opportunity for critical reflection and debate upon previously unquestioned assumptions is made possible.

These reflections are offered in relation to a reflection upon the political field, broadly conceived, but they might equally apply to any field. Any social field will entail a space for discourse which is, in turn, underwritten by a complex of assumptions and habits, some of which will have been fought over at an earlier time, and any field is liable to crisis if those assumptions are, for whatever reason, breached.

In moments of crisis, Bourdieu continues, doxic assumptions and the habits of everyday life are suspended, giving way to more critical and innovative forms of praxis. He argues this, for example, in respect of the growing tide of anti-capitalist demonstrations in France (and elsewhere):

> The habitus is a set of dispositions, reflexes and forms of behaviour people acquire through acting in society. It reflects the different positions people have in society, for example, whether they are brought up in a middle class environment or in a working class suburb.
>
> It is part of how society reproduces itself. But there is also change. Conflict is built into society. People can find that their expectations and ways of living are suddenly out of step with the new social position they find themselves in. This is what is happening in France today. Then the question of social agency and political intervention becomes very important.
>
> (Bourdieu 2000b: 19)

I have some reservations about the way in which Bourdieu sometimes develops this point (see Crossley 2001a, b). It can seem to suggest that the habitus is completely suspended in periods of crisis, giving way to another, unspecified principle of agency. This is problematic for a host of reasons (Crossley 2001a, b). I suggest, by contrast, that only certain habits are suspended in periods of crisis, albeit a sufficient number and range to generate a situation of 'social unrest' or generative 'collective effervescence'. Furthermore, I suggest that crisis situations allow for a different set of habits to kick in – perhaps those identified in Tilly's concept of 'repertoires of contention'. More problematic still, however, is the fact that Bourdieu seems here, as elsewhere, to posit a relatively simple crisis or strain theory of movements. He fails to attend to the other factors which mediate the emergence and development of movements, for example, or to the criticisms which strain theories have attracted. This does not negate the other important contributions which the theory of practice can make to our attempt to analyse and understand social movements but it does require that we attempt to modify this crisis theory by reference to the various arguments and studies discussed in this book. I suggest that the most fruitful way forward in this respect is to develop a reconstructed value-added model. This point needs to be unpacked. I will begin with a brief recap on Smelser and my arguments regarding his model.

Rethinking the value-added model

I outlined Smelser's value-added model of movement formation in Chapter 3. Although he is a 'collective behaviour' theorist and although there are many problems with his theory, particularly regarding agency and

Smelser's concept	The 'new' version
Structural conduciveness	Political opportunities (Tarrow, Tilly)
Structural strain	Generally ignored
Growth and spread of generalized belief	Frames (Snow et al.), grievance interpretation (Klandermans), attributions, cognitive liberation, insurgent consciousness and delegitimation (McAdam)
Precipitating factors	Suddenly imposed grievances (McAdam)
Mobilizing of participants for action	Resource mobilization (Jenkins), networks (Tilly, Tarrow), communication channels (Gamson)
Operation of social control	Social control (McAdam), media (McCarthy)

Figure 9.2

generalized beliefs, I noted, Smelser does not conform to the caricature of that approach, in which protest and movement formation are portrayed as reflex responses to situations of social strain. In part this is because Smelser has a sophisticated understanding of grievance interpretation and the intersubjective expectations which underlie it. More importantly, however, it is because he believes that successful movement formation depends upon the interaction (in any order) of six analytically distinct elements. As we have progressed through the book, considering later theories, I have attempted to show that and how these later theories, having misrepresented Smelser as a simple strain-reaction theorists, have tended to rediscover the same key elements that his model originally outlined. It has never been my intention to deny that these later theories provide more adequate accounts of these various elements but they are all there, in embryo, in Smelser. I have represented this diagrammatically in Figure 9.2. The left hand column of the table outlines the six basic value-added elements of Smelser's approach and the right hand column gives the reinvented version and (in brackets) one or two of its key pioneers.

If all that Smelser had done were to anticipate the later findings of movement theorists then this would be interesting but not particularly important, particularly if we admit, as I do, that the later theories generally provide a better account of each of these elements – albeit separately. However, this is not all that Smelser does. For all of its problems, his account has three distinct advantages over those of his successors. First, he keeps the issue of strains and their causes squarely in the picture, along-side the other value-added elements. This is important, even if its import-ance was overstated in some collective behaviour approaches, not least because strains and social divisions change as societies change (see Chapter 8). Moreover, strains provide the key to the intelligibility of movement activism. They might not explain activism but they are an essential focus if we are to understand it. Protests generally protest against something and we fail to grasp their meaning if we fail to consider what they protest against. Later theories threw the baby out with the bath water in respect of this matter and they are much weaker and less interesting as a consequence. Second, Smelser makes a distinction between the analytic elements specified in his model and concrete events, such that any one concrete event might register at different points in his schema. A single event may be both a trigger event and the response of social control agents, for example, and a strain may, at the same time, amount to shift in structural conduciveness. There is no comparable distinction or sophist-ication in later models. Finally, Smelser's model breaks with the tendency to explain movements and insurgency in mono-causal terms or in terms of a determinate order of causes. The succession of theories after collective behaviour have all, seemingly, been searching for the 'magic bullet' which explains all forms of movement formation. Some say 'resources', others 'opportunities', etc. Smelser, by contrast, identifies a range of conditions which may combine in any order, such that any one of them may serve as the 'final straw'. In some cases strains will persist for decades, only giving way to movement formation when a shift in opportunities or resources makes this possible. In other cases opportunities and resources may be in abundance, but there will be no movement until new strains emerge. In other cases still all the pieces may be in place save for a precipitating event which sets them alight, and so on. This, I contend, is a much more sophisticated view of movement formation than any other we have encoun-tered in this book.

To reiterate, I do not mean to deny, in saying this, that the newer theories have contributed a great deal to our understanding of the various precondi-tions of movement formation, both empirically and theoretically. They have. However, I believe that Smelser's conception of a value-added model for movement formation provides the most appropriate framework in which to combine and integrate this more recent work, and that the latter should be read as refinements to the former, albeit sometimes considerable refine-ments. Smelser may not have developed such ideas as 'structural conducive-ness' as well as the political opportunities advocates, and there is no question that his conception of generalized beliefs is deeply flawed, but he, more than anybody, had all the pieces of the puzzle in view. And he, more than anyone, recognized that the pieces may fit together in any order, with some events or processes, on some occasions, counting more than once.

The value-added model and the theory of practice

It is my contention that this value-added model must be brought to bear upon Bourdieu's theory of practice if we are to achieve the double goal of solving the agency/structure problem in movement theory and achieving a cogent model of movement formation within the parameters of the theory of practice. Bourdieu posits a persuasive general theory of practice which we may use to make sense of both social movements and the multiple differentiated contexts out of which they emerge and in which they wage their struggles. The weak link of his theory, however, is a tendency to explain movements in terms of social strains or crises alone. This is overcome if we are prepared to import the basic considerations of the value-added model, modified in accordance with the contributions which RM and PP theory have to make to it, into his account. A mismatch between expectations and outcomes in any one field may be sufficient to explain movement formation if all the other value-added pieces are in place but only under these conditions. Furthermore, the process and development of a movement will depend upon the continued interaction of these various value-added elements.

Durable struggle, the political field and resistance habitus

There is a further problem with the crisis theory of movements, however, in the respect that it tends only to convey the 'eruptive' aspect of movement formation and activism, neglecting the more durable forms which movement politics sometimes assumes. Mai '68 was an extremely short-lived eruption but, as I think Bourdieu recognizes in his more sustained reflections upon it (1986), it drew upon political resources which preceded it and it gave rise to a legacy which continued to have effects on (at least) French political life for much of the half-century that followed it. Mai '68 formed a generation of critical intellectuals, politicized agents and groups, who continued to agitate well into the seventies, eighties and nineties. My earlier reflections upon the political field provide one way of making more sense and doing more justice to this durable aspect of movement politics. The political field, broadly conceived, both offers (some) new movements support and affords them a space in which to operate in the longer term.

I would also like to add to this concept of the political field the notion of a resistance habitus (see also Crossley 1998a, 1999a, b; Crossley and Crossley 2001). The concept of the habitus seems very often to play a conservative role in Bourdieu's work. The habitus reproduces the conditions of its own production as habit is wont to do. Habitus are not always or just formed in periods and contexts of stability, however. They can be born in periods of change and discontent and can give rise to durable dispositions towards contention and the various forms of know-how and competence necessary to contention. Putting that another way, protests and insurgency do not arise out of nowhere and neither do they die away into nowhere. They persist in habits of resistance and political opposition. Movements and protests make habitus that make movements and protests. McAdam's (1988) aforementioned work on the biographical impact of freedom summer provides a fascinating example of this. He effectively shows how this event (among others) produced a whole generation of radical activists who continued to challenge their society for many decades to come. A theory of movements rooted in the theory of practice must, in my view, do more to explore the nature and significance of this radical habitus.

If we are to advance this concept of a resistance habitus, I further contend, then it is necessary for us to reconnect in a substantive way with some of Blumer's important insights on the culturally generative nature of movement activism (see Chapter 2). Blumer's concept of 'social unrest', and indeed Durkheim's notion of collective effervescence, both connect with Bourdieu's sense that the history of specific social arenas or groups periodically enters a turbulent period, what Bourdieu calls 'crises', where many features of the normal habitus are suspended. And all three share a conception of collective action which emphasizes the role of competent agency therein. What Durkheim and more particularly Blumer add to this, however, is a greater sense of the way in which new dispositions and forms of competence and know-how are generated at these times, which achieve a relative durability and thus force. He describes movement formation as a culturally generative process and outlines the various cultural phenomena that it generates. In addition, there is perhaps not quite enough 'agency' or 'creativity' in Bourdieu's conception of the habitus and a cross-reference to Blumer is necessary to rectify this (see also Crossley 2001a, b)

Summary and conclusion

Restrictions of space necessitate that this dialogue between movement theory and the theory of practice stops here. There is clearly much more that could be said, and there is much that should be done empirically (see also Crossley 1998a, b, 1999a, b, c, 2000a). For now it must suffice to recap my basic position. In this chapter I have attempted to offer a conclusion for the book as a whole. My concern has been twofold. On one hand I have sought to draw the various contributions of competing movement theories into an overarching value-added model. The conditions which give rise to movements and then later shape their history are multiple and complex and our theory must reflect this. If we were to maintain, in doing this, all the various epistemologies and theoretical assumptions of the models discussed this would amount to an incoherent eclectic hotchpotch. I do not propose to incorporate all this excess baggage. I propose, rather, to resituate the respective observations regarding movement dynamics offered by the various movement theories within the context of the theory of practice outlined by Pierre Bourdieu. My reason for selecting Bourdieu's approach, in particular, brings me to my second key conclusion. All theories of movements hitherto have been dogged by problematic conceptions of structure, agency or both. Bourdieu offers us a way to avoid these problems and, at the same time, his work connects with important themes from across the theoretical spectrum of movement analysis. Between Bourdieu and the canons of movement theory there is, in my view, a very fertile ground.

Further reading

The best introduction to Bourdieu's work, in my view, is Bourdieu and Wacquant's (1992) *An Invitation to Reflexive Sociology*. David Swartz's (1997) *Culture and Power* is also very good. I offer my own reflections on some of the weaknesses in Bourdieu's approach, at a level of general theory, in my book, *The Social Body: Habit, Identity and Desire* (2001a). I have also attempted to develop a Bourdieu-inspired approach to movements, empirically, in a range of papers. These are listed in the References; 'Working utopias and social movements' (Crossley 1999b) and also 'Fish, field, habitus and madness' (Crossley 1999a) are perhaps the most useful papers to start with.

References

Amenta, E. and Zylan, Y. (1991) It happened here: political opportunity, the new institutionalism, and the Townsend Movement, *American Sociological Review*, 56: 250–65.

Arendt, H. (1958) *The Human Condition*. Chicago, IL: University of Chicago Press.

Bagguley, P. (1992) Social change, the middle classes and the emergence of new social movements, *Sociological Review*, 40(1): 26–48.

Bagguley, P. (1995a) Middle class radicalism revisited, in T. Butler and M. Savage (eds) *Social Change and the Middle Classes*. London: UCL.

Bagguley, P. (1995b) Protest, poverty and power: a case study of the anti-poll tax movement, *Sociological Review*, 43: 693–719.

Barker, C. (1999) Empowerment and resistance: collective effervescence and other accounts, in P. Bagguley and J. Hearn (eds) *Transforming Politics: Power and Resistance*, pp. 11–31. London: Macmillan.

Barker, C. (2000) Robert Michels and the 'Cruel Game'. Proceedings of the sixth annual conference on Alternative Futures and Popular Protest, Manchester Metropolitan University, 25–7 April.

Barthes, R. (1973) *Elements of Semiology*. New York, NY: Hill and Wang.

Bateson, G. (1972) *Steps to an Ecology of Mind*. London: Paladin.

Beck, U. (1992) *The Risk Society*. London: Sage.

Bernstein, B. (1975) *Class Codes and Control* (3 vols). London: Routledge and Kegan Paul.

Blumer, H. (1969) Collective behaviour, in A. McClung-Lee (ed.) *Principles of Sociology*. New York, NY: Barnes and Noble.

Blumer, H. (1986) *Symbolic Interactionism*. Berkeley, CA: University of California Press.

Bourdieu, P. (1977) *Outline of a Theory of Practice*. Cambridge: Cambridge University Press.

Bourdieu, P. (1984) *Distinction*. London: Routledge.

Bourdieu, P. (1986) *Homo Academicus*. Cambridge: Polity Press.

Bourdieu, P. (1992a) *The Logic of Practice*. Cambridge: Polity Press.

Bourdieu, P. (1992b) *Language and Symbolic Power*. Cambridge: Polity Press.

Bourdieu, P. (1998a) *Practical Reason*. Cambridge: Polity Press.

Bourdieu, P. (1998b) *On Television and Journalism*. London: Pluto.

Bourdieu, P. (2000a) *Pascalian Meditations*. Cambridge: Polity Press.

Bourdieu, P. (2000b) The politics of protest (interview), *Socialist Review*, 18–20 June.

Bourdieu, P. and Haacke, H. (1995) *Free Exchange*. Cambridge: Polity Press.

Bourdieu, P. and Passeron, J-C. (1996) *Reproduction*. London: Sage.

Bourdieu, P. and Wacquant, L. (1992) *An Invitation to Reflexive Sociology*. Cambridge: Polity Press.

Bourdieu, P., Darbel, A. and Schnapper, D. (1991) *The Love of Art*. Cambridge: Polity Press.

Brockett, C. (1995) A protest cycle resolution of the repression/popular protest paradox, in M. Traugott (ed.) *Repertoires and Cycles of Collective Action*, pp. 117–44. Durham, NC: Duke University Press.

Byrne, P. (1997) *Social Movements in Britain*. London: Routledge.

Calhoun, C. (1994) (ed.) *Habermas and the Public Sphere*. Cambridge, MA: MIT Press.

Calhoun, C. (1995) 'New social movements' of the early nineteenth century, in M. Traugott (ed.) *Repertoires and Cycles of Contention*, pp. 173–216. Durham, NC: Duke University Press.

Chester, G. and Dickey, J. (1988) *Feminism and Censorship*. Dorset: Prism Press.

Cohen, J. (1983) Rethinking social movements, *Berkeley Journal of Sociology*, 28: 97–113.

Cohen, J. (1985) Strategy or identity: new theoretical paradigms and contemporary social movements, *Social Research*, 52(4): 663–716.

Crossley, M. and Crossley, N. (2001) Patient voices, social movements and the habitus: how psychiatric survivors speak out, *Social Science and Medicine*, 52(10): 1477–89.

Crossley, N. (1996) *Intersubjectivity*. London: Sage.

Crossley, N. (1998a) R.D. Laing and the British anti-psychiatry movement: a socio-historical analysis, *Social Science and Medicine*, 47(7): 877–89.

Crossley, N. (1998b) Transforming the mental health field, *Sociology of Health and Illness*, 20(4): 458–88.

Crossley, N. (1998c) Emotion and communicative action, in G. Bendelow and S. Williams (eds) *Emotions in Social Life*, pp. 16–38. London: Routledge.

Crossley, N. (1999a) Fish, field, habitus and madness: on the first wave mental health users in Britain, *British Journal of Sociology*, 50(4): 647–70.

Crossley, N. (1999b) Working utopias and social movements: an investigation using case study materials from radical mental health movements in Britain, *Sociology*, 33(4): 809–30.

Crossley, N. (1999c) Repertoire appropriation and diversity in (anti) psychiatric struggles: on habitus, capital and field. Proceedings of the fifth annual conference on Alternative Futures and Popular Protest, Manchester Metropolitan University, 29–31 March (Vol. 1).

Crossley, N. (2000a) New social movements, higher education and the habitus. Working paper, Department of Sociology, University of Manchester.

Crossley, N. (2000b) Radicals in retreat, *The Times Higher Education Supplement*, 22 September.

Crossley, N. (2000c) Emotions, psychiatry and social order, in S. Williams, J. Gabe and M. Calnan (eds) *Health, Medicine and Society*, pp. 277–95. London: Routledge.

Crossley, N. (2001a) *The Social Body: Habit, Identity and Desire*. London: Sage.

Crossley, N. (2001b) The phenomenological habitus and its construction, *Theory and Society*, 30: 81–120.

Crossley, N. (2001c) Citizenship, intersubjectivity and the lifeworld, in N. Stevenson (ed.) *Culture and Citizenship*. London: Sage.

Della Porta, D. and Diani, M. (1999) *Social Movements: An Introduction*. Oxford: Blackwell.

Della Porta, D. and Tarrow, S. (1987) Unwanted children, political violence and the cycle of protest in Italy, 1966–73, *European Journal of Political Research*, 14: 607–32.

Dewey, J. (1896) The reflex arc concept in psychology, *Psychological Review*, 3: 357–70.

Dewey, J. ([1922] 1988) *Human Nature and Conduct*. Carbondale, IL: Southern Illinois University Press.

Diani, M. (1990) The network structure of the Italian ecology movement, *Social Science Information*, 29(1): 5–31.

Diani, M. (1992) Analysing movement networks, in M. Diani and R. Eyerman (eds) *Studying Collective Action*, pp. 107–35. London: Sage.

Diani, M. (1996) Linking mobilisation frames and political opportunities, *American Sociological Review*, 61: 1053–69.

Diani, M. (1997) Social movements and social capital, *Mobilisation*, 2(2): 129–47.

Durkheim, E. ([1912] 1915) *The Elementary Forms of Religious Life*. New York, NY: Free Press.

Durkheim, E. ([1897] 1952) *Suicide*. London: Routledge and Kegan Paul.

Durkheim, E. ([1893] 1964) *The Division of Labour*. New York, NY: Free Press.

Durkheim, E. ([1895] 1965) *The Rules of Sociological Method*. New York, NY: Free Press.

Durkheim, E. ([1924] 1974) *Sociology and Philosophy*. New York, NY: Free Press.

Eder, K. (1985) The new social movements: moral crusades, political pressure groups, or social movements, *Social Research*, 52(4): 869–90.

Eder, K. (1993) *The New Politics of Class*. London: Sage.

Eisinger, P. (1973) The conditions of protest in American cities, *American Political Science Review*, 67(1): 11–28.

Elster, J. (1989) *Nuts and Bolts for the Social Sciences*. Cambridge: Cambridge University Press.

Evans-Pritchard, E. (1976) *Witchcraft, Oracles and Magic amongst the Azande*. Oxford: Clarendon.

Eyerman, R. and Jamison, A. (1991) *Social Movements: A Cognitive Approach*. Cambridge: Polity.

Feree, M. (1992) The political contest of rationality, in A. Morros and C. Mueller (eds) *Frontiers in Social Movement Theory*, pp. 29–52. New Haven, CT: Yale University Press.

Feree, M. and Miller, M. (1985) Mobilisation and meaning, *Sociological Inquiry*, 55(1): 38–61.

Foucault, M. (1980) *Power/Knowledge*. Brighton: Harvester.

Friedman, D. and McAdam, D. (1992) Collective identity and activism, in A. Morris and C. McClurg Mueller (eds) *Frontiers in Social Movement Theory*, pp. 156–73 New Haven, CT: Yale University Press.

Gadamer, H-G. (1989) *Truth and Method*. London: Sheed and Ward.

Gamson, W. (1992) The social psychology of collective action, in A. Morris and C. McClurg Mueller (eds) *Frontiers in Social Movement Theory*, pp. 53–76. New Haven, CT: Yale University Press.

Goffman, E. (1974) *Frame analysis*. Cambridge, MA: Harvard University Press.

Goldthorpe, J. (1998) Rational actor theory for sociology, *British Journal of Sociology* 49(2): 167–92.

Goodwin, J., Jasper, J. and Polletta, F. (2000) Return of the repressed, *Mobilisation*, 5(1): 65–82.

Gough, I. (1979) *The Political Economy of the Welfare State*. London: Macmillan.

Gramsci, A. (1971) *Selections from Prison Notebooks*. London: Lawrence and Wishart.

Green, D. and Shapiro, I. (1994) *Pathologies of Rational Choice Theory*. New Haven, CT: Yale University Press.

Habermas, J. (1981) New social movements, *Telos*, 49: 33–7.

Habermas, J. (1987) *The Theory of Communicative Action, Vol II: System and Lifeworld*. Cambridge: Polity Press.

Habermas, J. (1988) *Legitimation Crisis*. Cambridge: Polity Press.

Habermas, J. (1989a) *The Structural Transformation of the Public Sphere*. Cambridge: Polity Press.

Habermas, J. (1989b) *Toward a Rational Society*. Cambridge: Polity Press.

Habermas, J. (1991) *The Theory of Communicative Action: Reason and the Rationalisation of Society* (Vol. 1). Cambridge: Policy Press.

Habermas, J. (1992) *Moral Consciousness and Communicative Action*. Cambridge: Polity Press.

Hegel, G. ([1807] 1979) *The Phenomenology of Spirit*. Oxford: Oxford University Press.

Hindess, B. (1988) *Choice, Rationality and Social Theory*. London: Unwin Hyman.

Hobbes, T. ([1651] 1971) *Leviathan*. Harmondsworth: Penguin.

Hollis, M. (1994) *The Philosophy of Social Science*. Cambridge: Cambridge University Press.

Homans, G. (1961) *Social Behaviour*. London: Routledge and Kegan Paul.

Homans, G. (1973) Bringing men back in, in A. Ryan (ed.) *The Philosophy of Social Explanation*, pp. 50–64. Oxford: Oxford University Press.

Honneth, A. (1995) *The Struggle for Recognition*. Cambridge: Polity Press.

Jamison, A., Eyerman, R., Cramer, J. and Laessoe, J. (1990) *The Making of the New Environmental Consciousness*. Edinburgh: Edinburgh University Press.

Jasper, J. (1997) *The Art of Moral Protest*. Chicago, IL: Chicago University Press.

Jasper, J. and Nelkin, D. (1992) *The Animal Rights Crusade*. New York, NY: Free Press.

Jenkins, C. (1983) Resource mobilisation theory and the study of social movements, *Annual Review of Sociology* 9: 527–53.

Jenkins, C. and Perrow, C. (1977) Insurgency of the powerless farm workers movements (1946–1972), *American Sociological Review*, 42(2): 249–68.

Joas, H. (1985) *G.H. Mead*. Cambridge: Polity Press.

Johnson, H. and Klandermans, B. (1995) *Social Movements and Culture*. London: UCL.

Kant, I. ([1788] 1975) *Critique of Practical Reason*. New Jersey, NJ: Prentice-Hall.

Kant, I. ([1785] 1995) *The Moral Law: Groundwork of the Metaphysic of Morals*. London: Routledge.

Kerbo, H. (1982) Movements of 'crisis' and movements of 'affluence', *Journal of Conflict Resolution*, 26(4): 645–63.

Kerbo, H. and Shaffer, R. (1986) Unemployment and protest in the United States, 1890–1940, *Social Forces* 64(4): 1046–56.

Kitschelt, H. (1986) Political opportunity structures and political protest, *British Journal of Political Science*, 16(1): 57–85.

Klandermans, B. (1984) Mobilisation and participation, *American Sociological Review*, 49(5): 583–600.

Klandermans, B. (1989) Grievance interpretations and success expectations, *Social Behaviour*, 4: 113–25.

Klandermans, B. (1992) The social construction of protest and multiorganisational fields, in A. Morris and C. McClurg (eds) *Frontiers in Social Movement Theory*. New Haven, CT: Yale University Press.

Klein, N. (2000) *No Logo*. London: HarperCollins.

Koopmans, R. (1993) The dynamics of protest waves, *American Sociological Review*, 58: 637–58.

Kriesi, H. (1989) New social movements and the new class, *American Journal of Sociology*, 94: 1078–116.

Labov, W. (1969) The logic of non-standard English, *Georgetown Monographs on Language and Linguistics*, 22: 1–31.

Laver, M. (1997) *Private Desires, Political Action*. London: Sage.

Loftland, J. (1985) *Protest: Studies of Collective Behaviour and Social Movements*. New Brunswick: Transaction Books.

Luxemburg, R. (1986) *The Mass Strike*. London: Harper Torchbooks.

McAdam, D. (1982) *Political Process and the Development of Black Insurgency*. Chicago, IL: University of Chicago Press.

McAdam, D. (1983) Tactical innovation and the pace of insurgency, *American Sociological Review*, 48: 735–54.

McAdam, D. (1986) Recruitment to high risk activism: the case of freedom summer, *American Journal of Sociology*, 92(1): 64–90.

McAdam, D. (1988) *Freedom Summer*. New York, NY: Oxford University Press.

McAdam, D. (1989) The biographical consequences of activism, *American Sociological Review*, 54: 744–60.

McAdam, D. (1994) Culture and social movements, in E. Laraña, H. Johnson and J. Gusfield (eds) *New Social Movements*, pp. 36–57. Philadelphia, PA: Temple University Press.

McAdam, D. (1995) 'Initiator' and 'spin-off' movements, in M. Traugott (ed.) *Repertoires and Cycles of Contention*, pp. 217–40. Durham, NC: Duke University Press.

McAdam, D. and Paulsen, R. (1993) Specifying the relationship between social ties and activism, *American Journal of Sociology*, 99(3): 640–67.

McAdam, D., McCarthy, J. and Zald, M. (1988) Social movements, in N. Smelser, *Handbook of Sociology*, pp. 695–737. London: Sage.

McCarthy, J. (1994) Activists, authorities and media framing of drunk driving, in E. Laraña, H. Johnson and J. Gusfield (eds) *New Social Movements*, pp. 133–67. Philadelphia, PA: Temple University Press.

McCarthy, J. and Zald, M. (1977) Resource mobilisation and social movements, *American Journal of Sociology*, 82(6): 1212–41.

McKay, G. (1996) *Senseless Acts of Beauty*. London: Verso.

Mannheim, K. (1952) *Essays on the Sociology of Knowledge*. London: Routledge and Kegan Paul.

Mead, G. (1967) *Mind, Self and Society*. Chicago, IL: Chicago University Press.

Melucci, A. (1985) The symbolic challenge of contemporary movements, *Social Research*, 52(4): 789–816.

Melucci, A. (1986) *Nomads of the Present*. London: Radius.

Melucci, A. (1996) *Challenging Codes*. Cambridge: Cambridge University Press.

Merleau-Ponty, M. (1965) *The Structure of Behaviour*. London: Methuen.

Michels, R. (1949) *Political Parties*. Glencoe, IL: Free Press.

Morris, A. (1984) *The Origins of the Civil Rights Movement*. New York, NY: Free Press.

Morris, A. and McClurg Mueller, C. (1992) *Frontiers in Social Movement Theory*. New Haven, CT: Yale University Press.

Oberschall, A. (1973) *Social Conflict and Social Movements*. Englewood Cliffs, NJ: Prentice-Hall.

Offe, C. (1985) New social movements: challenging the boundaries of institutional politics, *Social Research*, 52(4): 817–68.

Oliver, P. (1984) If you don't do it, nobody else will, *American Sociological Review*, 49: 601–10.

Olson, M. (1971) *The Logic of Collective Action*. Cambridge, MA: Harvard University Press.

Opp, K-D. and Gern, C. (1993) Dissident groups, personal networks and spontaenous cooperation, *American Sociological Review*, 58(5): 659–80.

Parsons, T. (1951) *The Social System*. New York, NY: Free Press.

Parsons, T. (1966) *Societies*. New York, NY: Prentice-Hall.

Parsons, T. (1968) *The Structure of Social Action*. New York, NY: Free Press.

Piven, F. and Cloward, R. (1979) *Poor People's Movements*. New York, NY: Vintage.

Piven, F. and Cloward, R. (1992) Normalising collective protest, in A. Morris and C. McClurg Mueller (eds) *Frontiers in Social Movement Theory*, pp. 301–25. New Haven, CT: Yale University Press.

Popper, K. (1945) *The Open Society and its Enemies* (2 vols). London: Routledge.

Rootes, C. (1995) A new class? The higher educated and the new politics, in L. Maheu (ed.) *Social Movements and Social Classes*. London: Sage.

Rowbotham, S. (1973) *Woman's Consciousness, Man's World*. Harmondsworth: Penguin.

Sartre, J-P. (1969) *Being and Nothingness*. London: Routledge.

Sartre, J-P. (1993) *The Emotions: Outline of A Theory*. New York, NY: Citadel.

Savage, M. (2000) *Class Analysis and Social Transformation*. Buckingham: Open University Press.

Scott, A. (1990) *Ideology and New Social Movements*. London: Unwin Hyman.

Scott, J. (1985) *Weapons of the Weak*. New Haven, CT: Yale University Press.

Scott, J. (1990) *Domination and the Arts of Resistance*. New Haven, CT: Yale University Press.

Simon, H. (1979) *Models of Thought*. New Haven, CT: Yale University Press.

Simon, H. (1982) *Models of Bounded Rationality*. Cambridge, MA: MIT Press.

Smelser, N. (1962) *Theory of Collective Behaviour*. London: Routledge and Kegan Paul.

Snow, D. and Benford, R. (1992) Master frames and cycles of protest, in A. Morris and C. McClurg Mueller (eds) *Frontiers in Social Movement Theory*, pp. 133–55. New Haven, CT: Yale University Press.

Snow, D., Zurcher, L. and Ekland-Olson, S. (1980) Social networks and social movements, *American Sociological Review*, 45(5): 787–801.

Snow, D., Rochford, E., Worden, S. and Benford R. (1986) Frame alignment processes, micromobilisation and movement participation, *American Sociological Review*, 51(4): 464–81.

Snyder, D. and Tilly, C. (1972) Hardship and collective violence in France, 1830 to 1960, *American Sociological Review*, 37: 520–32.

Steinberg, M. (1995) The roar of the crowd, in M. Traugott (ed.) *Repertoires and Cycles of Contention*, pp. 57–88. Durham, NC: Duke University Press.

Steinberg, M. (1999) The talk and back talk of collective action: a dialogic analysis of repertoires of discourse among nineteenth-century English cotton spinners, *American Journal of Sociology*, 105(3): 736–80.

Swartz, D. (1997) *Culture and Power: The Sociology of Pierre Bourdieu*. Chicago, IL: Chicago University Press.

Tarrow, S. (1989) *Democracy and Disorder*. Oxford: Oxford University Press.

Tarrow, S. (1995) Cycles of Collective Action, in M. Traugott (ed.) *Repertoires and Cycles of Contention*, pp. 89–116. Durham, NC: Duke University Press.

Tarrow, S. (1998) *Power in Movement*. Cambridge: Cambridge University Press.

Taylor, V. (1989) Social movement continuity: the women's movement in abeyance, *American Sociological Review*, 54(5): 761–75.

Thompson, E. (1993) *Customs in Common*. Harmondsworth: Penguin.

Tilly, C. (1977) Getting it together in Burgundy, *Theory and Society*, 4: 479–504.

Tilly, C. (1978) *From Mobilisation to Revolution*. Reading: Addison-Wesley.

Tilly, C. (1986) European violence and collective violence since 1700, *Social Research*, 53: 159–84.

Tilly, C. (1995) Contentious repertoires in Great Britain, 1758–1834, in M. Traugott (ed.) *Repertoires and Cycles of Contention*, pp. 15–42. Durham, NC: Duke University Press.

Touraine, A. (1981) *The Voice and the Eye*. New York, NY: Cambridge University Press.

Traugott, M. (1995a) *Repertoires and Cycles of Contention*. Durham, NC: Duke University Press.

Traugott, M. (1995b) Barricades as repertoire, in M. Traugott (ed.) *Repertoires and Cycles of Contention*, pp. 43–56. Durham, NC: Duke University Press.

Tucker, K.(1991) How new are the new social movements?, *Theory, Culture and Society*, 8(2): 75–98.

Weber, M. ([1956] 1978) *Economy and Society* (2 vols). Berkeley, CA: University of California Press.

Whittier, N. (1997) Political generations, micro-cohorts and the transformation of social movements, *American Sociological Review*, 62: 760–78.

Wittgenstein, L. (1953) *Philosophical Investigations*. Oxford: Blackwell.

Zald, M. and Ash, R. (1966) Social movement organisations, *Social Forces*, 44: 327–41.

Zolberg, A. (1972) Moments of madness, *Politics and Society*, Winter: 183–207.

Index

abortion movements, 1, 85, 91,
110–11
action systems, 52
activism, 117–19, 126
  resources and, 78, 80–1, 87, 96,
  100–3
  see also agitation/agitators; protest;
  resistance
administrative structure/system, 161–2
advertising, 88–9, 160
agency, 71, 76, 104
  RAT model, 65–7, 72, 89, 101, 127,
  141
  value-added model, 48, 50–2
agency, structure and, 36, 54, 124–5
  habitus and, 177–82, 190
  problems of, 16, 168, 169–71, 189
agents, 38
  emotions and, 48–50, 108
  RAT model, 58–62, 65–7, 72–3
  social, 67–8, 174–7
AGIL schema, 154
agitation/agitators, 30, 34–5, 83,
  182
alienation, 45, 98
altruistic suicide, 102
Amenta, E., 110
animal rights, 2, 5, 8, 11, 67, 69, 72,
  73, 91, 132, 149
anomie, 11, 12, 45, 48, 98, 101–2

anti-psychiatry movement, 1, 5, 11, 15,
  97, 149, 179
Arendt, H., 28
Ash, R., 77, 85
association, 31, 94, 96, 98, 99
authority, 155–6
Azande, 72–3

Bagguley, P., 67, 121, 164
Barker, C., 15, 92, 144
Barthes, R., 19
Bateson, P., 133–4
Beck, U., 4
behaviourism, 18, 65
beliefs, 6, 43, 50–1, 53, 56
  see also generalized beliefs
beneficiaries, 87, 88
Benford, R., 136, 145–6
Bernstein, B., 140
biographical impacts, 117–18, 126,
  190
Blumer, H., 2, 5, 7, 15, 17–38, 39, 41,
  53, 58, 65, 69, 76, 83, 85, 89,
  101, 108, 113, 125, 147, 182, 190
Bourdieu, P., 2, 15–16, 73, 140, 168,
  171–4, 175, 176, 177–86, 189–91
bourgeoisie, 150–1
Brockett, C., 143
bureaucratic society, 158–9, 161, 162
Byrne, P., 3, 84, 164

Calhoun, C., 4, 150
capital, 171–2, 178–9, 181, 182–3
capitalism, 99, 124, 134, 150–1,
    157–9
categorical imperative, 22
'catnet' factor, 96
Chester, G., 164
civil privatism, 156, 161–2
civil rights, 10, 12, 67, 69, 83, 92–5,
    97, 99–100, 107, 113, 115–19,
    135–6, 145, 164
Cloward, R., 82–3, 92–3, 98–100,
    102, 114, 132
cognitive liberation, 105, 113–15, 122,
    126, 134–5, 144
Cohen, J., 100, 152
collective action, 79, 93
    psychodynamics of, 48–50
    RAT, 16, 56, 61–4, 69, 76–8, 100
collective behaviour approach, 10, 14,
    56, 99, 108, 113, 125
    Blumer, 17–38
    Smelser, 39–55, 137
    straw model, 11–12, 15, 35, 42, 54,
    80
collective effervescence, 15, 26–7, 36,
    102–3, 186, 190
collective enterprises, 3
colonization, 162, 165
    lifeworld, 154, 158–61, 166–7, 180
commodification, 159
communication, 19–21
communicative action, 155, 162
communicative rationality, 22, 23, 33,
    50, 69, 155–6, 161
communities, 93, 95, 96
conscience constituents, 87, 88, 89
constituents, 87, 88, 89
constraint, 43, 58, 65, 106, 109–13,
    124, 169
contention
    cycles of, 15, 16, 127, 143–7, 163
    framing, 16, 127, 133–43
    repertoires of, 16, 127–33, 176–7,
    186
cost–benefit analysis, 106, 125
cost–benefit ratio, 59–60, 63, 65–6, 72
costs, 57–60, 62–6, 121

counter-movements, 85, 110–11
craze, 11, 44, 45, 46
creativity, 4, 19, 36, 37, 190
crisis theory, 157–8, 183–6, 190
Crossley, M., 189
Crossley, N., 5, 17, 43, 49, 56, 66, 73,
    84–5, 90, 97, 100, 133, 138,
    171–2, 176, 186, 189–90
crowds, 25, 27, 28, 129
cultural capital, 178, 181
cultural codes/opportunities, 139
cultural drifts, 5–6, 29
cultures
    movement, 17–38, 90, 114
    resistance, 33, 112, 116–17
customs, 26, 28
cycles of contention, see contention

Darwin, C., 18
deliberation techniques, 70, 72–3
Della Porta, D., 6, 143
demand, 85–6, 90–1, 104
democracy, 9, 112, 120–1, 150, 164,
    171, 184
deontological ethics, 68
desires, 57–9, 66, 70, 74
Dewey, J., 18, 19
Diani, M., 6, 97, 110, 138
Dickey, J., 164
differentiation, 51–2, 67, 178
direct action, 90, 92, 165
disabilities movement, 86–7
discourse ethics, 23
discursive repertoires, 130, 140
distance, 24, 25, 27
domination, 23, 179, 183
doxa, 184–6
drink driving, 10, 138
Durkheim, E., 11, 15, 26, 36, 65–6,
    89, 98, 101, 130, 137, 147, 171,
    190
duties, 65, 66, 68–9

economic capital, 178
Eder, K., 175
Eisinger, P., 12, 105–9, 110, 126
elementary behaviour, 24–6, 30, 34,
    102

elementary groups, 27–8
elites, 4, 47–8, 80–4, 95, 99, 111, 113
Elster, J., 56, 57, 59
embeddedness, 67–8, 174–5
emotions, 48–50, 108, 136–7
empirical value (in RAT), 74–5
environmental movements, 1, 4, 5,
    7–8, 11, 48, 61, 69, 73, 84, 86,
    90, 91, 149, 164–5
esprit de corps, 27, 30, 31–2, 34, 35,
    37, 54, 125
Evans-Pritchard, E., 72
expectations, 34–6, 40, 42, 62
extra-movement networks, 96
Eyerman, R., 4, 5

family resemblance, 2, 7
farm workers study, 77, 80–2, 84
fascist movement, 1, 85, 136
feedback mechanism (protests), 109–10
feminism, 1, 5, 8, 11, 29, 86, 132,
    142, 145, 149, 164–5
Feree, M., 70, 100, 114
field, 171, 178–83, 185
Foucault, M., 140
frames, 16, 110, 127, 133–46, 170,
    174
free-rider problem, 61, 62–3, 87, 93
freedom summer project, 94, 115–19,
    141, 145, 190
French Revolution, 27, 102, 128
Friedman, D., 118
friendship networks, 94, 97, 99
full information, 59, 70
functionalism, 52, 57, 169
fundamental attribution error, 114
fuzzy logic, 2, 7

Gadamer, H-G., 37
game theory, 131, 176–83, 184
Gamson, W., 140–1, 187
general social movements, 29–30
generalized beliefs, 43, 45–8, 50, 54,
    122, 135, 137, 187–8
Gern, C., 94, 100
Goffman, E., 133
Goldthorpe, J., 59
Gough, I., 84, 158

Gramsci, A., 135–6
Green, D., 74
grievances, 135, 136
    NSM, 152–3, 161, 167, 170
    PP approach, 114, 121–5, 152–3
    RM, 81, 84, 95–6, 99, 103, 152–3
    theory of practice, 173, 179–80
group culture, 67–8
group ideology, 32

Haacke, H., 180, 184
Habermas, J., 16, 22, 28, 149–50,
    153–66, 167, 171, 180
habit, 8–9, 19–21, 24–5, 34, 67–8,
    116, 147, 171–2
habitus, 171–83, 184–6, 189–90
hardship, 11, 42, 95
Hegel, G.W.F., 18, 22
heterodoxy, 184
Hindess, B., 72
Hobbes, T., 63, 68
Hollis, M., 57
Homans, G., 57, 59, 60
Honneth, A., 18, 22, 139
horizontal differentiation, 52, 67, 178
hostile outburst, 44–5, 46, 47

identity movements, 67
identity politics, 152
ideology, 32, 34–5, 37, 54
incentives, 63–4, 78, 86, 89–90, 93
individuals, networks and, 100–3
industrial conflict, 133
industrial society, 150–1
information gathering, 59, 70–1
innovation, 19–21, 36, 37, 115
instrumental rationality, 49, 58, 69,
    156, 175–6
insurgent consciousness, 113–15, 122
integration, 40, 98, 101–2, 154–5, 157
interaction, 26–8, 31, 36–7, 40, 66,
    134
    see also symbolic interactionism
interpretation, 70–2
irrationalism, 46, 56, 135

Jamison, A., 4, 5
Jasper, J., 42, 69, 70, 72, 125

Jenkins, C., 11, 77, 80, 84, 87, 89, 187
Joas, H., 17, 18
Johnson, H., 125
juridification process, 158–9, 164

Kant, I., 18, 22, 23, 68
Kerbo, H., 53
Kitschelt, H., 110, 111
Klandermans, B., 114, 125, 135, 141, 174, 187
Klein, N., 121, 159, 166
Koopmans, R., 6–7, 144
Kriesi, H., 110

labour movement, 1, 29, 67, 69, 150–2, 157–8, 159, 179
Labov, W., 140
language, 19, 20–1, 66, 177–8
language games, 129
latency, 98, 112, 147, 149, 154
Laver, M., 56, 57–8, 63–4, 74–5
leaders (of movements), 78
legitimation, 9
    crises, 154–5, 156, 157–8, 183–5
lifeworld, 42, 53, 136, 165, 173
    colonization, 154, 158–61, 166–7, 180
    system and, 154–5, 157, 164
Loftland, J., 85
Luxemburg, R., 144

McAdam, D., 9, 11, 82–3, 85, 91–6, 99, 103, 105, 110, 113–19, 125–6, 135, 141, 143–6, 175, 187
McCarthy, J., 77, 85–92, 138, 169, 181–2
McClurg Mueller, C., 125
McKay, G., 121
Major government, 121
Mannheim, K., 132
market/market mechanism, 159, 165–6
Marx, K., 10, 11, 124–5, 151, 157, 158
Marxism, 10, 82, 124, 136, 150–1, 152–3
mass/masses, 28, 85
master frames, 136, 145–6

Mead, G.H., 17, 18–24, 31–2, 36, 65–6, 68, 76, 89, 90, 101, 155
mechanical–physical response, 18–19
media, 28, 43, 123–4, 137–8, 162, 180–1, 183
Melucci, A., 5, 97–8, 112, 139, 147, 149–50, 152–3, 159, 163, 167
mental health movements, 15, 51–2, 133, 138, 139, 180–1
mental health survivor movements, 1, 97, 132–3, 164, 179
Merleau-Ponty, M., 90
methodological individualism, 66, 90, 169
Michels, R., 3, 91, 92
micro-mobilization contexts, 94
Miller, M., 114
'milling', 25
mobilization, 110, 113, 114
    networks and, 94–6, 99, 103
    new social movements, 161–4
    participants, 43, 50–1, 122, 161, 187
    political, 9, 78–9
    value-added model, 43, 50–1, 52
mobs/mob psychology, 11
moral law, 23, 65
'moral shock', 42
moral theory, 68–9
morality, 22
morale, 32, 34–5, 54
Morris, A., 94, 125
motivation, 40–1, 44–5, 155, 157
movement cultures, 17–38, 90, 114
movement politics, 9, 78–9, 103, 150, 181–2
movement theories, 15–16, 168–91
mutual expectations, 40
mutual recognition, 22, 97

narratives, 32, 33, 37
nationalism, 1, 29, 136, 137
Nelkin, D., 72
networks, 4, 5, 6, 12, 14, 27, 36, 53, 77, 93–103, 105, 110, 112, 114, 118
new social movements, 4, 5, 10–14, 16, 68, 84, 118, 125, 149–67, 170, 180

norms, 22–4, 26, 40–1, 44–6, 48, 65, 66, 68–9

Oberschall, A., 11, 77–80, 84, 93, 95, 98, 100
Offe, C., 3, 7
Oliver, P., 96
Olson, M., 61–3, 77–9, 83, 86, 93, 100
Opp, K-D., 94, 100
opportunities, 114
  constraints and, 43, 58, 65, 106, 109–13, 124, 169
opportunity structures, political, 14, 105–15, 121, 123–6, 144–5
organization (value-added model), 40–1, 44–5
organizations
  networks and, 77, 93–103
  resource mobilization and, 77–104
  SMOs, 85–92
orthodoxy, 184
'outsiders', 26, 31, 32, 47, 132

pain (moral theory), 68
Parsons, T., 40, 52, 68, 154
Passeron, J-C., 174
Paulsen, R., 96
panic, 3, 11, 44, 45
peace movement, 2, 11, 84, 86, 91, 149
Perrow, C., 77, 80–1, 84, 87, 89
phenomenology, 50, 60–1, 171, 172–3
Piven, F., 82–3, 92–3, 98–100, 102, 114, 132
play-fighting (otters), 133–4
pleasure (moral theory), 68
political field, 181–3, 189–90
political mobilization, 9, 78–9
political opportunity structures, 14, 105–15, 121, 123–6, 144–5
political power, 82, 184
political process approach, 10, 11, 13, 16, 105–26, 127, 139, 143, 147–8, 149, 152–3, 170, 189
politics, 3, 4, 82, 132–3, 139
  movement, 9, 78–9, 103, 150, 181–2

Popper, K., 57, 59, 71
power, 9, 84, 113, 140, 155–6, 174, 179
  political, 82, 184
powerless groups, 80–3, 87, 104, 113–14
practice, theory of, 15–16, 168–91
praxis, 18, 20, 22, 186
precipitating factors, 43, 46, 50, 121, 122, 169, 187–8
preference, 70, 73–4, 85, 90–1
process (movement formation), 33–5
proletariat, 11, 99, 124, 150–1, 163
protest, 4–6, 11–12, 73, 90, 98
  farm workers (US study), 77, 80–2, 84
  feedback effect, 109, 110
  opportunity and, 105–9, 110–11, 120–1
  see also activism; agitation/ agitators; contention; resistance
psychiatric survivor movements, 1, 97, 132–3, 164, 179
psychodynamics, 48–9, 50, 169
psychology, 48, 59, 60
public goods, 61–2, 63–4, 67, 86
public sphere, 4, 6, 28, 155–6, 159–61, 162, 175, 183–4
publics/public opinion, 22

rank and file activists, 78
rational actor theory, 12–14, 16, 56–76, 77, 89–91, 100, 104, 108, 125, 127, 131, 141–3, 147–8, 169–70, 174–6
rational choice theory, 13–14, 49, 75–6, 130–1
rationality, 49, 50, 157
  communicative, 22, 23, 33, 50, 69, 155–6, 161
  instrumental, 47, 58, 69, 156, 175–6
  RAT's conception, 58, 69–70
rationalization, historical, 155–6
realism (RAT model), 60–1, 74, 90
reality, 19, 34–6, 90, 134, 142
reincorporation (new social movements), 164–5
'reinforcement', 31

religion, 3, 27, 32, 102–3, 136, 137
repertoires of contention, 16, 127–33,
    170, 176–7, 186
repression, 43, 45, 108–10, 111–12,
    143
resistance, 26, 121, 160, 165
    cultures, 33, 112, 116–17
    habitus, 189–90
resource mobilization, 10, 11, 12, 16,
    77–105, 122, 124, 135, 139, 143,
    147–8, 149, 152–3, 170, 182, 189
rewards, 63–4, 78, 86, 89–90, 93
Rhinehart, L., 72
roles, 21, 26, 31, 40, 48, 66
Rootes, C., 67, 84, 164
Rowbotham, S., 5
rules, 14, 40, 41
rules of the game, 25, 36, 37, 164

Sartre, J-P., 49–50, 172
Savage, M., 67
Scott, A., 100, 125
Scott, J., 112
segmentation/segmented communities,
    95–6
segregation, 98, 99, 100
selective incentives, 63–4, 78, 86
self, 20, 21–3
self-consciousness, 21–6, 37, 147
self-interest, 60, 63, 78, 83, 89, 100,
    159
Shaffer, R., 53
Shapiro, I., 74
shock, 37, 42, 116–17
short-circuit theory, 46–8
sign systems, 19, 71
Simon, H., 59, 70
situational facilities, 40–1, 44, 135
Smelser, N., 9, 15–16, 39–55, 56, 103,
    108, 113, 121–3, 169, 173, 179,
    186–8
Smith, A., 157
Snow, D., 3, 95–6, 135, 136, 140–1,
    142, 145–6, 187
Snyder, D., 12, 109
social capital, 97, 178, 181
social class, 11, 124, 150–1, 158, 164,
    172, 174–5

'social contagion', 25
social control, 5, 31, 33, 95, 180
    cognitive liberation and, 105,
        113–15, 126
    operation of, 43, 50, 122, 187–8
    self-consciousness, 21–6, 37, 147
social facts, 131, 173
social fields, 14, 36, 139
social integration, 22, 100–2, 157, 160
social interaction, see interaction
social movement industry, 86, 88–9,
    182
social movement organization, 85–92,
    104, 118, 124, 133, 135, 140,
    142, 174, 180–1
social movement sector, 86, 88, 89,
    182
social movements
    definitions, 1–7, 85, 169–70
    importance of, 7–9
    making sense of, 10–13
    sociology of, 9–10
social networks, see networks
social norms, see norms
social stability, 34, 51
social structures, 52, 66, 67–8
social systems, 40–1, 43–4, 46–7,
    51–3
social unrest, 15, 23–5, 30, 36–8, 103,
    108, 186, 190
socialism, 27, 102
sociality, 65–7
socialization, 32, 65, 66, 118, 160
solidarity, 6, 15, 37, 64, 93, 98,
    100–2, 114, 137
state, market and, 165–6
Steinberg, M., 130, 139–40, 141–2
stimulus-response model, 18–19
strains, 25, 30, 34–6
    NSMs, 153, 161, 167, 170
    PP approach, 122, 123–5
    RM approach, 81, 84, 99, 103
    social, 44, 53, 188, 189
    structural, 41–3, 45–6, 50, 52,
        124–5, 187–8
    theory of practice, 169, 173,
        179–80, 186–9
    value-added approach, 41–6, 50–3

strategy, habitus and, 176–7
structural conduciveness, 43, 50–1,
    122, 187–8
structural conflicts, 12, 14, 45
structural systems, 53
structuration, 177–8
structure, 14
    habitus and, 177–82, 190
    problems of, 16, 168–71, 189
    see also agency, structure and
subjectivity, 70–3, 141, 173
suicide, 102
supply, 85–6, 118
survival, 91, 97, 132–3, 164, 179
symbolic capital, 178, 181
symbolic interactionism, 3, 18–23, 36,
    76, 154
symbolic reality, 90
symbolism, 136–7, 140, 142, 143
synthetic framework (analysis), 168–91
system attributions, 114
systems, 40–1, 43–5, 47, 179
    differentiation and, 51–2
    integration, 157
    lifeworld and, 154–5, 157, 164

tactics, 32–3, 34, 54, 115
Tarrow, S., 4–6, 92, 105, 109–12,
    121–3, 126, 130, 136–8, 143–6,
    149, 187
Taylor, V., 112

Thatcher government, 120–1, 131
theory of practice, 15–16, 168–91
Thompson, E.P., 42
Thompson, Edward, 173
Tilly, C., 11–12, 15, 77, 96, 109–10,
    127–31, 176–7, 186, 187
Touraine, A., 149, 150–1, 153, 159,
    167
Trautgott, M., 127, 128
trigger events, 43, 46, 50, 121–2, 169,
    187–8
Tucker, K., 150

urbanization, 99, 124
utilitarianism, 65–9, 91, 101, 131, 141

value-added approach, 15, 39–55, 103,
    121, 122–3, 168, 180, 186–90
values, 24, 40–1, 44–5
vertical differentiation, 52, 67
violent protest, 106, 138

Weber, M., 68, 73, 143
welfare state, 84, 158, 159, 160, 166
Whittier, N., 132
Wittgenstein, L., 2, 66, 129
workers, 150–1, 157–8

Zald, M., 77, 85–92, 169, 181, 182
Zolberg, A., 143
Zylan, Y., 110

SOCIAL SOLIDARITIES
THEORIES, IDENTITIES AND SOCIAL CHANGE

Graham Crow

- What is the significance of social solidarity?
- Has social change undermined the potential for people to come together and act coherently?
- What can we learn from comparing the solidarities of families, communities and wider societies?

Social solidarity is important in many areas of our lives, or at least in how we wish our lives to be. Family and kinship relationships, community life, trade union activity and the identity politics of new social movements are just some of the numerous ways in which social solidarity features in contemporary social arrangements. This book explores the ways in which people strive to come together and act as a coherent, unified force. It considers the arguments of those who claim that solidarity is increasingly fragile, and of those who are concerned to revitalise solidarities in our unsettled societies. The author shows how social change can be understood in the context of the limitations as well as the potential of the pursuit of solidarity, drawing on research findings on social relationships in families, communities, and the post-communist world. Written with undergraduate students and researchers in mind, *Social Solidarities* will be an invaluable text for those studying social theory, and family, community or comparative sociology.

Contents
Introduction – Part One: Classical theories of social solidarity – Contemporary theories of social solidarity – Part Two: Family solidarities – Community solidarities – The solidarity of solidarity *– Part Three: Making sense of social solidarities in unsettled societies – References – Index.*

176pp   0 335 20230 6   (Paperback)   0 335 20231 4   (Hardback)

SURVEILLANCE SOCIETY
MONITORING EVERYDAY LIFE

David Lyon

- In what ways does contemporary surveillance reinforce social divisions?
- How are police and consumer surveillance becoming more similar as they are automated?
- Why is surveillance both expanding globally and focusing more on the human body?

Surveillance Society takes a post-privacy approach to surveillance with a fresh look at the relations between technology and society. Personal data is collected from us all the time, whether we know it or not, through identity numbers, camera images, or increasingly by other means such as fingerprint and retinal scans. This book examines the constant computer-based scrutiny of ordinary daily life for citizens and consumers as they participate in contemporary societies. It argues that to understand what is happening we have to go beyond Orwellian alarms and cries for more privacy to see how such surveillance also reinforces divisions by sorting people into social categories. The issues spill over narrow policy and legal boundaries to generate responses at several levels including local consumer groups, internet activism, and international social movements. In this fascinating study, sociologies of new technology and social theories of surveillance are illustrated with examples from North America, Europe, and Pacific Asia. David Lyon provides an invaluable text for undergraduate and postgraduate sociology courses, for example in science, technology and society. It will also appeal much more widely to those with an interest in politics, social control, human geography, public administration, consumption, and workplace studies.

Contents
Introduction – Part one: Surveillance societies – Disappearing bodies – Invisible frameworks – Leaky containers – Part two: The spread of surveillance – Surveillant sorting in the city – Body parts and probes – Global data flows – Part three: Surveillance scenarios – New directions in theory – The politics of surveillance – The future of surveillance – Notes – Bibliography – Index.

208pp   0 335 20546 1   (Paperback)   0 335 20547 X   (Hardback)

CITIZENSHIP IN A GLOBAL AGE
SOCIETY, CULTURE, POLITICS

Gerard Delanty

- What is citizenship?
- Is global citizenship possible?
- Can cosmopolitanism provide an alternative to globalization?

Citizenship in a Global Age provides a comprehensive and concise overview of the main debates on citizenship and the implications of globalization. It argues that citizenship is no longer defined by nationality and the nation state, but has become de-territorialized and fragmented into the separate discourses of rights, participation, responsibility and identity. Gerard Delanty claims that cosmo-politanism is increasingly becoming a significant force in the global world due to new expressions of cultural identity, civic ties, human rights, technological innovations, ecological sustainability and political mobilization. Citizenship is no longer exclusively about the struggle for social equality but has become a major site of battles over cultural identity and demands for the recognition of group difference. Delanty argues that globalization both threatens and supports cosmopolitan citizenship. Critical of the prospects for a global civil society, he defends the alternative idea of a more limited cosmopolitan public sphere as a basis for new kinds of citizenship that have emerged in a global age.

Contents
Introduction – Part 1: Models of citizenship – The liberal theory of citizenship: rights and duties – Communitarian theories of citizenship: participation and identity – The radical theories of politics: citizenship and democracy   Part 2: The cosmopolitan challenge – Cosmopolitan citizenship: beyond the nation state – Human rights and citizenship: the emergence of the embodied self – Globalization and the deterritorialization of space: between order and chaos – The transformation of the nation state: nationalism, the city, migration and muliticulturalism – European integration and post-national citizenship: four kinds of post-nationalization – Part 3: Rethinking citizenship – The reconfiguration of citizenship: post-national governance in the multi-levelled polity – Conclusion: the idea of civic cosmopolitanism – Bibliography – Index.

192pp   0 335 20489 9   (Paperback)   0 335 20490 2   (Hardback)